738.13
H342b

Harvey.

Building pottery equipment.

September 1975

A

BUILDING POTTERY EQUIPMENT

BUILDING POTTERY EQUIPMENT

BY ROGER HARVEY
AND
SYLVIA AND JOHN KOLB

WATSON-GUPTILL PUBLICATIONS / NEW YORK
PITMAN PUBLISHING / LONDON

First published in 1975 in the United States and Canada by Watson-Guptill Publications,
a division of Billboard Publications, Inc.,
One Astor Plaza, New York, N.Y. 10036

Published in Great Britain by Sir Isaac Pitman & Sons Ltd.,
39 Parker Street, Kingsway, London WC2B 5PB
ISBN 0–273–00855–2

Manufactured in U.S.A.

Library of Congress Cataloging in Publication Data
Harvey, Roger, 1943–
   Building pottery equipment.
   1. Pottery craft—Equipment and supplies. I. Kolb,
Sylvia, 1912–   joint author. II. Kolb, John,
1915–1974 joint author. III. Title.
TT921.5.H37 1974   681'.7666   74-16375
ISBN 0–8230–0540–2

First Printing, 1975

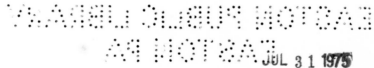
Edited by Sarah Bodine
Designed by Bob Fillie
Set in 9 point Helvetica by Gerard Associates/Graphic Arts, Inc.
Printed and bound by Halliday Lithograph Corp.

This book remembers, with love, Jack Kolb
who conceived and shaped it with us.

R.H. and S.K.

CONTENTS

PART 6. WORKSHOP LAYOUT

APPENDIX

Roger Harvey in His Ideal Pottery Shop by Andrea Grey

INTRODUCTION

The equipment and tools described in this book have been developed and constructed by a potter, largely for his own use. Some of the designs are the result of having to build many modified and improved versions. In this way, the book presents the traditional craftsman's approach to working, using tools he makes himself and constantly evolving better ones as every-day working experience demands. (Because of this process of evolution, not all photographs of finished equipment will look exactly like that presented in the text.)

The three major goals of this book are: (1) to make equipment to suit your individual needs; (2) to build equipment as economically as possible; (3) to make the equipment that you build as good or better than that commercially available.

We think that building specialized equipment is basic to good craftsmanship and good craft products. Therefore, we recommend modification of the equipment designs presented here whenever necessary to meet your individual needs. In Part 4 on kilns, in particular, design modifications are discussed at length.

You can make most of the pieces of equipment included at considerably less cost than commercially produced equivalents. All of the construction plans that have been included use parts and materials that are new. However, we have found that a small amount of searching can often turn up scrap or surplus items to substitute for some of the materials suggested. We encourage such substitution whenever it will reduce costs without diminishing quality or safety.

To the extent possible, the construction of the equipment presented here requires only those handtools and powertools found in many home work-shops. We assume that you know how to use these tools. Some pieces of equipment will require small amounts of assistance from tradesmen, such as welders or plumbers.

Although the drawings provided in the instructions are not made to scale, they are accurate enough to be easily followed. The system of drawings is sequential—one drawing builds on another. In many drawings, only detailed information is shown for the specific operations being performed while previously detailed parts are present in a simplified form. This has been done to keep the drawings as uncluttered as possible. The drawings and text together furnish the essential data for building the equipment.

Because we are actively concerned with environmental problems, there were inevitable discussions during the writing of this book about the desirability of giving instructions that will further encourage the use of raw materials and energy in these days of shortages and pollution. However, we believe that the crafts' contribution to the improvement of the quality of life justifies their demands on our environment.

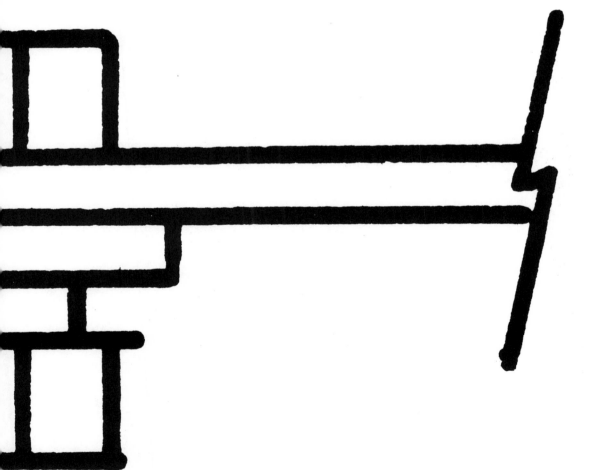

PART 1
CLAY
PREPARATION
EQUIPMENT

Mixing Clay

Perhaps it is best to begin by discussing briefly why clay must be mixed at all prior to use. Mixing is necessary in order to uniformly distribute all the ingredients throughout the clay body. Mixing also provides proper consistency for working the clay.

Mixing a clay body from dry ingredients is less expensive than buying the body premixed, because the supplier has been saved the mixing cost, and also, since wet clay contains considerable water by weight, you do not have to pay for shipping the water in the clay.

The two commonly used commercial methods of mixing clay require a great deal of mechanical energy or time and a lot of complicated equipment to do the job. In one mixing method, only enough water is added to the dry ingredients to achieve a workable clay body. For this method the potter could build a small pug mill or buy a used dough mixer (such as those used in bakeries), but to do so inexpensively requires luck in finding good used equipment and parts. Some potters have also made mixers from the gear box and auger of a stoking unit taken from an old coal-fired furnace. Such equipment can sometimes be found in junkyards. One limitation of dough mixers is that the heavy consistency of the clay tends to cause excessive wear on the mixing blades. Obviously, there are many variables in the design, construction, and power requirements of such

home-built mixers. Therefore they will not be included in this book.

In the other common mixing method, water is added to the dry ingredients until they are in a liquid or semi-liquid state. The excess water is then squeezed from the clay in an expensive filter press.

The mixer for which plans and instructions are provided in this book differs from the two methods just described in that the clay ingredients are blended in a completely dry state. This provides a number of advantages. The steel drum on which the mixer is based can be turned by hand by one or two people for the few minutes required to achieve a uniform

distribution of all the ingredients. Premixing the dry ingredients makes less stirring necessary when water is added after removing the clay from the dry mixer. Emptying and cleaning the dry clay mixer is also easy since the dry clay does not stick to the metal drum.

No plans for making the containers in which the dry clay mixture will be combined with water are provided since the equipment suggested for this step consists of inexpensive containers (garbage cans, a steel drum, or a wooden barrel) that are available ready-made. Enough water should be added to the clays in the wet mixer so that they attain a semi-liquid state—the consistency of soft ice cream. Although the clay must sit for several days to allow

Dry clay mixer on base with loading and emptying ports installed.

excess water to evaporate, the result will be a very plastic, easier-to-work material.

Drying Clay

Plans and instructions are provided for special clay-drying boxes, in which the semi-liquid clay is placed to get rid of excess water. These boxes represent a number of distinct improvements over the plaster bat normally used for drying clay. One advantage of these boxes is dramatically illustrated by the experience of a potter-friend. This potter had made a large number of pots from clay which had, as usual, been dried on a plaster bat. The pots had gone successfully through throwing, bisquing, glazing, and firing and were apparently in good condition when they were sold soon afterward.

Within a few weeks, purchasers began to complain about craters developing on the surfaces of the pots. When the potter examined some of the craters, he discovered small particles of plaster still imbedded in them. The particles were plaster chips picked up by the clay while drying on the plaster bat. The chips had gradually absorbed moisture through the walls of the pots. The moisture caused the chips to expand. When the pressure had built up sufficiently, it forced small fragments of the clay and glaze to pop out. The potter discovered that the plaster chips had come from his badly cracked plaster bat. Cracking is not an unusual condition when the plaster has been incorrectly poured or has

End view.

Electric gear drive adapted from stoker.

been in use too long. The potter had to replace several hundred dollars' worth of pots.

There is a second reason for suggesting a substitute for plaster bats. When large amounts of clay have been dried on a bat over a long period of time, the bat becomes sealed by clay ingredients leached out with the moisture absorbed by the plaster. When this happens, the potter must tackle the unpleasant chore of scraping off the nonabsorbent coating that has formed.

Another argument for using the clay-drying box is demonstrated by comparing its construction with that of a plaster bat drying table. The weight of the amount of clay being dried at any one time constitutes a heavy load for whatever kind of equipment is to be built. But adding the four to five inches of plaster required for a drying table at least doubles the weight involved. This, in turn, requires a heavy, expensive construction job. Such plaster drying bats also require substantial floor space. By comparison, the clay-drying boxes for which plans are given are lightweight and comparatively small. Yet they should prove large and strong enough to hold batches of clay weighing from 75 to 100 pounds. The boxes will dry clay as quickly as a plaster bat. The boxes are so easy and inexpensive to build that the potter will want to build at least four of them. Plans are provided in Part 6 for a drying rack to hold four of these boxes.

DRY CLAY MIXER

The steel drum used for this mixer should have the usual two reinforcing ribs formed in the sidewall and the ends should be permanently attached, not removable. *Do not* select a used drum, if at all possible, because it may contain residue of the former contents. Such residue can be hazardous, if flammable, and can also pose a contamination problem. If the screw-in plugs normally supplied with the drum are missing, it is possible to buy regular pipe plugs from a plumbing supply shop.

Tools

1. Drawing compass.
2. Tape measure or folding rule.
3. Metal-cutting torch or metal-cutting saber saw (not needed if cutting is done at welding shop).
4. Center punch.
5. Electric drill with 5/16″, 3/8″, 1/2″, and assorted smaller size metal-drilling bits.
6. Hacksaw.
7. Metal-cutting file and/or coarse-grit sandpaper.
8. Hammer.
9. Set of wrenches, for fastening 1″ and smaller nuts.
10. Carpenter's framing square.
11. Wood-cutting saw.

Parts and Materials for the Drum

Item No.

1. A 55 gal. steel drum, new or reconditioned.
2. A 9″ × 22″ piece of 16-gauge steel sheet metal.
3. A 12″ long piece of strap iron, at least 1/8″ × 1″.
4. Pieces of 2 × 4 lumber:
   a. Two 33 1/2″ lengths.
   b. Two 17″ lengths.
   c. Two 19″ lengths.
5. Two pieces of 1/4″ thick foam-rubber sheet, one 9″ × 22″, the other 10″ in diameter.
6. Contact cement.
7. A 1/2″ to 3/4″ thick plywood disk, 10″ in diameter.
8. Bolts:
   a. Four 3/8″ eyebolts, the shortest available, threaded the full length of the shank.
   b. Three 1/2″ × 6″ bolts.
   c. Eight 5/16″ × 1 1/2″ lag bolts.
   d. Two 1/4″ × 4″ eyebolts.
   e. Eight 1 1/2″ long lag bolts to fit caster mounting holes, two for each caster.

9. Washers:
   a. Eight 3/8″ washers.
   b. Four 3/8″ lock washers.
   c. Six 1/2″ washers.
   d. Three 1/2″ lock washers.
   e. Eight 5/16″ lock washers.
   g. Two 1/4″ fender washers.
10. Nuts:
   a. Four 3/8″ nuts.
   b. Six 1/2″ nuts.
   c. Eight 5/16″ nuts.
   d. Two 5/16″ wing nuts.
   e. Two 1/4″ wing nuts.
11. Pieces of 5/16″ threaded rod:
   a. Two 2″ lengths.
   b. Two 1 1/2″ lengths.
12. Three 4 1/2″ pieces of 1/2″ pipe.
13. One-half lb. 10D common nails.
14. Four heavy-duty, hard-wheel swivel casters.

Parts and Materials for the Hoist

Item No.

15. A boat winch (type used on boat trailers) with matching mounting bolts.
16. Three heavy-duty pulleys (either boat hardware or garage-door cable pulleys will do) with mounting hardware.

17. A piece of 3/8″ diameter nylon rope (rated for at least 1,500 lbs.) as long as required for your installation facilities.
18. A piece of 3/16″diameter steel cable, 40″ long, with two matching cable clamps.
19. Two 1/4″ S hooks.

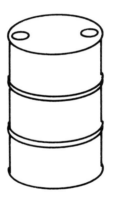

1

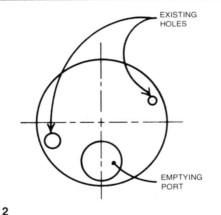

2

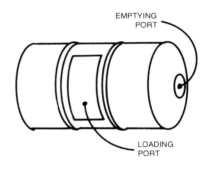

3

Cutting the Loading and Emptying Ports. Position the drum (item 1) so that the end with the threaded holes provided for filling and emptying is up. The holes should be tightly closed with screw-in plugs.

Draw a circle 8″ in diameter, whose center is 5 1/2″ from the edge of the drum. The location of this hole in relation to the existing plugs must be as shown in the drawing. Now cut out the hole, using a torch or saber saw. This is the emptying port.

Important: if you have never used a metal-cutting torch, you may want to have this job done by a professional welder. The job can also be done with a saber saw equipped with a metal-cutting blade if starting holes are drilled for each of the cutouts. If you use a saber saw, you may not be able to follow the guideline near the edge of the drum because the saw's base plate will hit the rim. The resulting undersized emptying port will still be adequate.

Next, turn the drum on its side and draw a rectangle 7″ wide by 15″ long. Locate this rectangle on the side of the drum opposite the emptying port, as indicated in the drawing. Center the rectangle between the drum's reinforcing ribs. Cut out this rectangular hole. This is the loading port.

4

5

Drilling. The next step is to drill the holes required in the parts that will later be attached to the drum. First locate and mark with a pencil the positions of the four holes shown in the drawing of the 9″ × 22″ sheet metal

cover (item 2), which will serve as the loading port. Center the holes 1″ from the long sides and 1/2″ from the ends. Next mark these hole locations with the center punch. Then drill the four 3/8″ holes in the sheet metal cover.

Locate, center punch, and drill two 3/8″ holes in the 12″ long strap iron (item 3) that will be used to clamp the plywood cover over the emptying port.

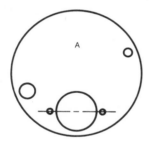

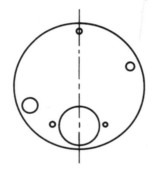

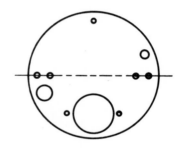

6

7

8

Now stand the drum on end with the emptying port up. All holes required in this end should be located, center punched, and drilled. This end of the drum is labeled A in the drawings. Use the strap-iron cover clamp you have just finished drilling as a template to mark the two holes, as shown in the drawing. Locate the two holes so that they are evenly spaced on each side of the emptying port. Center punch and then drill the two 5/16" holes.

Next, on the same end of the drum, 1 1/2" from the edge opposite the emptying port, mark and center punch the position for one hole, as shown in the drawing. Drill a 1/2" hole for one of the drum-turning handles.

Now locate and mark two pairs of holes on opposite sides of the drum-head, arranged as in the drawing. The outer hole of each pair should be 3" from the edge of the drum. The holes in each pair are 2" apart. Center punch and drill the four 5/16" holes. These holes are for bolting the 2 × 4 mixing vanes (item 4a) to the drum head.

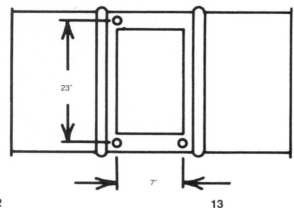

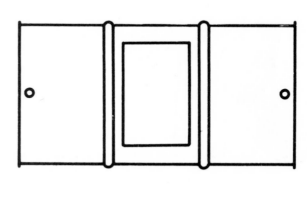

12

13

Locate and drill two 3/8" holes 7" apart and 23" from the 5/16" hole at the other end of the loading port in the position shown.

Next locate and mark two holes about 1 1/2" from the ends of the drum, as shown in the drawing. Center punch and drill the two 3/8" holes. These are for the eyebolts which will be used for hoisting the mixer to empty it.

Before beginning the assembly of the dry mixer, file or sand all edges of the loading and emptying ports to

remove burrs. This step is necessary for safety reasons and to assure tight seals at all ports. Then cement the foam-rubber seals (item 5) to one side of the loading port cover (item 2) and the emptying port cover (item 7) respectively, using contact cement (item 6).

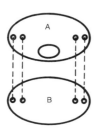

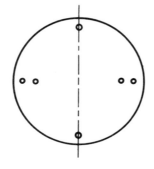

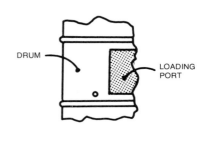

9

Use 2 × 4s as straightedges to help locate the four holes which will be required in the opposite end (labeled B) of the drum (see drawing). The position of these holes should be located as closely as possible to the four matching holes in drumhead A. Center punch and drill the four 5/16" holes.

10

In drumhead B, mark, center punch, and drill two 1/2" holes 1 1/2" from the edge of the drum, arranged as in the drawing. These are for the remaining two turning handles.

11

Turn the drum on its side with the loading port up. Mark the location for a hole, as indicated in the drawing. The hole is in line with the long edge of the loading port and 2 1/2" from its end. It is for one of the threaded-rod studs which will hold one end of the loading port cover in place. Center punch and drill a 5/16" hole.

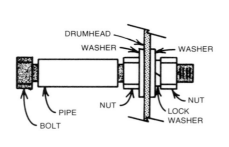

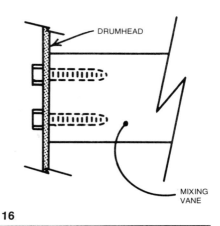

14

Drum Assembly. For hoisting the mixer, install the eyebolts, washers, lock washers, and nuts (items 8a, 9a, 9b, 10a) in the holes near the ends of the side of the drum, as shown in the drawing.

15

For turning the mixer, install the bolts, 1/2" pipe, washers, lock washers, and nuts (items 8b, 12, 9c, 9d, 10b), as shown in the drawing. The first nut you put on the bolt should be as tight as possible without being too tight to keep the piece of pipe from turning freely on the bolt.

16

For mixing, bolt the 2 × 4 mixing vanes (items 4a, 8c) to the drumheads, as shown in the drawing. The best way to install these mixing vanes is as follows.

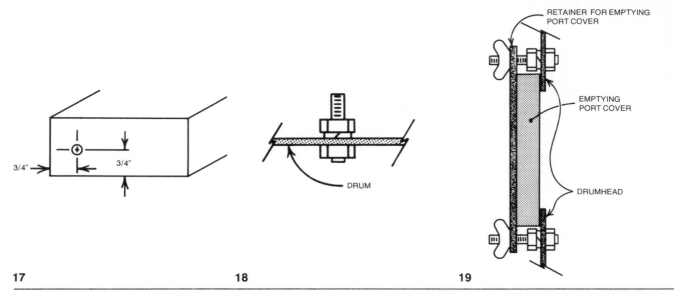

17

Mark and drill one 3/16″ lead hole in each end of the four ends of the 2 × 4s, as shown in the drawing. Now bolt the 2 × 4s in place. Next, drill the second lead hole in each end of the 2 × 4s through the mounting holes you previously drilled in the drumheads. Install the other four lag bolts.

18

To install the cover on the emptying port, insert the 5/16″ × 2″ threaded-rod studs (item 11a) into the previously drilled holes and secure them with washers, lock washers, and nuts (items 9e, 9f, 10c), as shown in the drawing.

19

Now center the plywood cover (item 7) over the emptying port and fasten it in place with the strap-iron clamp and 5/16″ wing nuts (items 3, 10d), as shown.

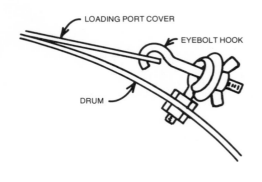

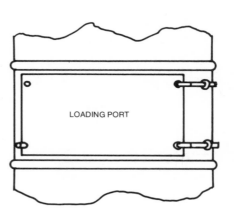

23

Then slip the threaded ends of the eyebolts through the holes of the eyebolts already installed near the end of the loading port. Install the fender washers and wing nuts (items 9g, 10e).

24

To attach the loading port cover, position it so that you can fit one of the drilled holes in one end over the threaded-rod stud (it should not be necessary to use a nut to hold the cover in place on the threaded-rod stud), and insert the eyebolt hooks in the holes in the other end of the cover as shown. Tighten the wing nuts un-

til the cover is pressing tightly against the drum. Center punch through the remaining hole in the cover. Remove the cover and drill the 5/16″ hole for the remaining 1 1/2″ threaded-rod stud (item 11b). Install this threaded-rod stud as you did the first. Reinstall the cover.

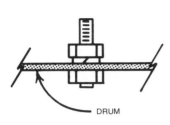

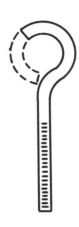

20

Before beginning to install the cover on the loading port, position the drum on its side so that the end with the emptying port is on your right; first install a 5/16″ × 1 1/2″ threaded-rod stud, washer, lock washer, and nuts (items 11b, 9e, 9f, 10c) in the hole above the loading port, as shown in the drawing.

21

Install two 3/8″ eyebolts, washers, lock washers, and nuts (items 8a, 9a, 9b, 10a) in the two holes at the other end of the loading port, as shown in the drawing.

22

Before installing the 1/4″ × 4″ eyebolts (item 8d), it will be necessary to hacksaw out a portion of the ring section of each bolt, as shown.

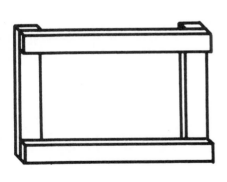

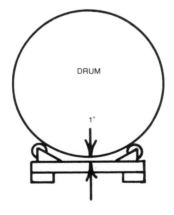

25

Base for Dry Mixer. To make the frame for the base on which the dry mixer will rotate, nail (item 13) together four 2 × 4s (item 4b, 4c), as shown in the drawing. Position the casters (item 14) at each corner of the frame and nail them temporarily into position.

26

Place the dry mixer on the casters and adjust the position of the casters until the mixer clears the frame by about 1″ when turned. Mark the locations for the caster bolts (item 8e), two bolts should be sufficient to hold each caster, and drill lead holes. Install the casters with the lag bolts.

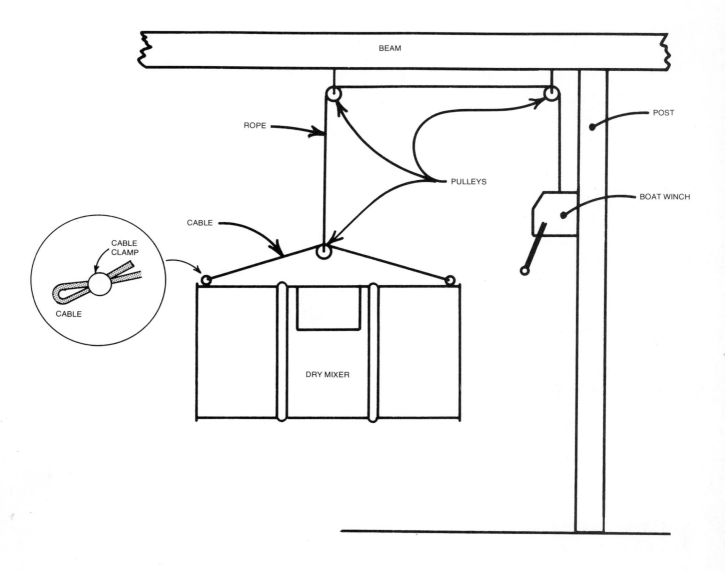

27

Hoist for Dry Mixer. The dry mixer can weigh well over 300 pounds when loaded, so it is necessary to have a means of hoisting it for emptying. The hoisting arrangement shown in the drawing should prove adequate for lifting both the mixer and other heavy objects around the workshop. Be sure, however, that the beams, rafter, and flooring in the workshop area where the pulleys and winch (items 15, 16) are to be mounted can withstand the maximum load expected. It is equally important that the mounting hardware (item 16) used for attaching the pulleys and winch is strong enough to handle the load.

Make a loop in each end of the cable (item 18), as shown above, and attach the cable to the hoisting loops with S hooks (item 19).

The cable passes through the pulley (item 16) on the end of the rope (item 17) so the mixer can tilt to pour the mixed clay out of the emptying port, as shown at right.

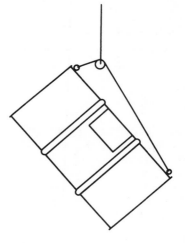

WET CLAY MIXER

When the ingredients for a clay body have been mixed in the dry mixer, the process of adding water is a relatively simple one. The equipment recommended here is correspondingly simple, inexpensive, and readily available. You can choose from a 26 gallon galvanized steel garbage can, a 30 gallon steel drum of the type which comes with a corrosion-resistant interior coating, and a 30 gallon wooden barrel, of the type made to hold liquids.

The easiest choice, of course, is the garbage can, because it will probably be the most readily available.

The coated drum is a good choice, if available, so long as no sharp tools which might harm the protective finish are used.

The wooden barrel, of course, will never rust. On the other hand, it will have to be kept wet even when not in use, in order to prevent the wooden staves from drying out and opening up, permitting leaks to develop. When the barrel is not in use, keep a few inches of water in it and slip a large plastic bag over it to retain the moisture.

How to Use the Dry Clay Mixer and the Wet Clay Mixer

Pour all dry ingredients for the clay being prepared (as much as 230 pounds) into the loading port in the side of the dry mixer.

Install the cover on the loading port, making sure it is securely fastened. Check the emptying port cover to make sure it is also in place and tightly closed.

Use the turning handles (preferably with the help of an assistant), to rotate the dry mixer on its base about 20 times.

Fill the wet mixer about one-third full with water. Attach the hoist and lift the dry mixer, using the winch, until the emptying port cover is positioned directly over the wet mixer.

Remove the emptying port cover and pour the mixed clay into the wet mixer (one 27 gallon garbage can should hold one dry-mixer load). Stir the clay for five or 10 minutes with a 4' long 1 1/2" square oak stick, a shovel handle, or a length of 1" pipe. If necessary, add water at this point. Only enough water should be used to make the clay thin enough to stir. Excess water will only prolong the time required to dry the clay.

Then allow the clay to sit for at least 12 hours to allow the water to thoroughly soak through. Put the wet clay in the drying boxes in the hottest, dryest place available, and allow it to dry to a wedgeable consistency.

CLAY DRYING BOXES AND STORAGE RACK

As explained earlier, the large bench-type plaster bat widely used for drying clay is not recommended by the authors. Instead, you are urged to make the clay-drying boxes described below. They require substantially less time and are less expensive to build than a plaster bat. Each box, as specified below, will hold from 75 to 100 pounds, or about as much as one or two people can carry. Four of these boxes fit into a storage rack which can be constructed from 2 × 4s.

Tools

1. Hammer.
2. Wood-cutting saw.
3. Drill with masonry bit and screwdriver, if you have a concrete floor.

Parts and Materials for Four Boxes

Item No.

1. Pieces of 2 × 4 lumber:
   a. Eight 28″ lengths.
   b. Eight 19″ lengths.
2. Pieces of 1 × 2 lumber:
   a. Eight 28″ lengths.
   b. Eight 19″ lengths.
3. Nails:
   a. One-half lb. 16D nails.
   b. One-half lb. 6D nails.
4. Four 20 1/2″ × 28″ pieces of aluminum window screening.
5. Staple gun with staples at least 5/16″ long.
6. Four 20 1/2″ × 28″ pieces of galvanized hardware cloth (1″ × 1″ mesh).
7. Electrical staples, of the type used to fasten electrical cable to a structural framework, at least 1″ long.

Parts and Materials for the Drying Rack

Item No.

8. Pieces of 2 × 4 lumber:
   a. Four lengths to reach from floor to ceiling.
   b. Eleven 23″ lengths.
9. One-half lb. 8D nails.
10. Four shields with 2 1/2″ screws to fit, if you are installing the rack on a concrete floor.

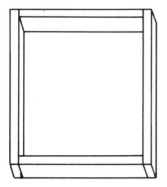

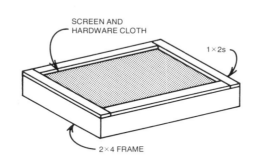

SCREEN AND
HARDWARE CLOTH

1×2s

2×4 FRAME

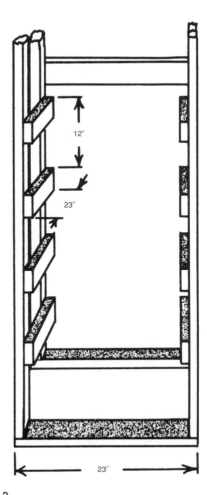

12"

23"

23"

1

Assembling the Clay Boxes. Nail the
2 × 4s (item 1) together with 16D
nails (item 3a), as shown in the
drawing, to form four boxes.

2

Stretch one piece of window screening (item 4) over each box and staple
it in place with the staple gun (item 5).

Stretch one piece of hardware cloth
(item 6) over each box, directly on
top of the window screening. Fasten
it in place with the electrical staples
(item 7). The function of the hardware
cloth is to support the weight of the
clay. The function of the aluminum
screening is to keep the hardware
cloth from cutting into the clay. Nail
(item 3b) the 1 × 2s (item 2) directly
over the hardware cloth to form
smooth surfaces on the bottom of the
boxes so they will slide easily into the
racks.

3

Building the Drying Rack. Build the
frame as shown in the drawing. Nail
the top ends of the vertical 2 × 4s to
the ceiling joists. If you have a wood
floor, nail the bottom 2 × 4s directly
into the floor. For a concrete floor,
drill holes in the floor to accept plastic shields and screw the bottom
2 × 4s into the shields.

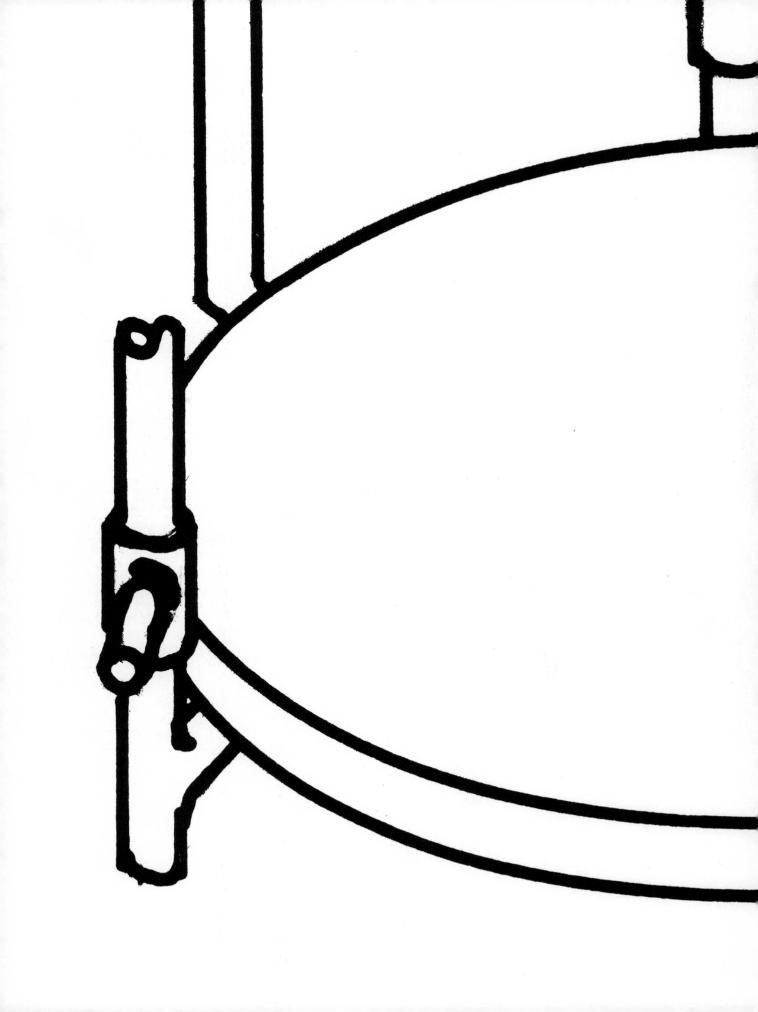

There are many varieties of ready-made potter's wheels on the market. Many of them offer distinct advantages, but few, if any, are without certain disadvantages that limit their usefulness. The plans and instructions for potter's wheels provided in this section attempt to combine those features that have proved the most desirable, while eliminating or minimizing limitations.

Perhaps the most important aspect of these plans is that they should make it possible for any potter generally skillful at using hand tools for wood and metalworking to construct a wheel for considerably less money than it would cost to buy comparable ready-made equipment. This should be true even if the more difficult parts of the construction job, such as welding, must be done by a professional.

If the plans and instructions are followed carefully, the potter should have not only a less expensive wheel, but also one that is as good or better than those commercially available.

Kickwheels and Treadle Wheels

Only two varieties of the oldest types of wheel are in general use—the kickwheel and the treadle wheel. These wheels share certain advantages and disadvantages. Both are relatively simple in design and easy to build. They are often said to provide the greatest intimacy with the clay itself and with the process of turning a mass of clay into a finished form. Also, of course, they avoid the problem of supplying a motor to drive them. Among the disadvantages of these wheels are their greater weight and size, which make them practically non-portable. Also the potter must exert energy just to operate the wheel, and therefore production rates are likely to be lower than with an electrically powered wheel. Plans for the kickwheel are given in this book, since it is more popular than the treadle wheel and because it is easier to build. Also, it can be motorized later, if desired.

Electrically Powered Wheels

There are three categories of powered wheels; the principal difference among them is the method used to control the speed of rotation. The simplest type is the motorized kick-

Welded frame wheel, without pan, similar to the one for which plans are provided.

Completed pipe frame wheel similar to the one for which plans are provided (the back of the pan is not slanted in the instructions).

wheel, for which plans are given in this part. Besides being easy to construct, this wheel also provides an exceptionally wide range of speed and plenty of power. It is also durable and comfortable to use.

Either the welded frame or the pipe-frame wheel can be built for use as a motorized kickwheel. Whereas the welded frame is stronger and more rigid, the pipe frame is easier to build and can be taken apart for moving or shipping, if necessary. Both frames provide durable, high-performance wheels.

The second category of powered wheels uses mechanical means to vary speed. Such wheels are generally too complicated for the potter to build himself, since they often require special parts that cannot be purchased ready made. Wheels of this type are light in weight and small in size. Disadvantages vary from one make to another. Most often, the available speed range is too narrow (20 to 180 r.p.m., the minimum desirable range). Adjustment of mechanical parts is frequently necessary, and there is sometimes a lack of steady sustained power because of slippage in the drive systems. Furthermore, speed controls are sometimes awkward to use.

A third kind of electrical wheel varies speed by altering the speed of the motor. Of these, the oldest and most widely used type is based on a two-speed motor; the problem here is that the slowest operating speed always seems to be too fast and the top speed too slow. In other words, again, the available speed range is too narrow.

The DC-Powered Wheel

Another type of wheel that varies rotation speed by altering motor speed uses a permanent magnet DC motor. This kind of motor speed control is the best. A good DC motor provides smooth speed variation from near zero to maximum; it also provides plenty of torque (turning power), even at low speeds. DC-motor-driven wheels can be small and light-weight while still possessing plenty of power. Their basic construction is relatively simple, and adjustments are seldom necessary.

The principal disadvantage of this wheel is the cost of the motor and related components. Still, the DC-powered wheel for which plans are given here can be built for half to two-thirds the cost of a ready-built one; or, about twice the cost of a motorized kickwheel. Also, the adjustable seat and the large pan suggested for all the wheels in this book are not available on any commercial DC-powered models at the present time.

Not only is the pan presented here larger, it is also unbreakable. In addition its side walls are high enough to prevent clay and water from spattering the potter or the area around the wheel. The built-in leakproof tube that surrounds the drive shaft prevents water and abrasive clay from running down the shaft into the bearings. This pan should hold at least two gallons of clay and water before it has to be emptied.

Although the bench-type seat suggested for all the wheels in this book is simple in design, it should provide a sufficiently large and comfortable support. Because a potter at work sits only on the front edge of the seat, the tractor seat used on many wheels is not really necessary. However, if you prefer that type of seat, it can be adapted for use on the wheels described in this book. More important is the fact that all the wheel designs

presented here allow whatever type of seat is used to be adjusted, up and down and forward and backward. Some parts of these wheels, such as the seat, are a matter of personal preference, while other features that must be built and installed for safety reasons are mandatory. For example, the drive belt enclosure intended for the DC-powered wheel must be made up and attached properly to avoid the possibility of clothing, hair, or fingers (particularly those of little children) getting caught in the belt and pulleys. The drive-belt guard also serves to protect the belts from most of the water and clay that would otherwise drip down onto them, shortening their service life.

Proper safety precautions must also be taken when installing all electrical components. Consult a qualified electrician if you are not sure of proper electrical installation procedures.

Square steel tubing is used on several wheels in this book mainly because it is easy to cut so that joints fit properly. While more expensive than pipe, the greater ease of forming and welding square tubing makes it well worth the difference in cost. To some potters, the more attractive appearance of the square tubing is reason enough for the added expense.

DC-powered wheel.

WELDED FRAME WHEEL

Even if you do not know how to handle welding equipment, you may still want to build this kind of frame if you feel competent to handle the job of laying out and cutting notches in steel tubing and bending the tubing into shape. These tasks must be done with exactness, following carefully the instructions and measurements provided. If you can do a workmanlike job of making the parts of the frame, the costs of having them welded together should not be too high. Considering the prices asked for wheels with this type of frame today, it may even pay to have a welder do the entire job of cutting, bending, and welding. Some welders would probably prefer to do the job from scratch; so, before doing any cutting, check with the welder you have in mind.

When you shop for the square steel tubing recommended for the frame, you may be surprised at the high cost. This kind of tubing, however, provides a particularly sturdy structure; it is also easier to form and weld than round tubing. Moreover, square tubing makes a better-looking frame. This welded frame, if well made, will be in every way as good as any on the market.

Tools

1. Two straight 10' long boards, 4" or 5" wide.
2. Measuring tape or folding rule.
3. Pencil.
4. A 45° triangle.
5. Hacksaw or cutting torch.
6. Drill with assorted metal-cutting bits, up to 3/8".
7. C clamps (at least two which must open at least 4").
8. Flat steel bar about 1/8" × 1" × 12".
9. Carpenter's framing square.
10. Welding equipment (unless welding is to be done by a professional welder).
11. A 3/8"–16 threading tap with handle.
12. Spirit level.
13. Center punch.
14. Hammer.
15. Two wrenches to fit 3/8" hex-head bolts.
16. Pliers (2 pairs).
17. Paint brush (if you are going to paint the wheel).

Parts and Materials

Item No.

1. Pieces of 2" × 2" × 1/8" square steel tubing:
   a. One 86" length.
   b. One 107" length.
   c. One 11" length.
2. Bolts:
   a. One 3/8"–16 × 2".
   b. Two 3/8" × 1" hexhead with nuts.
   c. Two 3/8" × 3" with nuts.
3. One 1/4" wing nut.
4. Steel rod :
   a. One 3/8" × 2".
   b. One 3/16" × 34 1/2".
   c. One 3/16" × 7".
5. Threaded steel rod:
   a. One 1/4" × 4 1/2".
   b. One 1/4" × 1".
6. Black pipe:
   a. Two 6" lengths of 1/2" (only one for a motorized wheel).
   b. One 1" length of 1/4".
7. Cast-iron, ball-bearing, self-aligning, pillow blocks:
   a. One 1" rigid mount.
   b. One 1" flange mount (two mounting holes).
8. One 30" length of cold-rolled steel shaft (both ends should be saw cut).
9. Flywheel, seat, and pan assemblies (see instructions later in this part).
10. A pint of rust-inhibiting paint (optional).

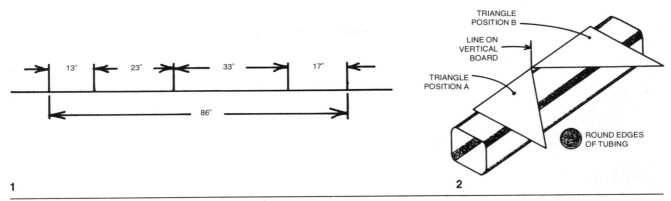

1

2

Laying Out the Tubing for Cutting. It is necessary to cut V-shaped notches in the square steel tubing in order to bend it and weld it into the shapes required. Two methods for measuring and laying out these notches will be given. The cutting must be done carefully and accurately. If the notching is not exact, it will be difficult, or even impossible, to achieve a good fit when welding the frame parts together. To make the measurements for the first method (which is more difficult but can be used for any size

tubing), you will need a long, horizontal, level surface that meets a flat, vertical surface. Two 10′ boards nailed together at right angles will work very well.

Begin by marking on the vertical board the points at which the cuts are to be made in the tubing. The spacing must be as shown in the drawing. Lay the tubing (item 1a) on the boards with one end at the first mark.

Now lay a 45° triangle, flat, on the top surface of the tubing in position A, so that one of its short sides is flush against the vertical board, with the point of the narrow angle at one of the marks you made on the vertical board, as in the drawing. Along the slanted side of the triangle draw a line across the tubing. This marks one side of the V notch.

Now, reverse the triangle so that it is in position B. Again, following the slanted side, draw a line across the tubing. This marks the other side of the V.

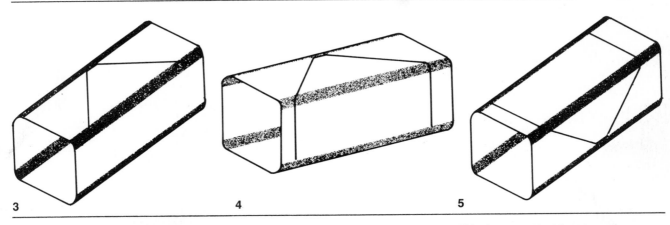

3

4

5

Next, connect the two lines with a third line near the back edge of the top surface of the tubing at the point where the curve forming the rounded corner begins. You will now have drawn a flat-bottom V on the tubing, as indicated in the drawing.

Repeat this process all along the tubing at each of the points you have marked on the board.

Then rest the triangle on the horizontal board so that it stands upright against the tubing. Along its straight side, draw vertical lines, extending the tops of the V's onto the vertical face of the tubing, as shown.

Next, rotate the tube, a one-quarter turn backward, so that the V-shaped mark is against the vertical board and the straight lines extending the V are on the top horizontal surface. You are now going to continue the lines to make another flat-bottom V on the vertical surface.

This time, rest the triangle on the horizontal board upright against the tubing. Then draw the lines for this V just as you did for the first one. Again, repeat this marking procedure at each of the points at which notches are to be cut in the tubing.

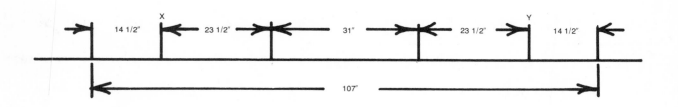

6

Next, lay out and mark the 107″ length of tubing (item 1b) in the same way.

Note: lay out the V's at points X and Y on the 107″ tubing so that these notches can be cut slightly wider than the others.

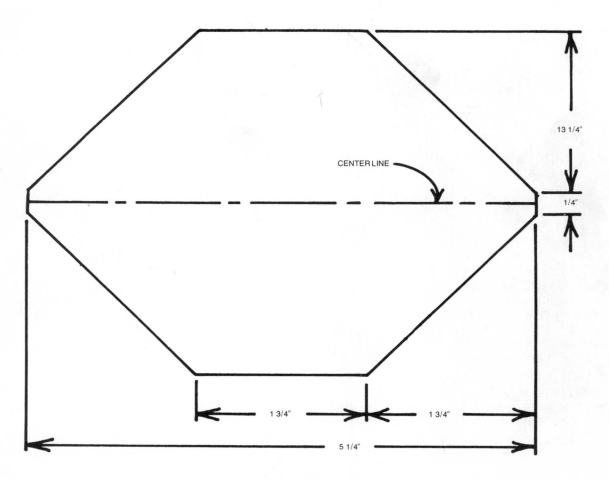

TEMPLATE SHOWN ACTUAL SIZE

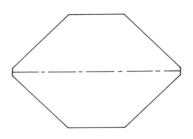

7

8

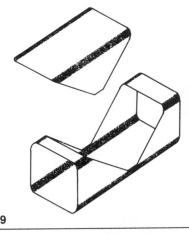

9

The second method for laying out the notches (which can be used for 2″ square tubing only) is to use a template. Make the measurements for the notches directly on the square tubing (see drawings 1 and 6). Make the template from heavy paper and tape it perpendicular to the tubing so the center line is on the mark. Trace around the template. Remove the template and cut out the area inside the lines.

Cutting the Notches. The notches can be cut in the tubing with either a hacksaw or a metal-cutting torch. If you use a hacksaw, it will not be possible to make the cuts across the bottoms of the V's. Instead, make these cuts by drilling enough interconnected small holes (about 3/16″ diameter) across the bottom of each V to permit separating these cutouts from the tubing, as shown.

All the notches must be cut wide enough to remove the guidelines. This will leave narrow gaps between the edges of the metal after bending (see drawing 10). These gaps make welding easier and provide stronger joints.

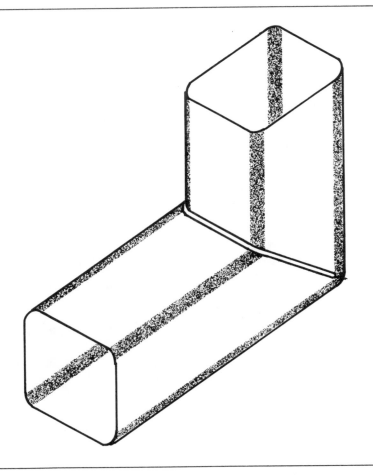

10

Bending the tubing. The next step is to bend the tubing into the required shapes. Begin with the smaller, 86″ length of tubing. Position the tubing flat on the workbench surface (or floor) with the cuts facing you. Bend each notched area until the tubing forms a 90° angle, making sure to keep the tubing on both sides of the bend flat on the work surface. If the tubing is not kept flat, it is likely to twist or otherwise deform at the bends. After each bend is completed, there should be a narrow gap between the two sides of the cutout, as shown in the drawing.

Repeat this bending procedure at each notch. When the bending is finished, the shape of the 86″ long tubing should be the same as the one with dimension A in drawing 12. This completes the first of the two major sections of the frame.

Before you begin bending the longer, 107″ tubing, note that the angles at points X and Y are to be a little less than 90°. This is why you were instructed to lay out these cuts so that they would be a little wider than the others. Use the same method for bending the longer tubing as you did for the 86″ length.

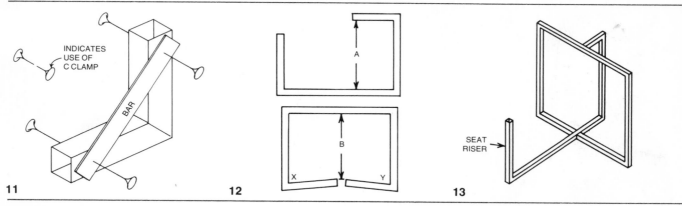

11

12

13

Welding the Frame. It is best to weld all the 90° bends first. Before welding, C clamp a steel bar across each joint to act as a brace. Check each joint with a carpenter's square before welding to be sure it is square (90°).

Before welding the bends at X and Y, check again to make sure that dimensions A and B are equal. Clamp these bends, also, before welding.

Now weld together the two parts of the frame, as shown in the drawing.

Locate the top (pillow block) bearing (item 7a) so that it is centered on the 11″ mount tubing, as in the drawing. The top surface of the bearing must not be higher than the top surface of the frame. With the bearing in position, mark the location of the center of the bearing mounting holes on the frame. Center punch and drill two 3/8″ holes at the marks. Bolt the bearing in place with the two 3/8″ hex head bolts (item 2b).

To determine the proper position for the bottom bearing (item 7b), slide the shaft (item 8) through the top bearing and slip the bottom bearing onto the lower end. Put the wheelhead (see *Wheelhead* plans) on the top end of the shaft, as shown. With the frame positioned on a level surface, move the bottom bearing around on the bottom frame member until the wheelhead is level in all directions. (Use a carpenter's spirit level to determine this.)

Mark the proper location for the mounting holes for the bottom bearing with a center punch. Remove the shaft and drill the holes all the way through the bottom frame member. Bolt the bottom bearing in place with 3/8″ × 3″ bolts (item 2c), as shown. Insert the bolts from under the frame.

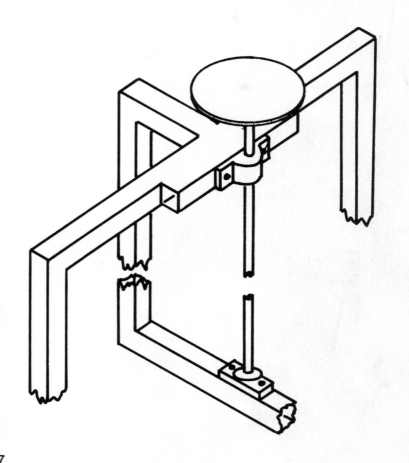

17

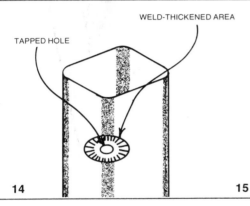

TAPPED HOLE

WELD-THICKENED AREA

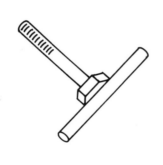

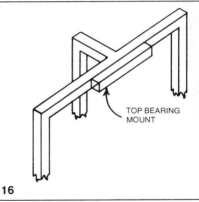

TOP BEARING MOUNT

14

15

16

Preparing the Seat Riser. In order to make the seat riser, indicated in the drawing, strong enough to support the seat assembly and the weight of the potter, it is necessary to increase the thickness of one of its rear corners. This is accomplished by adding weld metal about 2″ from the top of the riser, as shown. The built-up area should be flat and about 3/4″ in diameter. Drill a 5/16″ hole through the built-up area and thread the hole with a 3/8″–16 tapping tool.

To make the seat-support bolt that will be used to adjust the height of the seat, weld the 3/8″ × 2″ bolt (item 2a) to the piece of 2″ steel rod (item 4a), as shown. This will make a tee-handled bolt that can be screwed into the threaded hole you have already made in the seat riser.

Slide the free end of the 1 1/4″ pipe of the seat support into the seat riser and tighten the tee-handled bolt at any position desired (see *Seat* plans).

Installing the Top and Bottom Bearings. The 11″ long piece of 2″ square tubing (item 1c) provides a mounting surface for the top bearing. It must be welded to the side of the long horizontal frame member in the position shown. Be sure that the center line of the 11″ tubing is lined up exactly with the center line of the short horizontal frame member. Clamp the tubing securely in position and weld it to the frame. You can now paint the frame, if you wish, with a rust-inhibiting paint (item 10).

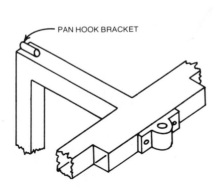

PAN HOOK BRACKET

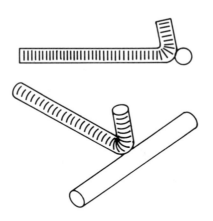

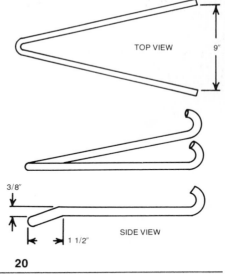

TOP VIEW

9″

3/8″

SIDE VIEW

1 1/2″

18

19

20

Making and Attaching the Pan-Mounting Hardware. First weld the 1″ length of 1/4″ pipe (item 6b) to the top of the front frame member, locating it as shown. This is the anchor for the hook that holds the pan bracket in place.

Bend the end of the 4 1/2″ length of 1/4″ threaded rod (item 5a) to form a hook, as shown (see the *Appendix* for instructions on bending steel rod). Next, weld the 1″ long piece of 1/4″ steel rod (item 5b) onto the hook, as shown.

Install the hook by slipping the straight end through the pan-hook bracket previously welded to the top frame member. Install a 1/4″ wing nut (item 3) on the straight end of the hook at the front of the frame.

Make the bracket that holds the pan in place by bending the 34 1/2″ length of 3/16″ steel rod (item 4b) in the sequence shown in the drawing. The bends can be made by using two pairs of pliers.

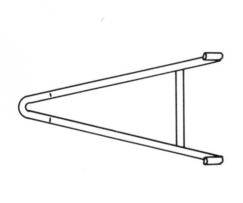

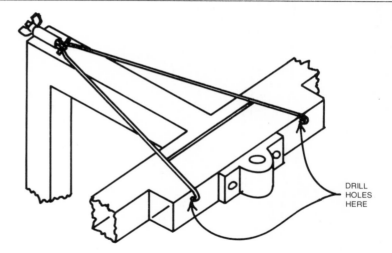

DRILL HOLES HERE

21

22

Now to reinforce the bracket, weld the 7″ length of 3/16″ steel rod (item 4c) in the position shown, linking the two sides of the V. The bracket is now completed.

Next, locate two 1/4″ holes in the square tube on which the top bearing is mounted by putting the pan-mounting bracket, just finished, in place and marking the location of the hooked ends, as shown. Center punch and drill these holes.

Now fit the hooks formed on the ends of the rod snugly into the holes in the tube just drilled at each side of the top bearing. Hook the other end of the bracket assembly onto the curved end of the pan-mounting hook that is already installed at the front of the frame. Tighten the wing nut until the entire assembly is securely seated on the frame except for the bent-up part that attaches to

the tightening hook. One or another of the parts may have to be bent slightly to achieve a tight fit.

Install the flywheel, seat, and pan (item 9) following the plans and instructions later in this section. These plans are presented separately because they apply to more than one wheel in this book.

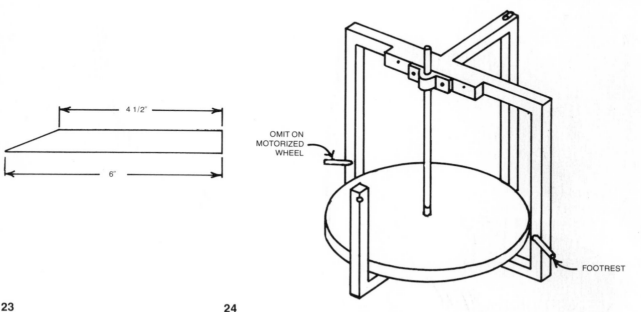

4 1/2″

6″

OMIT ON MOTORIZED WHEEL

FOOTREST

23

24

Installing the Footrests. Cut two pieces of 1/2″ pipe (item 6a), as shown (the motorized wheel requires only one).

Weld the footrests to the frame about 2″ above the top surface of the flywheel, in the position shown.

MOTOR LINKAGE FOR THE WELDED FRAME WHEEL

The welded frame wheel is made to turn by a rubber drive wheel powered by an electric motor hung on the frame. When the foot pedal controlling the position of the motor is depressed far enough to bring the rubber wheel into contact with the flywheel, the motor drives the flywheel, shaft, and wheelhead. The speed of turning and the amount of turning power (torque) imparted to the wheel by the motor depend on how long the two wheels are engaged and on how much pressure is applied. Light pressure allows slippage between the rubber wheel and the flywheel; but, as more pressure is applied, slippage is decreased, and both speed and power are steadily increased. When all pressure is removed, inertia will cause the flywheel to continue turning for a time.

The motor is mounted so that its weight will automatically keep it disengaged from the flywheel so long as no pressure is applied to the foot pedal. When the foot pedal is depressed the two wheels are brought into contact and the flywheel begins to turn. The simple motor mount described below eliminates springs and switches (except for a single on-off motor switch) found on some wheels with this type of drive.

It is important to note that for the rubber wheel to drive the flywheel efficiently and with minimum wear, a flat metal ring is required on the flywheel (see *Flywheels* for information on this ring). This is true whether this wheel is being converted from use as a kickwheel or is being built as a motorized wheel from scratch. The thickness and weight of the flywheel to be used depend on whether or not the wheel is to be motorized (see *Flywheels*).

Tools

1. Tape measure or folding rule.
2. Center punch.
3. Welding and cutting equipment.
4. Hacksaw.
5. Drill with 1/2″, 3/8″, 5/16″, 1/4″ metal drilling bits.
6. Adjustable wrench.
7. Allen wrench to fit set screw in rubber drive wheel.
8. Miscellaneous wood blocks.
9. Screwdriver.
10. Knife.

Parts and Materials

Item No.

1. One 9″ length of 1″ × 1″ × 1/8″ angle iron.
2. Steel:
   a. One 1″ × 1/2″ × 1/8″ piece.
   b. One 1″ × 3″ × 1/4″ piece.
3. Steel rod:
   a. One 3 1/2″ length of 3/8″ rod.
   b. One 2″ length of 1/2″ threaded rod.
   c. Two 1″ lengths of 5/16″ threaded rod.
   d. One 2 1/2″ length of 1/4″ threaded rod.
4. Black pipe:
   a. One 7″ length of 1 1/4″ pipe.
   b. One 10″ length of 1″ pipe.
   c. One 6″ length of 1″ pipe.
   d. One 7″ length of 1/2″ pipe.
5. Bolts:
   a. One 1/2″ × 8″.
   b. One 5/16″ × 1″.
6. Two 1/4″ machine screws, 3/4″ long.
7. Washers:
   a. Three 5/16″.
   b. Three 5/16″ lock washers.
   c. One 1/4″.
8. Nuts:
   a. Three 5/16″.
   b. Three 1/4″.
   c. One 1/2″.
9. One 1/2 horsepower 1750 r.p.m. motor (when facing the shaft, this motor rotates clockwise).
10. One rubber drive wheel, 2″ in diameter, with mounting hole to fit motor (item 9).
11. One single pole toggle switch with housing. The housing replaces the cover on the wiring opening on the motor.
12. One 10′ length of three-wire electrical cord.
13. One three-prong electrical plug.

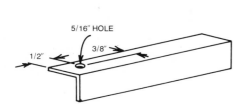

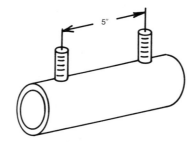

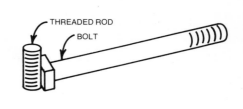

1

Motorizing the Wheel. Many of the parts needed to motorize this wheel must be specially made. Therefore, the best way to start the job is to make these parts first.

Begin by drilling a 5/16" hole in the 9" piece of angle iron (item 1), located as shown in the drawing.

2

Next, weld the two 1" long pieces of 5/16" threaded rod (item 3c) to the 7" piece of 1 1/4" black pipe (item 4a), as shown in the drawing. This will be the motor hanger.

3

Weld the 1/2" × 8" bolt (item 5a) to the 2" length of 1/2" threaded rod (item 3b), as shown.

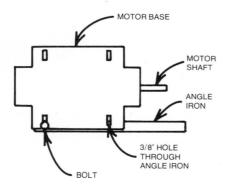

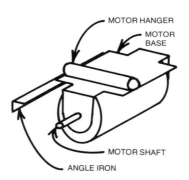

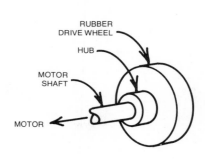

7

Assembly. Start the assembly and installation of the motor-and-drive system by using the 5/16" × 1" bolt, washer, lock washer, and nut (items 5b, 7a, 7b, 8a) to fasten the 9" piece of angle iron (item 1) to the base of the motor (item 9), as shown. Next, using the other slotted hole in the same side of the motor base as a guide, drill a 3/8" hole through the angle iron, as shown.

8

Now join the motor and the motor hanger shown in drawing 2, with washers and nuts (items 7a, 7b, 8a), as shown.

9

Next install the rubber drive wheel (item 10) on the motor shaft. The shaft should go all the way into the mounting hole on the rubber drive wheel until the end of the shaft is flush with the other side of the wheel, as shown.

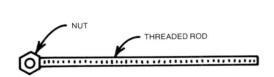

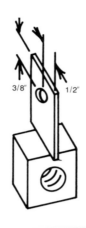

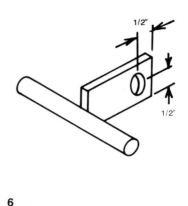

4

Weld the 1/4″ nut (item 8b) to the 2 1/2″ length of 1/4″ threaded rod (item 3d) to make the motor link as shown. A machine screw (item 6) should be in the nut to protect the threads while the weld is made.

5

Drill a 1/4″ hole in the 1″ × 1/2″ × 1/8″ thick piece of steel (item 2a), located as shown. Weld this piece of steel to the 1/2″ nut (item 8c).

6

Finally, for the foot pedal, drill a 1/2″ hole in the 1″ × 3″ × 1/4″ thick piece of steel (item 2b), and weld it to the 3 1/2″ piece of 3/8″ steel rod (item 3a), as shown.

The entire motorizing system is composed of three sub-assemblies: (1) the motor support, which consists of two pieces of black pipe welded to each other and to the wheel frame; (2) the motor and the parts used to connect it to the support; (3) the movable linkage, which connects the motor and foot pedal.

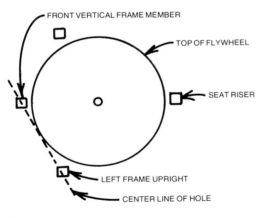

10

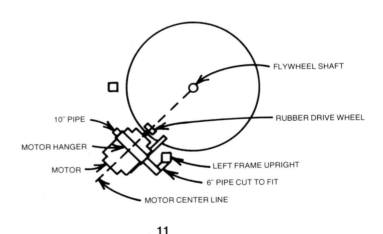

11

Attaching the Motor to the Frame.

First cut a 1″ diameter hole in the left frame upright, indicted in the drawing. Locate the center of the hole in the upright about 1 1/2″ above the top surface of the flywheel. Make sure that the hole lines up with the front upright, as shown in the drawing.

Now use wood blocks, clamps, or any other means of temporarily propping the motor assembly so that its shaft is positioned 5″ away from the left frame upright. The motor shaft should point directly at the flywheel shaft and the rubber drive wheel should rest in the center of the metal drive ring on the flywheel. Be sure that the motor shaft is horizontal.

Now slip the 10″ length of 1″ pipe (item 4b) through the motor-hanger pipe mounted on the motor base. Cut the 6″ pipe (item 4c) to the length necessary to fit between the left frame upright and the 10″ pipe just inserted in the motor hanger, as shown.

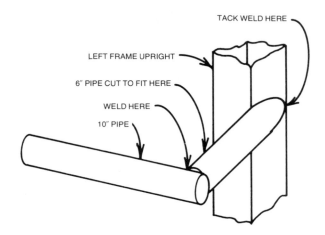

TACK WELD HERE

LEFT FRAME UPRIGHT

6" PIPE CUT TO FIT HERE

WELD HERE

10" PIPE

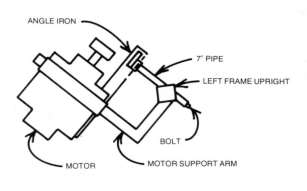

ANGLE IRON

7" PIPE

LEFT FRAME UPRIGHT

BOLT

MOTOR

MOTOR SUPPORT ARM

12

Now weld the two pieces of pipe together in the position shown. This is the motor-support arm.

After checking the position of the motor to make sure it is still in the position specified above, tack weld the 6" pipe to the left frame upright, as shown. Remove the props that have been holding the motor in place. Again check the motor's position. Also make sure that the support arm is parallel with the top surface of the

flywheel. At this point, the motor should be hanging on the support arm so that the rubber drive wheel is slightly above the flywheel surface. The motor should also move freely on the support arm, and the rubber drive wheel should contact the flywheel when the motor is in a horizontal position.

When all these conditions have been satisfied, weld the support arm securely to the frame member.

13

Linking the Foot Pedal to the Motor.
Insert the 8" bolt (item 5a) into the 7" long piece of 1/2" pipe (item 4d). Now put the 1/2" pipe into the hole previously cut in the left frame upright. The threaded rod should be on the motor side of the frame member.

Hold the bolt head tight against the end of the 7" pipe. Position the pipe so that the threaded rod welded to the bolt head is centered directly below the angle iron that is bolted to the motor base, as in the drawing (the motor shaft must point directly at the flywheel shaft). Note that the 1/2" pipe must also be parallel to the surface of the flywheel, and lined up with the front vertical frame member.

Weld the 1/2" pipe to the frame member through which it passes.

Installing the Electrical Switch and Wiring.

The simplest kind of switch (item 11) for this wheel fits in a small housing that replaces the cover on the wiring opening of the motor. Cut a length of black wire about 4" long from the cord (item 12). Peel the insulation off about 1/2" of each end of the wire. Connect one end to one terminal on the switch and the other end to the copper-colored motor terminal.

Peel off about 2" of the outer covering of the three-wire cord (item 12) and 1/2" of the insulation on each wire. Connect the wire with the black insulation to the remaining switch terminal and the white-insulated wire to the silver-colored motor terminal. (*Note to British readers:* see the *Appendix* for information on British color coding.) The green-insulated wire should be connected to a screw that holds the switch cover on the motor. This last connection is of particular importance, because it grounds the wheel's electrical system and helps to minimize shock hazard. You will have to remove some of the cord covering and insulation from each wire in order to connect the plug (item 13). Attach the black wire to the brass-colored screw, the white wire to the silver-colored screw, and the green wire to the hexhead screw.

Important: use only a grounded wiring system to avoid electrical shocks and possible motor damage. Three-hole electrical outlets generally indicate that the system is grounded. If in doubt as to the safety of the system, have it checked by a qualified electrician. It is possible to have a three-hole outlet that has been improperly installed and not grounded; this condition is likely to exist only if the wiring system has been installed by an amateur.

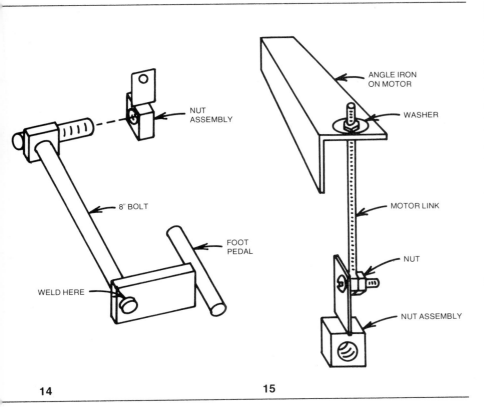

14

15

To join the foot pedal to the motor linkage, begin by putting the threaded end of the 8" bolt into the hole already drilled in the foot pedal. Push the bolt far enough into the hole so that the bolt will no longer be able to slide back and forth in the pipe but will still be able to turn freely. Weld the bolt end to the foot pedal in the position shown.

Now screw the nut assembly shown in drawing 5 onto the threaded rod on the end of the 8" bolt, as shown in the drawing. Position the foot pedal so that the threaded rod welded to the bolt head is parallel to the top surface of the flywheel. Position the motor so that the rubber drive wheel touches the flywheel.

On the top surface of the angle iron bolted to the motor, locate a point directly above the hole in the nut assembly. Drill a 3/8" hole at this point. Use the motor link shown in drawing 4 to connect the foot-pedal assembly to the angle iron bolted to the motor base, as shown in the drawing. First insert a machine screw (item 6) through the hole in the nut assembly, and then turn the machine screw into the nut on the end of the motor link. This joint between the nut assembly and the motor link should be loose enough to permit the parts to move freely. Screw a nut (item 8b) onto the end of the machine screw and tighten it against the nut on the motor link. Next, insert the threaded end of the motor link through the 3/8" hole drilled in the angle iron. Put a washer and a nut (items 8b, 7c) on the end of the motor link.

Sit at the wheel and try the foot pedal. Adjust it to a comfortable pressure position by loosening or tightening the nut on the motor link.

PIPE FRAME WHEEL

This pipe frame design produces an excellent, easy-to-build wheel that requires little welding. The design is especially suitable for the potter who does not know how to weld or who must have a wheel that can be easily disassembled for moving and storing. The pipe frame wheel provides all the performance characteristics of the welded frame wheel, although it is slightly less rigid in use.

Construction is relatively simple, and much of it does not require sophisticated tools or techniques. Cutting pipe to length, for example, is most easily accomplished with a plumber's pipe cutter, but an ordinary hacksaw can do a satisfactory job, if you are willing to invest the time and effort.

Cutting the pipe is the first step in building the pipe frame. All the lengths should be cut to size and any sharp burrs filed off before assembly begins.

The pipe fittings specified are the standard slip-on type often used to make stair railings, storage racks, and other structures. These are held in place by set screws, and they need only an allen wrench to install them. They are easy to remove if you want to disassemble the wheel.

Galvanized pipe is recommended for this frame because it is more resistant to rust in the wet conditions prevailing in most pottery workshops. However, if you plan to paint the frame, use black pipe. Also, if you think you may decide at some future time to weld additional elements to this frame, you should use black pipe because galvanized metal generates poisonous fumes when it is welded.

Parts and Materials

Item No.

1. Pieces of 1 1/4″ galvanized pipe (*Note:* Some hardware stores, plumber's supply stores, or plumbers will cut pipe to length and thread it.):
   a. One 15″ length, threaded on one end.
   b. One 28″ length, threaded on both ends.
   c. One 18″ length, threaded on both ends.
   d. One 13 1/2″ length, threaded on one end.
   e. Two 22″ lengths, not threaded.
   f. Two 25″ lengths, not threaded.
   g. Two 4″ lengths (only one for motorized wheel), not threaded.

2. One 17″ length of 1″ galvanized pipe, threaded on one end.

3. Miscellaneous 1 1/4″ threaded galvanized fittings as follows:
   a. Two tees.
   b. Two close nipples.
   c. One elbow.
   d. One floor flange.

4. Railing fittings, 1 1/4″ (these fittings are not threaded, they are held in place with set screws):
   a. Two elbows.
   b. Two cross-over fittings (see drawing 12).
   c. Five tees.
   d. One collar.
   e. One flange (see drawing 11).

5. Galvanized pipe fittings:
   a. One 1″ × 6″ threaded nipple.
   b. One 1″ threaded elbow.
   c. One 1″ flange railing fitting (see drawing 10).

6. One tube of Loctite or two small tubes (one resin, one hardener) of epoxy cement.

7. One pint lacquer thinner (only if epoxy is used in 6).

8. One 3/8″–16 × 6″ bolt.

9. One 8″ length of 2″ × 2″ × 3/16″ angle iron.

10. Two 1/4″ × 3/4″ machine screws with nuts and lock washers.

11. Three 1 1/2″ no. 14 flat-head wood screws.

12. Hexhead bolts with nuts.
   a. Two 3/8″ × 1″.
   b. Two 3/8″ × 2 1/2″.

13. A 29″ length of 1″ cold-rolled steel shaft.

14. Cast-iron, ball-bearing, self-aligning pillow blocks:
   a. One 1″ rigid mount.
   b. One 1″ flange mount (two mounting holes).

15. Steel rod:
   a. One 5″ length of 1/4″ threaded rod.
   b. One 34 1/2″ length of 3/16″ rod.

16. One 1/4″ wing nut.

17. Flywheel, seat, and pan assemblies (see instructions later in this part).

Tools

1. Pipe cutter (optional, not needed if pipe is cut by supplier).

2. Pipe threader (optional, not needed if pipe is threaded by supplier).

3. Hacksaw.

4. Vise.

5. A pipe wrench (12″ minimum size).

6. Allen wrenches to fit set screws in railing fittings.

7. Tape measure or folding rule.

8. Spirit level.

9. Hammer.

10. Center punch.

11. Power drill with 1/2″, 3/8″, 5/16″, 1/4″, 1/8″ bits.

12. Large and small screwdrivers.

13. Wrench set or two adjustable wrenches.

14. A 6″ length of 3/8″ pipe (a 6″ nipple will do).

15. Two pairs of pliers.

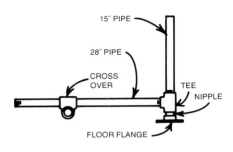

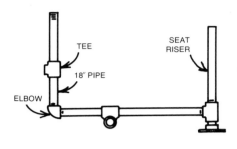

1

2

Frame Assembly. All of the threaded pipe joints in this wheel must be assembled so that they cannot be taken apart. The simplest way to do this is to use a product called Loctite (item 6), applied according to the manufacturer's instructions, on each joint. Another way to lock the joints is to clean the parts in a non-oily solvent, like lacquer thinner (item 7), and then coat the threads with a thin coat of epoxy (item 6), before assembly. Follow up which-

ever of these methods you use by tightening each joint as much as possible with a pipe wrench to provide maximum strength.

Begin assembling the frame by joining five threaded parts (items 1a, 1b, 3a, 3d), as shown in the drawing. Slip a cross-over fitting (item 4b) on the 28″ pipe (item 1b) and tighten the set screws enough to hold it in place until it can be properly located later.

Proceed with the frame assembly by adding the elbow (item 3c) and the 18″ length of pipe (item 1c), as indicated in the drawing. The 18″ pipe should be parallel to the seat riser. If the wheel is to be motorized, or if it is likely to be motorized at some future time, it is necessary to add the tee (item 4c) now. It cannot be added later. Tighten a set screw in the tee enough to hold it in the position shown until it can be properly located.

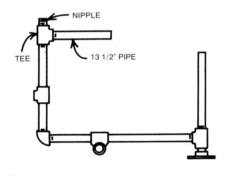

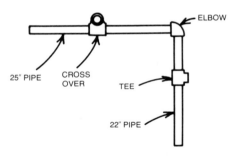

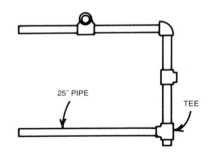

3

4

5

Complete the threaded-pipe assembly by adding another tee, nipple, and 13 1/2″ pipe (items 3a, 3b, 1d), as shown. The 13 1/2″ pipe should be parallel with the 28″ one. The nipple-tee joint does not require Loctite or epoxy.

To make the second section of the frame, slip an elbow (item 4a) on the piece of 22″ pipe (item 1e) as far as possible and tighten the set screw. Put an end of one of the 25″ pipes (item 1f) into the open end of the elbow and tighten the set screw. Slip a tee (item 4c) onto the 22″ pipe and tighten enough to keep it in place until it can be properly located later. Slip a cross-over fitting (item 4b) onto the 25″ pipe and tighten it enough to hold it in place; this fitting, too, will be properly located later. This assembly should now look like the one in the drawing.

Proceeding with the same assembly, slide a tee (item 4c) onto the end of the 22″ pipe, but do not tighten it; slip the remaining 25″ pipe (item 1f) into the tee and tighten it. The assembly should now look the way it does in the drawing.

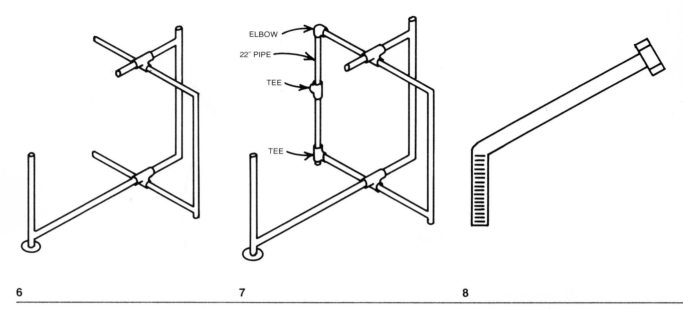

6

Now you are ready to put the two major parts of the frame together. Loosen the cross-over fitting on the threaded-pipe assembly. Through this fitting, slide the 25″ pipe that is the bottom one in drawing 5. Next, slide the cross-over fitting that is on the top 25″ pipe onto the 13 1/2″ pipe of the threaded-pipe assembly. When the pipes are in about the positions shown in the drawings, tighten the cross-over fittings, temporarily.

7

Now, slip an elbow (item 4a) as far onto the remaining 22″ (item 1e) as possible and tighten it securely. Slip two tees (item 4c) onto the pipe, but do not tighten them. Join these parts to the frame by slipping the elbow onto the top 25″ pipe and the bottom tee onto the other 25″ pipe, and tighten both joints. The basic frame, now completely assembled, is shown in the drawing.

Place the basic frame on a level surface and adjust the locations of the cross-over joints and bottom tees on the 22″ uprights until all of the following conditions are met: (1) the bottom pipe of the threaded assembly is centered between the 22″ uprights; (2) the bottom 25″ pipe is 10″ from the 18″ front riser, measured from the center of one pipe to the center of the other; (3) the 13 1/2″ pipe is centered on the top 25″ pipe; (4) both 22″ uprights are plumb.

8

Installing the Seat. Assemble the seat support by tightly screwing the 17″ and 6″ lengths of pipe (items 2 and 5a) into the elbow (item 5b). Apply Loctite or epoxy to both joints.

Bend a 3/8″–16 × 6″ bolt (item 8) to about the angle shown in the drawing. To make the bend, put 2″ of the threaded end of the bolt in a vise. Slip a piece of pipe over the protruding end. Then, grip the pipe firmly and apply enough pressure to produce the desired angle. Be sure not to damage the threads on the end of the bolt as you bend it. This bolt will serve to adjust the height of the seat.

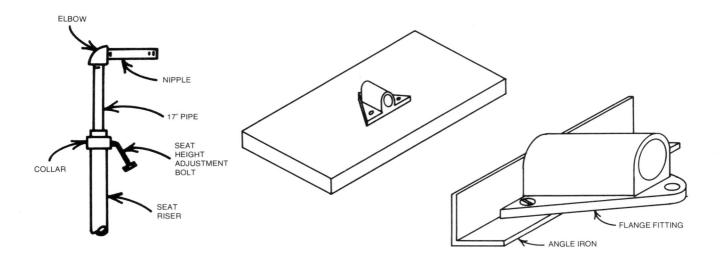

ELBOW

NIPPLE

17″ PIPE

COLLAR

SEAT
HEIGHT
ADJUSTMENT
BOLT

SEAT
RISER

FLANGE FITTING

ANGLE IRON

9

Drill a 1/2″ diameter hole 2″ from the top of the seat riser. The hole should be on the back of the riser. Replace the set screw in the collar (item 4d) with the height-adjusting bolt you have just made. Put the collar on the seat riser so that the end of the adjusting bolt passes through the hole drilled in the riser. Tighten the remaining set screw.

Slip the long pipe of the seat support into the seat riser, as shown, and secure it in any position by tightening the height-adjusting bolt.

Next, make the padded seat (item 17), following the seat instructions later in this part.

10

Turn the completed seat over and screw the flange fitting (item 5c) to the center of the bottom with three 1 1/2″ No. 14 flat-head wood screws (item 11), as shown. You will have to drill 1/8″ guide holes for the screws.

Slip the flange fitting, now secured to the seat, onto the 6″ pipe of the seat support. Tighten the set screws to hold in the seat in any position desired.

11

Installing the Bearings. Make the top bearing mount by fastening an 8″ long piece of 2″ × 2″ × 3/16″ angle iron (item 9) to a flange fitting (item 4e) with machine screws (item 10) as shown. Slip this assembly onto the 13 1/2″ pipe at the top of the frame.

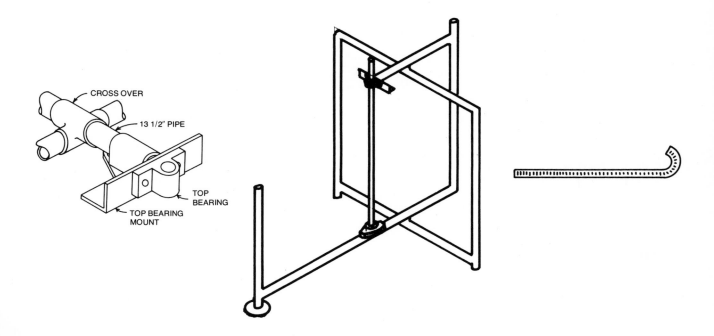

12

Now place the bearing (item 14a) in the center of the face of the angle iron with the top of the bearing even with the top of the angle iron. Mark the center of the bearing-mount holes. Center punch and drill two 3/8″ mounting holes at the marks. Then bolt the bearing to the angle iron with two 3/8″ bolts (item 12a) as shown.

13

To determine the proper position for the bottom bearing (item 14b), slide the shaft (item 13) through the top bearing and slip the bottom bearing (item 14b) onto the lower end. Position the bottom bearing so that the two mounting holes are centered on the 28″ pipe that forms the front-to-back member of the base of the frame. Slide the bearing back and forth on this pipe until the shaft is plumb on all sides. It is possible that the 28″ pipe may have to be moved to one side to achieve the proper position for mounting the bearing so that the shaft is plumb. If this is so, you can move the pipe by loosening the cross-fitting and tapping the pipe with a hammer. Mark the proper location for the mounting holes for the bottom bearing on the 28″ pipe.

Remove the shaft, center punch and drill two vertical 3/8″ holes through the 28″ pipe for mounting the bottom bearing. Bolt the bottom bearing in place with 3/8″ × 2 1/2″ bolts (item 12b). Insert the bolts from the underside of the frame.

14

Making the Pan-Mounting Assembly
The hook for mounting the pan is made by bending a 5″ long piece of 1/4″ threaded rod (item 15a), to the shape shown. (See the *Appendix* for instructions on bending steel rod. In this case, use method 1.)

Drill a 5/16″ hole all the way through the nipple that protrudes from the top of the tee at the top front of the frame. The hole should be as close to the tee as possible and should be parallel to the 13 1/2″ pipe, as in drawing 16. To install the hook, slip it through this hole and put a 1/4″ wing nut (item 16) on the straight end. The hooked end should be on the bearing side of the nipple, also indicated in drawing 16.

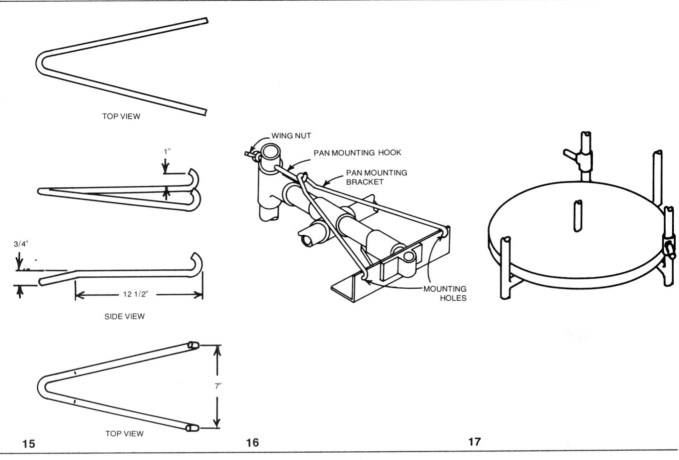

TOP VIEW

1"

3/4"

12 1/2"

SIDE VIEW

7"

TOP VIEW

WING NUT

PAN MOUNTING HOOK

PAN MOUNTING BRACKET

MOUNTING HOLES

15

16

17

To make the pan-mounting bracket, bend a 34 1/2" long piece of 3/16" steel rod (item 15b) in the sequence shown in the drawing. These bends can be made with two pairs of pliers.

The next step is to drill two 1/4" holes in the angle iron on which the top bearing is mounted. These holes can be located by putting the pan-mounting bracket in place and then marking the position of the hooked ends, as shown.

The pan-mounting assembly should fit firmly onto the frame so that the hooks on the ends of the rods fit into the holes in the angle iron. Cut the hooked ends of the bracket to length so that they fill the holes in the angle iron but do not extend beyond it. Now tighten the wing nut on the mounting hook until the entire assembly is securely seated. The parts may have to be bent slightly to achieve a good, tight fit.

Now you are ready to install the pan, the flywheel, and the wheelhead (item 17) on the frame. Instructions for making these parts are presented later in this part.

The footrests for the kickwheel are made by slipping a 4" length of 1 1/4" pipe (item 1g) in each of the tees on the 22" uprights and tightening them in a comfortable-to-use position on the outside of the frame, as shown.

To prepare the wheel frame to hold a motor foot control pedal, begin by center punching and drilling a 1/2" hole through the left 22" upright of the frame. This hole must be centered 2" above the top surface of the flywheel and must be drilled parallel to the flywheel surface on an imaginary line connecting the 22" upright with the 18" front upright. The motor foot control will be mounted in this hole, as shown in drawing 7 in the next section.

MOTOR LINKAGE FOR THE PIPE FRAME WHEEL

The operating principle of the motor-mount linkage is the same for the pipe and welded frame wheels. However, the parts are different because the rail fittings for the pipe frame cannot be joined to the square tubing of the welded frame wheel and because no welding is used in the process of motorizing the pipe frame wheel.

Tools

1. Tape measure or folding rule.
2. Center punch.
3. Two C clamps that will open at least 2″.
4. Hacksaw.
5. Drill with 1/2″, 3/8″, 5/16″, 1/4″ metal drilling bits.
6. Adjustable wrench.
7. Allen wrench to fit set screw in rubber drive wheel.
8. Miscellaneous wood blocks.
9. Screwdriver.
10. Knife.

Parts and Materials

Item No.

1. Galvanized pipe fittings:
   a. One 3/8″ × 2″ threaded nipple.
   b. Two 3/8″ threaded tees.
2. One 1/8″ × 1″ × 2″ piece of steel.
3. One 7″ length of 1/2″ threaded steel rod.
4. Four 1/2″ nuts.
5. One 1/4″ split steel pin.
6. Pieces of 1 1/4″ galvanized pipe:
   a. One 2 1/2″ length.
   b. One 4 3/4″ length.
   c. One 15″ length.
7. Two 1 1/4″ elbow rail fittings.
8. One 9″ length of angle iron, 1/8″ × 1 1/4″ × 1 1/4″.
9. Hexhead bolts:
   a. One 3/8″ × 1″.
   b. Two 3/8″ × 2″.
10. One 1/2″ coarse thread self-locking nut.
11. One rubber drive wheel, 2″ in diameter, with mounting hole to fit motor (item 13).
12. One 1/8″ turnbuckle.
13. One 1/2 horsepower, 1750 r.p.m. motor (when looking at the shaft, this motor rotates clockwise).
14. One single-pole toggle switch with housing. The housing replaces the cover on the wiring opening on the motor.
15. A 10′ length of three-wire electrical cord.
16. A three-prong electrical plug.
17. Lubricating oil.

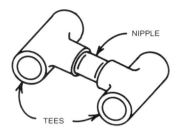

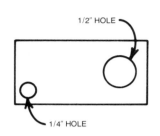

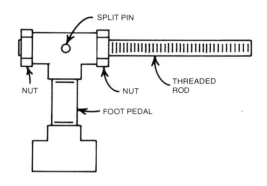

1

2

3

Making and Mounting the Foot Control. The foot pedal is made up of a number of small assemblies that are put together before they are joined to the wheel. Assemble the nipple (item 1a) and the two 3/8" tees (item 1b), as shown. These should be tightly screwed together, but they need no Loctite or epoxy.

To make the pedal arm, cut and drill a 1/8" × 1" × 2" piece of steel (item 2), as shown.

Begin making the foot pedal assembly by cutting a 7" length of 1/2" threaded steel rod (item 3). Then insert the threaded rod into the foot pedal and secure it with two nuts (item 4) as shown. The nuts should be very tight against the ends of the tee. Drill a 1/4" hole through the tee and the threaded rod enclosed in it. Then drive a split pin (item 5) into the hole so that the foot pedal cannot turn on the threaded rod.

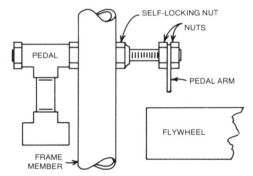

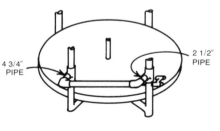

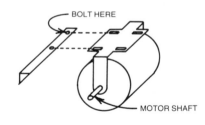

4

5

6

Slip the foot-pedal assembly through the hole drilled in the 22" upright of the frame so that the pedal is on the outside. Install a self-locking nut (item 10) so that the pedal can turn freely but cannot slide in and out.

Then secure the pedal arm on the free end of the threaded rod with the two nuts (item 4) as shown. The nuts must be very tight against the flat steel pedal arm so that it cannot turn on the threaded rod.

Mounting the Drive Motor. The mounting for the drive motor consists of the 2 1/2", 4 3/4", and 15" pipes (items 6a, 6b, 6c) and two elbows (item 7), as shown.

Tighten the set screws in the tees enough to keep the mounting together and in place. The screws holding the 15" pipe can be removed because it must be able to turn freely in the elbows.

Drill the two 3/8" holes in the 9" long piece of 1 1/4" × 1 1/4" × 1/8" angle iron (item 8) to match holes on one side of the mounting plate of the motor (item 13). Bolt (item 9a) the angle iron to the underside of the motor's mounting plate, using the (one) hole indicated in the drawing.

Next, install the rubber drive wheel (item 11) on the motor shaft. The shaft should go all the way into the mounting hole on the rubber drive wheel until the end of the shaft is flush with the other side of the wheel, as shown.

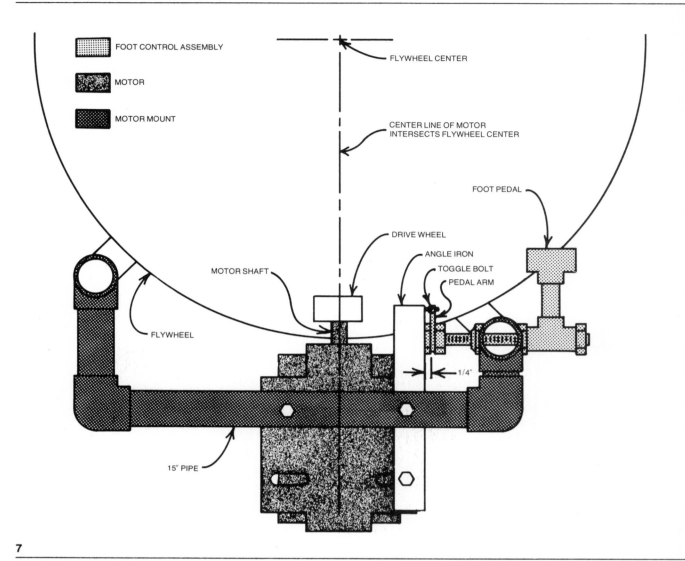

FOOT CONTROL ASSEMBLY

MOTOR

MOTOR MOUNT

FLYWHEEL CENTER

CENTER LINE OF MOTOR
INTERSECTS FLYWHEEL CENTER

FOOT PEDAL

DRIVE WHEEL

ANGLE IRON

TOGGLE BOLT

PEDAL ARM

MOTOR SHAFT

FLYWHEEL

1/4"

15" PIPE

7

Using C clamps, hang the motor underneath the 15" pipe, as shown from the top view in the drawing. Position the motor so that the outer edge of the angle iron is about 1/4" to the left of the pedal arm. The motor should be clamped so that the front mount holes are directly under the 15" pipe.

Once the correct position is established, mark the points at which the 15" pipe and the motor-mount holes intersect. The hole on the right side should coincide with the hole in the angle iron. You will next have to center punch and drill mounting holes all the way through the pipe. Then bolt the motor and angle iron assembly to the 15" pipe with 3/8" × 2" bolts (item 9b).

Next, adjust the angular position of the pipe mounting so that the motor shaft points directly at the flywheel center. Also, the rubber drive wheel must be positioned directly over the metal ring on the flywheel when the motor shaft is parallel to the top surface of the flywheel.

Both of these adjustments can be accomplished by loosening the set screws in the elbows and tees and securing the 2 1/2" and 4 3/4" pipes to the frame uprights. Move the two pipes in and out, as necessary; you may also need to rotate the tees on the uprights in order to get the right fit. If necessary, you can also replace the 2 1/2" or 4 1/2" pipes with longer or shorter ones to achieve the proper fit. When all adjustments are com-

pleted, be sure to re-tighten all set screws securely.

Loosen all set screws holding the left upright and rotate the upright so that the threaded rod of the foot control is parallel to the pipe the motor is mounted on. Tighten the set screws.

The last adjustment is also the easiest. The motor must be positioned so that the drive wheel touches the flywheel when the motor shaft is parallel to the top surface of the flywheel. This is accomplished by loosening the tees holding the motor mount to the frame uprights and then moving the entire assembly up or down to the proper position. Again, be sure to re-tighten the set screws securely when the adjustment is completed.

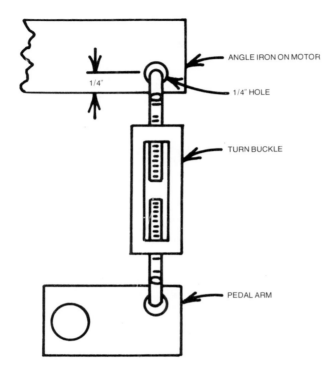

ANGLE IRON ON MOTOR

1/4" HOLE

1/4"

TURN BUCKLE

PEDAL ARM

8

Linking the Foot Pedal to the Motor.

Locate and drill a 1/4" hole in the angle iron on the motor directly above the 1/4" hole in the pedal arm in the foot-control assembly. While you are locating this hole, the pedal arm must be parallel to the flywheel surface and the rubber drive wheel must be in contact with the flywheel.

A turnbuckle (item 12) is used to link the foot pedal to the motor. Begin by taking the turnbuckle apart and bending the ends open enough so they will hook into the hole in the angle iron on the motor and the hole on the pedal arm of the foot control. When the end pieces of the turnbuckle are in place, bend the loops back to the original position and reassemble the turnbuckle, as shown.

Now, sit at the wheel. Adjust the length

of the turnbuckle so that the drive wheel is brought into contact with the flywheel when the foot pedal is depressed a comfortable distance. If the turnbuckle does not permit full adjustment, loosen the nuts securing the pedal arm and re-position it in relation to the foot pedal. When the adjustment is correct, apply epoxy cement between the arm and nuts. Retighten the nuts. By its weight the motor should automatically pull the drive wheel up and away from the flywheel when pressure on the foot pedal is removed. Oil (item 17) the joints where the motor-mount pipe enters the two elbows to make it easy for the motor to move.

Wire and install the motor and switch (items 13, 14, 15, 16), using the same method given for the *Welded Frame Wheel* in the previous section.

DC MOTOR POWERED WHEEL

A wheel powered by a direct-current motor provides a wide speed range with excellent continuous control and torque (turning power) at all speeds. Because this wheel requires no fly-wheel, it is lighter in weight than others described in this book. It is also more compact and therefore more portable.

The DC-powered wheel for which building instructions are given here has a large pan and a fully adjustable seat. At this writing, no commercially produced wheel offers these features.

If you want to build this wheel, however, you must consider two important factors. First, the frame must be welded, which may be an inconvenience. Secondly, the DC motor costs about four times as much as the constant-speed motor commonly used on other wheels. This raises the total cost of the DC unit to more than twice that of a motorized kickwheel. However, for many potters, these considerations are more than counterbalanced by the DC wheel's excellent speed control and compact lightweight design.

Tools

1. Tape measure or folding rule.
2. Hacksaw or cutting torch.
3. Welding equipment.
4. Carpenter's framing square.
5. C clamps that will open 4″.
6. Drill with 1/8″, 3/16″, 5/16″, 3/8″, 1/4″, 9/64″, 5/32″, 5/64″, 7/32″, 1/2″ metal drilling bits.
7. A 3/8″–16 threading tap with handle.
8. Allen wrenches to fit pulley and bearing set screws.
9. Saber saw.
10. Screwdriver.
11. Sheet metal shears or metal-cutting blade for saber saw.
12. Center punch.
13. Hammer.
14. Vise.
15. Pliers.
16. Pop rivet tool.
17. Adjustable wrench.
18. Pencil compass (see the *Appendix*).
19. Some small nails.
20. Paint brush (if you are going to paint the wheel).

Parts and Materials

Item No.

1. Square steel tubing, 13′ of 2″ × 2″ × 1/8″:
   a. Five 17″ lengths.
   b. Two 30 1/2″ lengths.
   c. One 7″ length.
2. One 15″ length of 1″ cold-rolled steel shaft.
3. Steel rod (can be welding rod), 3/16″:
   a. One 31″ length.
   b. One 6 1/2″ length.
4. Black pipe:
   a. One 3″ length of 1/4″.
   b. One 12″ length of 3/4″.
5. Bolts:
   a. One 3/8″ × 2″.
   b. Four 3/8″ × 3″ with nuts.
   c. Four 5/16″ × 3″ with nuts.
6. Four 1″ No. 10 sheet metal screws.
7. Twenty 5/8″ No. 6 round-head wood screws.
8. One 5″ length of 1/4″ threaded steel rod.
9. One 1/4″ wing nut.
10. Two cast-iron pillow blocks (rigid mount, ball bearing, self-aligning type).
11. One double-groove cast iron V-belt sheave (pulley) with 10.75″ outside diameter (10.0″ A belt pitch diameter) and 1″ split taper bushing.
12. One double-groove cast-iron V-belt sheave (pulley) with 2.50″ outside diameter (2.1″ A belt pitch diameter) and 5/8″ bore.
13. Two 42″ long V belts, type 4L.
14. One 1″ shaft collar with set screws.
15. One 1/2 horsepower, 1200 r.p.m. permanent-magnet field, direct-current motor with integral bridge rectifier—NEMA 48 motor frame—for 115 volt, 60 cycle current source (when facing the end of the shaft, this motor rotates counterclockwise.)
16. One 3/16″ × 1 3/8″ long square steel key (this should come with the motor).
17. One piece of 5/8″ plywood, 12 3/4″ × 24″.
18. One piece of 18 to 24 gauge sheet steel with both of the long edges rolled (flat hem). Finished

dimensions should be 5 3/4" × 54". The edges can be rolled in a sheet metal or heating and air conditioning shop.

Note: items 19 through 31 are for the foot-operated speed control.

19. One 10" length of 3" iron channel.

20. One 5 1/2" length of 1/8" × 1" steel strap.

21. One 3/4" × 3" × 10" hardwood board.

22. One 1" No. 10 round-head wood screw.

23. One 1/4" × 2" bolt with two nuts.

24. One 1/4" × 3 1/2 " bolt with a self-locking nut.

25. One 2 1/2" long looped-end coil spring —8 oz. pull strength—for 1" extension.

26. Epoxy cement.

27. A 1' length of braided stainless steel fishing leader-wire, about 20 lb. test strength.

28. Two 3/16" × 1" round-head machine screws with nuts.

29. One 2 1/2" × 3" piece of 1/8" sheet steel.

30. One 250K on-off rotary potentiometer with metal shaft at least 1" long.

31. One empty wooden sewing-thread spool, 1" long × 1" dia.

32. One 6" × 10" piece of plastic or rubber sheet with non-slip texture.

33. One 4 1/2" × 9 3/8" piece of 22 to 28 gauge aluminum or galvanized sheet steel.

34. One grommet to fit around the wire used to connect the foot control.

35. A pint of rust-inhibiting paint (optional).

36. Seat and pan assemblies (see instructions later in this part).

37. One 10 amp. extended range power module (this varies the A.C. voltage supplied to the motor)—Cutter- Hammer SX4KD2 or equivalent.

38. One fuse holder with 5 amp. slow-blow fuse.

39. One waterproof single switch to fit electrical box.

40. One waterproof bell box (outdoor type electrical box).

41. Two 2" rubber feet to fit on 2" square steel tubing (item 1).

42. Two 2" long pieces of 1" rubber auto heater hose.

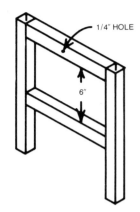

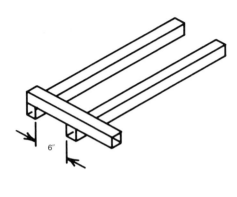

1

2

Frame Assembly. This frame is built by making and joining together two separately welded assemblies.

To make the first assembly, prepare to weld together four of the 17" lengths of square steel tubing (item 1a) by arranging them, as shown in the drawing, on a flat work surface that can withstand the heat of welding. Make certain that all four pieces of tubing are lying perfectly flat and that all joints are square. Then weld them.

Drill a 1/4" hole through the frame member as indicated in the drawing.

To make the second assembly, arrange the remaining 17" length of tubing (item 1a) across the ends of the two 30 1/2" pieces (item 1b), as shown. Again, make sure that all joints are flat and square and also that the long pieces are parallel. Clamp and weld these pieces together.

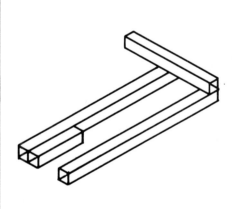

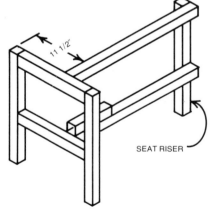

3

4

Next, weld the 7" piece of tubing (item 1c), to one of the 30 1/2" pieces, as shown. You are now ready to join the two welded assemblies. Arrange them as shown in the drawing.

Note: The assembly containing the two 30 1/2"pieces of tubing is *not* to be centered on the other assembly. It is to be positioned 11 1/2"from one end of the first assembly, as shown. When the assemblies are in place, check to make sure that all joints are square. Then clamp and weld the two assemblies together.

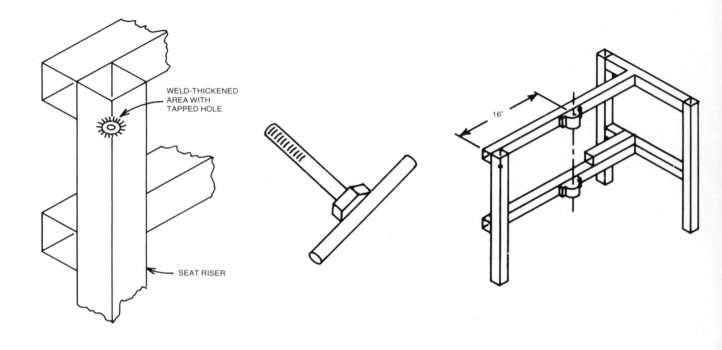

WELD-THICKENED
AREA WITH
TAPPED HOLE

SEAT RISER

5

Assembling and Attaching the Seat Support. In order to make the seat riser strong enough to support the seat assembly and the weight of the potter, it is necessary to increase the thickness of one of its corners. About 2″ from the top of the rear corner of the seat riser, build up an area of weld metal about 3/4″ in diameter, as shown. The surface of this welded area should be flat. Drill a 5/16″ hole through the weld metal and then tap the hole for 3/8″–16 threads.

6

To make the seat-support bolt that will be used to adjust the height of the seat, weld the 3/8″ × 2″ bolt (item 5a) to the 3″ long piece of 1/4″ pipe (item 4a), as shown. This will make a tee-handled bolt that can be screwed into the threaded hole in the seat riser.

Slide the free end of the 1 1/4″ pipe of the seat support into the seat riser and tighten the tee-handled bolt at any position desired (see plans for the *Seat* later in this part.)

Stand the frame on its three legs. Lay the pipe (item 4b) on the floor so that it is centered at the back of the seat support. Weld the pipe to the seat support. This will make the wheel more stable.

Paint the frame, if desired, with rust-inhibiting paint (item 35).

7

Mounting the Bearings, Pulleys, and Motor. Drill two 3/8″ holes in each of the 30 1/2″ frame members in order to mount the two pillow blocks (item 10) for the wheel shaft. It is important that these pillow blocks be positioned so that the center line of the wheel shaft is exactly 16″ from the rear of the seat riser.

The best way to make sure this dimension is accurate is to measure 16″ from the seat riser along the two 30 1/2″ frame members and mark the locations with a pencil. Temporarily slip the wheel shaft (item 2) into the two pillow blocks and position the assembly on the two frame members so that the 16″ marks are in line with the center line of the shaft. Next, make certain that the top surface of the bearing in both of the pillow blocks is flush with the top surface of the frame member on which it is to be mounted.

Once the locations of the four bolt holes are established, center punch them and then, using a 3/8″ bit, drill the holes all the way through the frame.

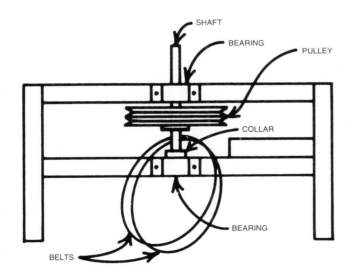

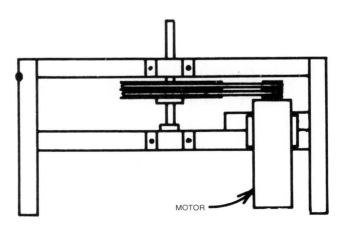

8

Remove the wheel shaft from the pillow-block bearings and mount the bearings with 3/8″ × 3″ bolts (item 5b), making sure that the set screws of both are on the upper side of the bearings. Now, reinsert the wheel shaft (item 2) through the top bearing. Next, slip the pulley, drive belts, and collar (items 11, 13, 14) on the shaft and insert the shaft into the bottom bearing until the shaft end is flush with the bottom of the bearing. Before securing the pulley on the wheel shaft, as shown, make sure that it is as close as possible to the underside of the top frame member without rubbing against it. Make sure the collar is tight against the top of the lower bearing. Now, tighten all set screws.

9

Next, mount the other pulley (item 12) on the motor shaft as close as possible to the housing of the motor (item 15). You will notice that there are grooves in both the wheel shaft and the pulley. When these grooves are aligned, you can slip the key (item 16) into them to keep the pulley from turning on the shaft. Make sure that the set screw is on the side away from the motor. Tighten the set screw.

Slip the drive belts onto both the pulley on the wheel shaft and the pulley on the motor shaft.

Then, using the C clamps (or with the help of an assistant), position the motor at its mounting location on the frame, as indicated in the drawing. To determine the proper location, slide the motor along the frame member until the drive belts are stretched taut;

then mark the points on the frame member at which the four holes for mounting the motor should be drilled.

Note: in locating these holes there are three important factors to bear in mind: (1) be sure to situate the holes in the ends of the motor-mount slots farthest away from the wheel shaft. This will make it possible to adjust the motor's position by tightening the belts further, if necessary; (2) the motor must be positioned so that the pulley on its shaft is level with the one on the wheel shaft; (3) the motor shaft and the wheel shaft must be parallel in order for the belts to run true and to avoid excessive wear. Once these conditions are established, center punch and drill the four 5/16″ holes all the way through the frame member. Then bolt the motor in place with the 5/16″ × 3″ bolts (item 5c).

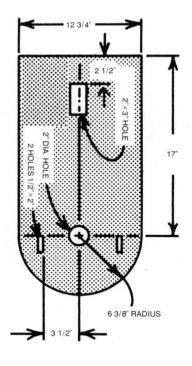

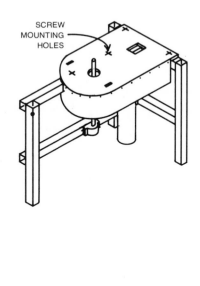

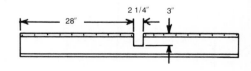

10

Enclosing the Drive Belts. As soon as the pulleys and drive belts are properly installed, they should be enclosed in the safety housing. To make this housing, begin by marking a half-circle on one end of the 12 3/4″ × 24″ piece of 5/8″ plywood (item 17) with a pencil compass. (Instructions for making the compass for drawing this half-circle are in the *Appendix*.) Saw along the half-circle to complete shaping the plywood, as shown.

Next, locate and mark on the plywood the three rectangular holes and the one round hole shown in the drawing. The round hole should be centered on the same point at which you placed the nail for the pencil compass. The best way to cut out these large holes is to drill starter holes first, inside the line marking the edge of each hole. Make the starter holes large enough to accept the wood-cutting saber saw blade. Then use a saber saw to cut out the holes.

11

Now you are ready to drill the holes required to fasten the plywood to the frame. Position the plywood on the frame so that the wheel shaft is centered in the round hole and the 12 3/4″ edge is parallel to the front frame member, as in the drawing. C clamp the plywood in place.

Drill through the plywood and the top surface of the frame members beneath it at the four points indicated with X's in the drawing. Use a 5/32″ bit. Lift the plywood off and enlarge the four holes you have just drilled with a 7/32″ bit. Put the plywood back in position and fasten it in place with the sheet metal screws (item 6).

12

Now, take the prepared piece of sheet metal (item 18) and notch one edge with metal shears, as shown. About 3/8″ from the notched edge, drill 9/64″ holes at 3″ to 4″ intervals the length of the piece.

Bend the sheet metal around the outer edge of the plywood so that the frame member fits in the notch. Lightly tack the sheet metal in place with a few small nails and drill 5/64″ pilot holes into the plywood through the holes you have just drilled in the edge of the sheet metal. These holes will keep the plywood from splitting when the screws are inserted. Install the 5/8″ screws (item 7) in the holes.

Now paint the top and sides of the belt guard with rust-inhibiting paint (item 35).

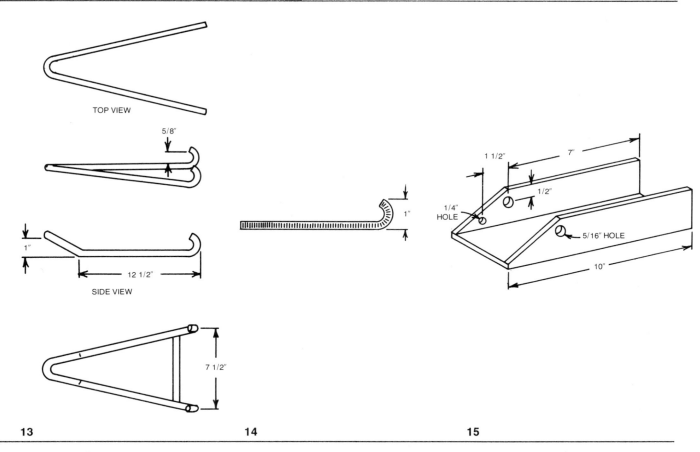

TOP VIEW

SIDE VIEW

5/8"

1"

12 1/2"

7 1/2"

1"

1 1/2"

7"

1/2"

1/4" HOLE

5/16" HOLE

10"

13

14

15

Making the Pan-Holding Bracket.
The bracket that holds the pan on the plywood top of the drive-belt enclosure is made by bending the 31" piece of 3/16" rod (item 3a) into the shape indicated in the sequence shown in the drawings. (See "How to Bend Steel Rod", Method 1, in the *Appendix.*) Weld a 6 1/2" length of steel rod (item 3b) between the hooked ends to keep them 7 1/2" apart, as shown.

The completed bracket should lie on the plywood top of the drive enclosure so that the hooked ends fit into the 1/2" × 2" holes and the V-shaped end of the bracket fits into the 2" × 3" hole (see drawing 10).

The bracket is held in place by a hook made from 1/4" threaded rod (item 8), bent to the shape shown in the drawing. (See "How to Bend Steel Rod," Method 1, in the *Appendix.*)

The hook fits through the 1/4" hole in the center of the top front frame member (see drawing 1), and the hooked end attaches to the V-shaped end of the pan bracket. Put a wing nut (item 9) on the straight end of the hook at the front of the frame to secure the bracket. The bracket should lie flat against the plywood. If the bracket does not fit firmly into place, bend it further to achieve a good fit.

See instructions for making and installing the pan (item 36) and the wheelhead later in this part.

Making the Foot Control. A great advantage of the DC motor is its infinitely variable speed. A foot-operated control pedal is required to regulate the speed of the motor.

Begin making the foot control by locating, center punching and drilling two 5/16" holes 7" from one end of the 10" long iron channel (item 19). These holes should be 1/2" from the top edge of each flange of the channel, as shown. Also drill the 1/4" hole indicated in the side of the channel. Cut the channel to the shape shown.

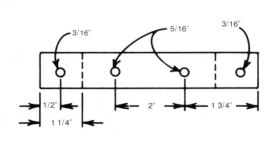

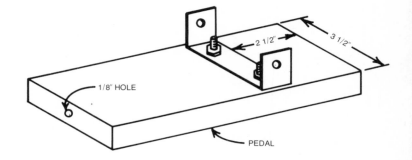

16

17

Next, for the pedal mounting, take the 5 1/2" length of 1/8" × 1" steel strap (item 20). Locate, center punch, and drill the two 5/16" and the two 3/16" holes in the steel strap, as shown. This will be the pedal-mounting strap. Next, bend the strap by C clamping it to the bottom of the channel iron that forms the foot-control base. Make certain that the two protruding ends of the strap are the same length, then, force the ends down over the edges of the channel with a hammer.

Remove the strap from the channel, and bend the ends a little more, making sure that the bent ends are perpendicular to the center section. The mounting is now complete.

The 3" × 10" hardwood board (item 21) will serve as the pedal. Locate two holes in it to accept the bolts for attaching the mounting strap by using the mounting strap as a template. Then drill the two 5/16" holes and attach the strap to the pedal with machine screws (item 28), as shown. Also drill the 1/8" hole in the end of the board. Then drive the wood screw (item 22) into this hole so that all but about 1/8" of the shank is inside the wood pedal.

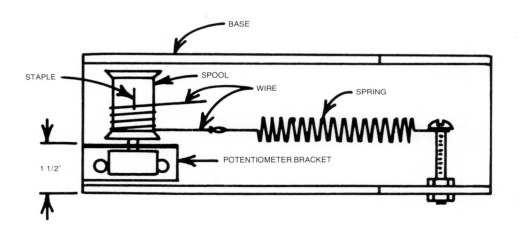

20

Now slide the wooden spool (item 31) on the potentiometer shaft and cement it in place using the epoxy (item 26). The spool should go all the way onto the shaft, but not quite touch the mounting nut.

Locate the bracket on the base, as shown. Mark the position of the two 1/8" holes on the base. Center punch and drill two 1/8"holes. Pop rivet the bracket in place. The heads of the pop rivets should be on the underside of the base.

Tie one end of the leader wire (item 27) to one end of the spring (item 25). Slip the 2" long bolt (item 23) through the other eye of the spring and screw a nut about 1/2" onto the bolt. Put the bolt into the 1/4" hole in the side flange of the base and install the second nut. Tighten the nuts against the sides of the flange, as shown.

Turn the potentiometer shaft all the way clockwise (while you are facing the end of the spool farthest from the potentiometer). Extend the spring about 1/2" by pulling on the wire; and, while holding the spring in that extended position, wrap the wire around the spool about two times. Double-check this part of the foot-control assembly by comparing it carefully with the illustration to make sure that you have wrapped the fish-line around the spool in the right direction.

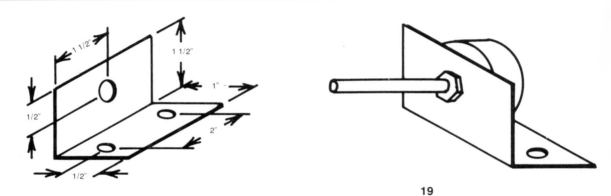

18

19

Because this wheel is electronically controlled, it uses a potentiometer (a variable resistor) in the foot control to vary its speed. The bracket for the potentiometer is made from the 2 1/2" × 3" piece of sheet metal (item 29). Locate, countersink, and drill the two 1/8" holes and the single 1/2" hole. Then draw a line on the bracket,

dividing it in two parts so that the 1/2" hole is centered in the 1 1/2" part and the two 1/8" holes are centered on the 1" part.

To bend the sheet metal, position it in a vise so that the dividing line you have drawn is just barely visible above the vise jaws. Strike the metal with a hammer until the two halves are bent perpendicular to each other, as shown.

Next, cut the shaft of the potentiometer (item 30) with a hacksaw so that it is only 1" long. Mount the potentiometer on the bracket by removing the nut from its shaft and inserting the shaft in the 1/2" hole in the bracket, as shown. Secure the potentiometer in place by reinstalling the nut and tightening it with pliers.

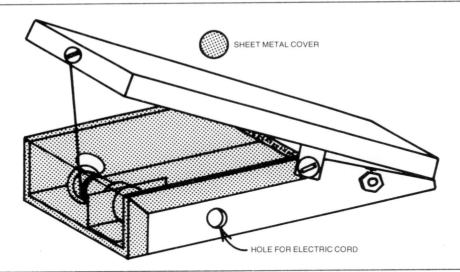

SHEET METAL COVER

HOLE FOR ELECTRIC CORD

21

Mount the pedal on the base by inserting the 3 1/2"bolt (item 24) through one side of the pedal-mounting strap, then through the 5/16" hole in the base flange, and then through the other 5/16" hole in the strap. Install the self-locking nut (item 24) on the bolt.

Wrap the wire one more turn around the spool, and then pull on the end of the wire in order to rotate the spool counterclockwise as far as possible.

Then, keeping the spool in the full counterclockwise position, and with the end of the pedal that has the screw in it raised as high as it will go, wind the wire around the screw shank. Fasten the wire securely to the screw. Then, turn the screw the rest of the way into the pedal.

If the assembly has been completed successfully, it will look as it does in the drawing, except that the cover

and hole for the electric cord will not yet be in place. The foot-control pedal will now be positioned so that its longer end (in relation to the mounting strap) is normally raised as far as the base will allow. When the wiring is completed, this will be the *on* position for the wheel. Depressing the foot pedal will cause the spool to turn the potentiometer, which will cause the DC motor to increase its speed.

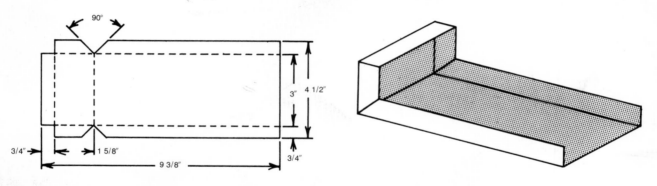

22

Making the Pedal Cover. Cut out a piece of 22 to 28 gauge sheet metal (item 33) in the shape shown.

Bend the metal as shown by the dotted lines to form the cover. Remove the woodscrew that holds the wire to the end of the foot pedal. Also remove the bolt that holds the foot pedal to the base. Mark and drill holes in the cover to match the foot-pedal mounting holes in the base. Locate and cut a hole in the cover so the wire can pass freely through it when the pedal is operated. Drill a hole in the side of the base large enough to install a wire

grommet (item 34). The hole should be located approximately as shown in drawing 21. Wire the foot control and reassemble the unit. Tighten the nut on the bolt that holds the pedal to the base just enough so that the pedal is held in any position by friction and must be moved with the foot to change speed.

You may wish to staple a piece of rubber or plastic sheet (item 32) onto the pedal cover to prevent your foot from slipping when the control is in use. For the same reason, it is advisable to cement (item 26) the same

material to the bottom of the base so that the base will not slide on the floor.

Mount the power module (item 37), fuse holder (item 38), and switch (item 39) in the electrical box (item 40). Mount the box at a convenient place on the wheel frame with pop rivets or self-tapping screws.

To make the wheel quieter, put rubber feet (item 41) on the front legs and slip short pieces of rubber hose (item 42) on the ends of the pipe at the bottom of the seat riser.

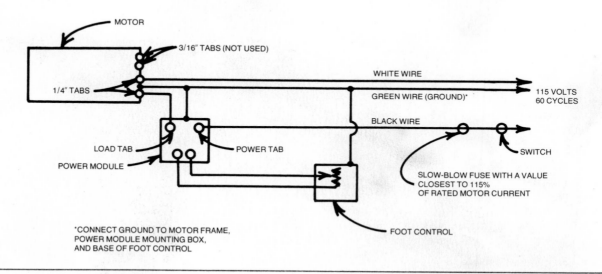

23

We strongly recommend that you get a professional to do the job of wiring the motor, power module, and foot control unless you have the required tools and are experienced at wiring electronic equipment. The motor is too expensive to risk damage caused by improper wiring.

This wiring diagram illustrates a typical wiring plan for the DC-powered wheel. However, the exact wiring required can vary according to the make of motor purchased. Therefore, make sure you obtain the manufacturer's wiring instructions and follow them.

FLY WHEELS

The flywheels used on all the potter's wheels, motorized wheels and kickwheels, in this book are nearly identical. All have the same diameter. All are made of concrete. All are cast in place on the shafts of the potter's wheels on which they will be used.

The principal difference between the flywheel for motorized wheels and that for kickwheels is that the latter must be heavier. This extra weight increases the inertia of the flywheel so that the kickwheel can be kept spinning with minimum exertion. To obtain this added weight, a deeper mold is used. This heavier flywheel cannot be used on a motorized unit.

Besides being lighter, the flywheel for a motorized unit requires the attachment of a metal ring to its top side. The function of this ring is to provide a smooth surface for the rubber drive wheel.

Some parts of these flywheel assemblies must be welded together. If you are not an experienced welder, you will probably want to have this part of the work done by a professional.

Tools

1. Hacksaw.
2. Drill with 5/16″ bit.
3. A 3/8″–16 threading tap (with handle).
4. Center punch.
5. Welding equipment.
6. Saber saw.
7. Pencil.
8. Pop rivet gun (optional).
9. Allen wrenches for 3/8″ set screws and bearing set screws.
10. Adjustable wrench.
11. Pliers.
12. Screwdriver.
13. Hammer.
14. Two C clamps that will open at least 3 3/4″.
15. Hoe.
16. Concrete mixing box, or child's rigid plastic wading pool.
17. Shovel.
18. Trowel or thin board.
19. Pencil compass (see *Appendix*).
20. Thin piece of straightedge wood or metal about 6″ long.

Parts and Materials

Item No.

1. Two 6″ lengths of 1″ black iron pipe. (Use a saw to cut the pipe to length. Do not use a pipe cutter.)
2. Four 3/8″–16 × 2″ bolts.
3. Three 12″ lengths of angle iron, 3/16″ × 1″ × 1″.
4. Two pieces of 3/8″ steel reinforcement rod, 23″ long.
5. One 5/8″ or 3/4″ thick plywood disk, 26″ in diameter.
6. One stainless steel pipe clamp for a 2″ plastic pipe.
7. Sheet metal, 18 to 24 gauge:
   a. For kickwheel, 6″ × 86″ strip.
   b. For powered wheel, 3″ × 86″ strip.
8. Three 1/2″ #8 flathead machine screws with nuts, or three 1/8″ × 1/8″ pop rivets.
9. One piece of 1″ × 1″ mesh hardware cloth, 25″ in diameter.
10. Two 3/8″ × 3/8″–16 set screws.
11. Soft clay, 2 or 3 lbs.
12. A length of 20 gauge tie wire, 3′ long.
13. Six nails, 1 1/2″ long, with heads.
14. Three pieces of 2 × 4 lumber:
   a. Two 6″ lengths.
   b. One 45″ length.
15. Gravel-filled concrete:
   a. For kickwheel, 2/3 cu. ft. (9 1/2 gal. wet or 180 lbs. dry).
   b. For motorized wheel, 1/3 cu. ft. (4 2/3 gal. wet or 90 lbs. dry).

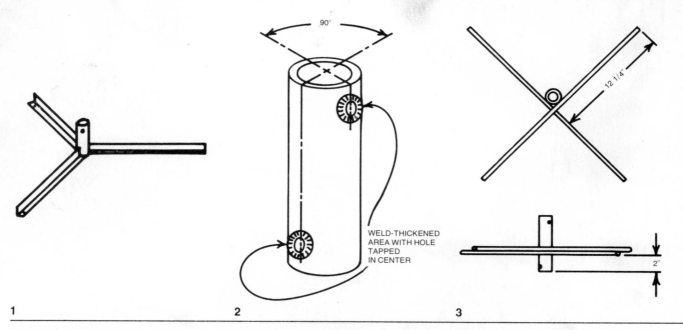

WELD-THICKENED
AREA WITH HOLE
TAPPED
IN CENTER

90°

12 1/4"

2"

1　　　　**2**　　　　**3**

Making the Flywheel Support. Before building the flywheel mold itself, it is necessary to make a device to support it during casting. This device will also be used to level the mold.

The first step in making this support is to drill one hole 5/16" in diameter in the side of the black iron pipe (item 1) about 1" from the end. This piece of pipe will serve as the hub of the support. Thread the hole with the 3/8"–16 tap. This threaded hole is for a bolt (item 2) that will hold the support in place on the shaft of the potter's wheel.

Next, make the same kind of threaded hole about 1" from one end of each of the pieces of angle iron (item 3).

Stand the piece of black iron pipe upright, keeping the end containing the threaded hole up. Make sure that the surface on which you stand the pipe is flat and suitable for welding. Now, arrange the three pieces of angle iron so that they are equally spaced radially around the pipe. The ends of the angle-iron pieces that were drilled and tapped should be outward with the tapped holes against the welding surface; the other ends should touch the hub, as shown in the drawing. Weld the four parts together.

Now screw a 3/8" bolt (item 2) into each of the holes in the ends of the three angle-iron pieces and into the tapped hole in the hub. The casting support is now complete.

Making the Flywheel Hub. Locate and drill two holes in the second piece of 1" pipe (item 1). It is most important that these two holes be perpendicular to each other—that is, the two holes should be positioned in the pipe 90° apart, as indicated in the drawing. Both holes should be about 1/2" from the ends of the pipe. Since these holes will have to withstand a considerable amount of stress, it is best, before drilling, to increase the wall thickness of the hub at these two locations by welding up a mound about 3/4" in diameter and 3/16" thick. After this is done, drill the two 5/16" holes and tap them with the 3/8"–16 threading tool.

Next, in the crossed position shown in the drawing (notice that the rods are not crossed at the center), weld the two pieces of 23" long reinforcing rod (item 4) to each other and then to the hub, about 2" from one end.

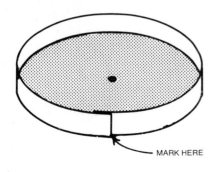

MARK HERE

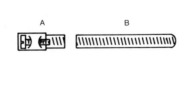

A   B

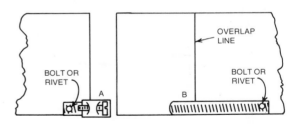

OVERLAP LINE

BOLT OR RIVET

A

B

BOLT OR RIVET

4

Constructing the Flywheel Mold.

Begin by drilling or cutting a hole in the exact center of the plywood disk (item 5) large enough to accept the 1″ pipe of the flywheel. The hole must be large enough to allow the welded-up area around the tapped hole to slip through.

The next step is to attach the pipe clamp (item 6) to the sheet-metal band (item 7a or 7b, depending on the wheel you are making). Lay the plywood disk on a floor or on any even, flat surface. Pull the metal band tightly around the plywood disk so that the ends of the metal overlap. Mark the band as in the drawing so that you will be able to tell where the overlap occurs.

5

Cut the strap of the pipe clamp as shown in the drawing.

6

Use either the flathead machine screws (heads must be on the inside) or the pop rivets (item 8) to fasten the two parts of the clamp to the two ends of the metal band. As indicated in the drawing, part A of the clamp is to be fastened to the outer end of the band; part B is to be fastened to the inner end. Do *not* assemble the disk and the metal band at this point. Put them aside until later.

Cut a 1 1/2″ hole in the center of the hardware cloth (item 9).

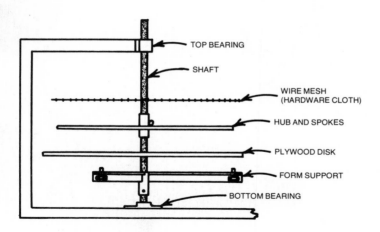

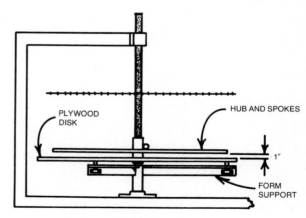

7   **8**

Assembling the Flywheel Mold.
Start mounting the mold assembly on the shaft of the potter's wheel by putting the shaft through the top bearing. Then put the parts of the mold and the support on the shaft in the following order: (1) the hardware cloth (item 9); (2) the hub of the mold —the end with the reinforcing rods should be down; (3) the plywood disk; (4) the support—the end with the three arms should be up.

Complete the assembly by putting the end of the shaft into the bottom bearing. The hub of the support should rest on top of the bearing. Tighten the bolt inserted in the hole tapped earlier, so that the support cannot move on the shaft.

The plywood disk that is to serve as the base of the mold must now be adjusted until it is level and will run true. To make the adjustment, grasp the frame of the potter's wheel so that with one extended finger you can almost touch the top surface of the plywood disk. Spin the shaft slowly. Notice which points on the disk touch your finger; these points will be high spots. Adjust the bolts in the ends of the three angle-iron arms of the support hub to level the disk. Repeat the finger test and adjust until the plywood disk runs as true as possible.

Next, position the hub of the flywheel so that the reinforcing spokes are about 1″ above the plywood base, as in the drawing. Install and tighten the set screws (item 10) in the hub so that it cannot move on the shaft. Plug any gap between the plywood disk and the hub with soft clay (item 11). Now fasten the hardware cloth to the reinforcing spokes with short lengths of the tie wire (item 12) twisted tightly together.

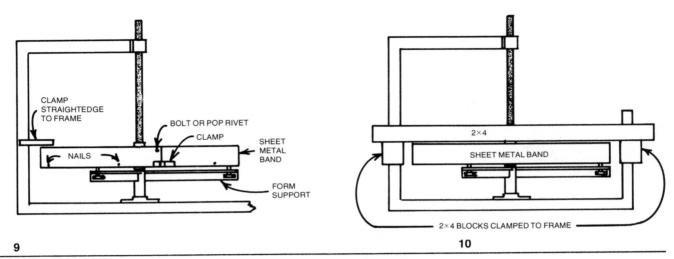

9

10

Now you are ready to secure the sheet-metal band around the plywood disk of the mold. The bottom of the band should be even with the bottom of the disk. When the band is in place, tighten the clamp only enough to hold it in position.

Next, using a C clamp, attach a straight-edged piece of wood or metal to the frame of the potter's wheel so that its bottom edge almost rests on the top edge of the sheet-metal band, as in the drawing. Turn the shaft slowly and note where the straightedge contacts the sheet-metal band. Adjust the band up or down until it runs true, with its top edge maintaining the same distance from the straightedge at all points.

When the adjustment is completed, the bottom edge of the band should be about even with the bottom surface of the plywood base.

Now tighten the clamp until the band cannot move. To strengthen the mold structure further, drill about six nail-size holes through the band, and nail (item 13) the band to the plywood disk. With a machine screw or the pop rivet (item 8), fasten the top edges of the band together where they meet. Plug any gaps between the band and plywood disk with clay (item 11). Then remove the straightedge and the clamp.

Casting the Flywheel. Use C clamps to fasten short lengths of 2 × 4 (item 14a) to the front and back uprights of the frame of the potter's wheel. Position them so that a longer piece of 2 × 4 (item 14b) laid on top of them just clears the top edge of the metal band, as in the drawing.

Mix the concrete (item 15) for the fly-wheel according to the instructions provided in the *Appendix*. You will need approximately 2/3 cubic foot (9 1/2 gallons wet or 180 pounds dry) for a kickwheel. For a powered wheel, you will need approximately 1/3 cubic foot (4 2/3 gallons wet or 90 pounds dry).

While a helper holds the 2 × 4 in place, shovel concrete into the mold, using a thin board or trowel to make sure that it is tamped uniformly into all sections of the mold. Continue to add concrete until the mold is full. Now rotate the shaft, permitting the 2 × 4 to scrape off any excess concrete and smooth the surface. Any gravel that strikes against the 2 × 4 should be pushed below the surface of the concrete, and the surface smoothed again.

When the concrete has dried completely (this will take a day or two), remove the shaft support and the mold. Remove the mold from the flywheel. Install the flywheel so that it rests on the bottom bearing when the shaft is in place, as shown. Tighten the set screws in the hub of the fly-wheel so that it cannot turn on the shaft. Tighten the set screws in the bearings.

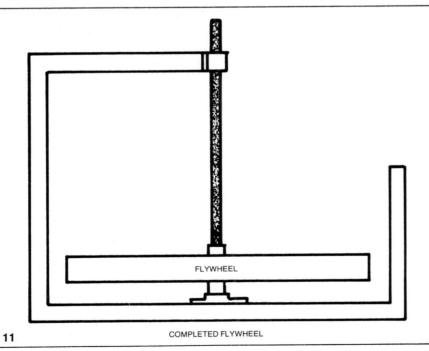

11

COMPLETED FLYWHEEL

MODIFYING THE FLYWHEEL TO BE MOTORIZED

The flywheel for a motorized wheel must be lighter than that for a kick-wheel, as discussed in the previous section.

Installing a friction drive requires that the flywheel must run true and its top surface must be hard and smooth. These conditions can be met rather simply by cementing a metal ring to the top of the flywheel.

Tools

1. Saber saw with fine-toothed metal cutting blade.
2. File.
3. Coarse sandpaper.
4. C clamp that will open 2 1/2".
5. Allen wrench for 3/8" set screw and for set screws in bearings.
6. Wax paper.
7. Ten or twelve bricks or other weights.
8. Coarse file.
9. Drill with bit large enough to make a hole to accommodate the metal-cutting blade.

Parts and Materials

Item No.

1. One 16 to 24 gauge sheet steel ring, 25" in diameter.
2. One pint of paste-type epoxy.
3. Straight-edged bar of metal about 1/8" × 1" × 8".

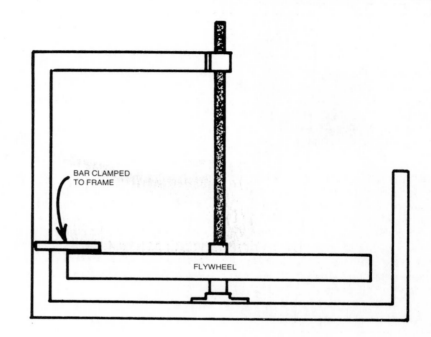

BAR CLAMPED TO FRAME

FLYWHEEL

Adding the Metal Ring. Using a saber saw equipped with a metal-cutting blade, cut out a flat ring of 16 to 24 gauge sheet steel (item 1). The ring should have an outside diameter of 25", an inside diameter of 19", as shown. Drill a hole in the sheet through which to insert the metal-cutting blade to make the cut. To improve the bond between the sheet-metal ring and the flywheel to which it is to be cemented, roughen one side of the ring with a file or coarse sandpaper.

Clamp a straight-edged metal bar (item 3) to one upright of the frame of the potter's wheel so that it just clears the flywheel, as in drawing. Make sure also that the surface of the flywheel to which the cement will be applied has been swept clean and is dry.

Apply a layer of paste-type epoxy (item 2) to the outer 4" of the top surface of the flywheel. Now rotate the flywheel; the metal bar will spread an even coating of paste over the outer 4" surface of the flywheel.

Remove the metal bar and allow the epoxy to harden, following the manufacturer's instructions. After the epoxy is hard, take out the kickwheel's shaft so that you can lay the sheet-steel ring

WHEELHEADS

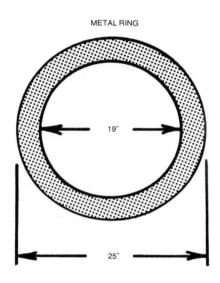

METAL RING

19"

25"

on top of the flywheel. Put the shaft back in place. Apply a *thin* coat of epoxy to the underside of the metal ring and a second thin coat to the dry epoxy on the flywheel.

Center the ring on the flywheel and then cover it and any exposed epoxy with wax paper. Place weights (bricks are good) evenly around the entire surface of the metal ring. When the epoxy is dry, remove the weights and the wax paper and file off any sharp or rough areas of epoxy.

With the flywheel completed, you can now mount the motor on the frame (see instructions for installing the motor under each separate wheel section).

Aluminum wheelheads are available from a number of ceramic suppliers at prices low enough to make it inadvisable for a potter to make them himself. There is, however, some variation among makes. Some models are made with holes too small to fit onto the drive shafts of the potter's wheels described in this book. To install one of these models, it is necessary to turn down the end of the drive shaft to fit the hole in that wheelhead, a job best done by a machine shop. The easiest models to install are those that simply slip onto a 1" diameter drive shaft (which is the shaft size used on all wheels in this book). These wheelheads require a steel pin in the shaft to prevent the wheelhead from turning.

Installing Purchased Wheelheads.
To install the steel pin, begin by putting the purchased wheelhead on the shaft on your wheel. Make sure that it is pushed down as far as it will go. You will notice that there is a slot in the side of the wheelhead hub. Make a mark on the shaft where the top end of that slot occurs. Then, remove the wheelhead.

Center punch the spot you have marked on the shaft and drill a 1/4" diameter hole about 3/4" deep. Drive a 1/4" × 1" split steel pin into the hole with a hammer. Slide the wheelhead back onto the shaft so that the pin is located at the base of the slot in its hub, as shown. The wheelhead can now be used as it is or slotted to accept screws that hold bats in place (see *Bats*).

Another type of wheelhead can be made from the kind of sanding disk used on a stationary disk sander. If the disk screws onto the shaft, the end of the potter's wheel shaft will have to be threaded to match.

BATS

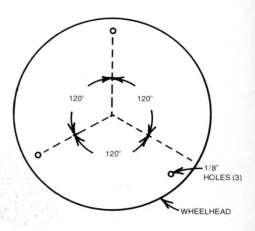

1/8″
HOLES (3)

WHEELHEAD

Bats can be made from a variety of materials. Exterior-grade plywood is good becuse it is durable and easy to cut. The method for attaching a bat given here holds it securely in place and makes it possible to throw a pot on the bat, remove both from the wheel, and then replace the bat so that the pot is again centered.

The plaster bats often used on wheels are inexpensive but are breakable and often cannot be removed and then replaced on the wheel so that a pot remains centered. Plaster is also easily gouged or chipped by tools used in throwing. In this way plaster chips can get into the clay and cause cratering in fired pots.

Tools

1. Drill with 1/8″, 3/16″, 3/8″, and 1/2″ bits.
2. Saber saw with metal-cutting blade.
3. Coarse file.
4. Hammer.
5. Screwdriver.
6. Center punch.

Parts and Materials

Item No.

1. A sheet of 5/8″ thick exterior-grade plywood, size depends on the number of bats you want to make.
2. Wheelhead.
3. Three (for each bat) No. 10 round-head brass wood screws, 1/2″ longer than the thickness of the wheelhead at the mounting slots, see text.

Securing Bats to the Wheelhead.

A plywood bat can be secured to the wheelhead by installing anchor screws in the bat and slots in the wheelhead in which the screws lock.

Begin by locating, center punching and drilling three 1/8″ lead holes in the upper surface of the wheelhead, about 1/2″ in from the outer edge, as shown in the drawing. Drill these lead holes all the way through the wheel-head. Note that these holes are *not* equally spaced from one another; this variation is important because it allows the bat to be installed in only one position.

Turn the wheelhead upside down. (From this point on, all drilling will be done from the underside of the wheelhead).

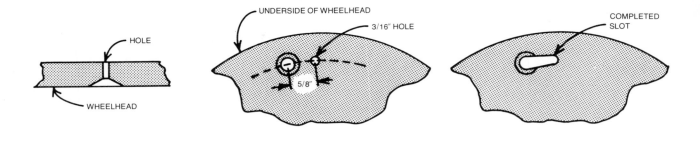

HOLE

WHEELHEAD

UNDERSIDE OF WHEELHEAD

3/16" HOLE

5/8"

COMPLETED SLOT

2

Using a 1/2" bit, redrill the 1/8" holes from this underside down only to the depth of the cone-shaped end of the bit. The holes will now be shaped as in the drawing. Then, with a 3/8" bit, again using the 1/8" holes as centers, enlarge these holes by drilling all the way through the wheelhead.

3

Locate and drill one 3/16" hole alongside each of the previously drilled holes in the positions shown in the drawing.

4

Next, slots must be cut in the wheelhead to connect each pair of holes. This cutting job is best done with a saber saw fitted with a metal-cutting blade. Saw out the metal between the holes and file the edges of the slots until they are shaped as shown.

Make as many bats as you want by cutting disks about 1" larger in diameter than the wheelhead. Center the wheelhead upside down on a bat. Place a screw in the narrow end of each of the slots in the wheelhead. With a screwdriver, drive each screw far enough into the plywood of the bat so that they hold the wheelhead and the bat together with light pressure. Repeat this procedure on each bat.

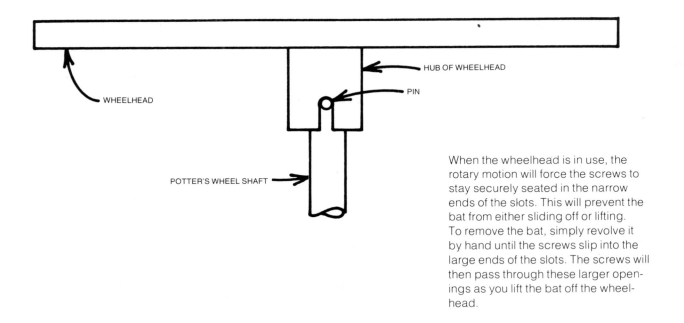

WHEELHEAD

HUB OF WHEELHEAD

PIN

POTTER'S WHEEL SHAFT

When the wheelhead is in use, the rotary motion will force the screws to stay securely seated in the narrow ends of the slots. This will prevent the bat from either sliding off or lifting. To remove the bat, simply revolve it by hand until the screws slip into the large ends of the slots. The screws will then pass through these larger openings as you lift the bat off the wheelhead.

PAN

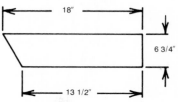

1

A satisfactory pan should be durable, convenient, and comfortable to use. To meet these requirements, certain specifications are advisable. First, the pan should be made of a non-corrosive material. Next, it should be large enough so that it does not need to be emptied too often; and, when it does need emptying or cleaning, it should be easy to remove from the wheel. The sides of the pan should be higher than the top surface of the wheelhead, so that the water and clay flung off during throwing will not spatter the potter or the surrounding area. Finally, the pan should make it possible for the potter to keep a supply of water at his fingertips and should provide shelf space for the hand tools he uses most often.

The pan described below meets all of these requirements. Also, it is not too difficult to make, and the materials required for it should be readily available. This pan design is suitable for all the wheels in the book. Please note, however, that the bracket for mounting the pan is different for each type of wheel. Therefore, directions for making brackets are included in the instructions for specific wheels. In each case, the bracket must be permanently attached to the pan.

Tools

1. Wood-cutting saw.
2. Pencil compass (see *Appendix*).
3. Saber saw or jig saw.
4. Staple gun.
5. Hammer.
6. Sharp knife.
7. Four throw-away paint brushes.
8. Metal shears.
9. Drill.

Making the Pan. Draw a half-circle with a 8 1/2″ radius at one end of the plywood panel (item 1a). Use a pencil compass (described in the *Appendix*) to draw the arc. Then, with a saber saw or jig saw, cut along the penciled curve to make the half-circle shape shown. This piece is the bottom, or base, of the pan.

Next, in the center of the half-circle, saw a hole in the plywood large enough so that the piece of 3″ pipe (item 9) fits tightly in it, as shown.

Cut the two shapes for the side pieces from the 1/4″ (or thinner) plywood (item 1b), as shown.

Parts and Materials

Item No.

1. Plywood:
   a. One 17″ × 22″ piece of 1/2″ exterior.
   b. Two 6 3/4″ × 18″ pieces of 1/4″ or thinner.
2. One 17″ length of 1 × 6 lumber.
3. One 17″ length of 1 × 5 lumber.
4. One 6 3/4″ × 29″ piece of 1/4″ mesh hardware cloth.
5. Nails:
   a. Three 4D common.
   b. 1/2 lb. sheet rock.
6. Wire staples, 3/4″, 1/4 lb.
7. One 54″ length of 1/2″ garden hose.
8. One 4″ length of 3″ plastic pipe.
9. Polyester resin, 1 qt., with hardener and pigment of desired color.
10. A 10 sq. ft. piece of fiberglass cloth.

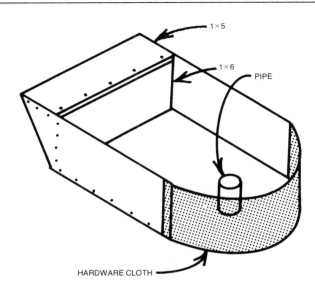

1×5

1×6

PIPE

HARDWARE CLOTH

2

You are now ready to nail (item 5b) the rectangular pieces of wood board (items 2, 3) and plywood bottom and side pieces together to form part of the pan, as shown.

The rounded end of the pan is formed of the 6 3/4″ × 29″ piece of hardware cloth (item 4). Position the cloth, as shown in the drawing, with the selvage or finished edge down, and staple it to the edge of the plywood base and the outside surfaces of the side walls.

About 1/4″ from the end of the plastic pipe (item 8), drill three nail-sized (item 5a) holes in the pipe. These holes should be equally spaced around the circumference of the pipe. Insert the pipe in the hole prepared for it so that the end with the drilled holes is flush with the bottom of the plywood pan base. Drive small nails (item 5a) through the holes in the pipe into the plywood base. This will serve to anchor the pipe securely in place.

Installing the Pan Mounting Bracket.
Put the pan-mounting bracket in place on the wheel. Then position the pan on the wheel so that the shaft is centered in the cylindrical hole. The round end of the pan should face the seat. On the bottom of the pan, mark the position of the pan-mounting bracket. Remove the pan and the mounting bracket. Position the bracket on the marks you made on the pan and lightly staple (item 6) it in place. Put the pan back on the wheel and see if the mounting hardware holds it in the proper position in relation to the shaft and the rest of the frame. Adjust the position of the pan on the bracket, if necessary.

Remove the pan and staple the bracket firmly to the bottom. Bend over the ends of the staples and pound them flat on the inside of the pan. It is advisable to apply a coat of resin over the area where the bracket joins the pan to further strengthen this assembly.

To provide a continuous and uniform top edge to the pan, slit the piece of garden hose (item 8) lengthwise and slip it over the top edges of the side walls and the hardware cloth. The hose will also make the pan more comfortable if you like to rest your arms on the edge while throwing.

The next step is to mix a pint of the resin (item 9) according to the manufacturer's instructions. Paint a coat of resin on the inside surfaces. While the resin is wet, cover all the inside surfaces with fiberglass cloth (item 10). Make sure that the fiberglass cloth laps up and over the garden hose and joins the outside surfaces of the pan. When all the fiberglass cloth is lying smoothly in place, coat it liberally with resin.

Cover the section of the pan formed from hardware cloth with an additional layer of glass cloth and resin, both inside and out.

When the resin is stiff and dry, paint the entire pan with two coats of colored resin. Pigments to color the resin come in tubes; use as much coloring as necessary to achieve the color you want.

The resin must make a smooth, continuous surface around the joint on the inside where the plastic pipe enters the pan. If there are still any openings or crevices, fill them with silicone-rubber bathtub caulking (item 7).

The completed pan should look like the one in the drawing.

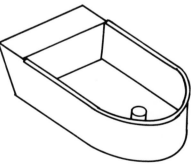

COMPLETED PAN

SEAT FOR POTTER'S WHEEL

This seat, together with the attachment hardware which is an integral part of it, is for use with all the wheels described in this book (except for the pipe frame kickwheel where the attachment hardware is different. Instructions for this hardware are included in the pipe frame wheel section). As the introduction to this section pointed out, this type of seat is really just a padded bench. However, it does provide all the support a potter needs at the wheel, because his working posture generally limits him to the front edge of whatever kind of seat he uses. An important feature of this seat is that it is designed to be adjustable, both up-and-down and forward-and-backward.

Tools

1. C clamp that opens at least 1".
2. Welding equipment.
3. Cutting torch or hacksaw with a silicon carbide rod blade.
4. Pencil.
5. Carpenter's framing square.
6. Drill with 3/8" bit.
7. Hammer.
8. Staple gun (optional).

Parts and Materials

Item No.

1. Two 8" lengths of 1" × 1" angle iron.
2. Two 1" lengths of steel rod 7/16" in diameter.
3. One 16" length of black pipe 1 1/4" in diameter.
4. One 20" length of 2" × 10" wooden board.
5. Two 3/8" × 3" carriage bolts.
6. One 1" thick piece of foam rubber, 14" × 24".
7. Staples or carpet tacks.
8. One 18" × 28" piece of vinyl upholstery material.
9. Two 3/8" wing nuts.

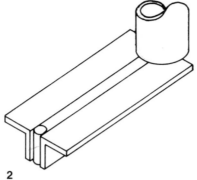

1

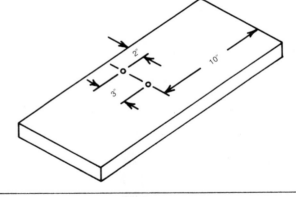

2

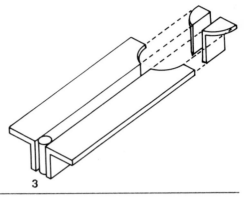

3

Making the Seat Support. Arrange the two 8″ pieces of 1″ × 1″ angle iron (item 1), with the two 1″ lengths of 7/16″ steel rod (item 2) between them, in the position shown in the drawing. Use a C clamp to hold the pieces in this position. Then, at *one end only,* weld the angle irons and the one piece of rod together.

Remove the clamp and the piece of steel rod that was not welded. This second piece of rod, which has served as a spacer, can be discarded.

Next, position the 16″ long piece of pipe (item 3) on the flat surface of the angle iron at the unwelded end of the assembly so that the angle iron overhangs half the diameter of the pipe, as shown. Draw a line around the outside of the pipe on the two pieces of angle iron.

Then, along this line, using a cutting torch or hacksaw with a rod-type blade, cut out the corner ends of the angle iron pieces as shown.

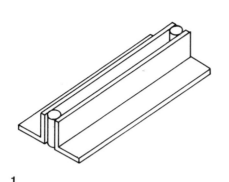

4

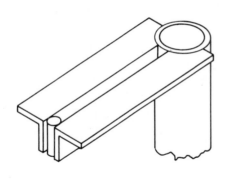

5

Lay the angle-iron assembly on a flat surface upside down. Stand the 1 1/4″ pipe in the cut-out section, as in the drawing, and tack weld the pieces together. Check with a square to make sure that the pipe and the flat surfaces of the angle-iron pieces are perpendicular (at a 90° angle) to each other. Make any necessary adjustment by tapping the pipe with a hammer. Finish welding the pieces together, as shown, and the seat support is completed.

Making the Seat. Drill two 3/8″ holes in the 20″ long piece of 2″ × 10″ wooden board (item 4), as shown.

Drive a 3/8″ × 3″ carriage bolt (item 5) into each hole until the underside of the head is tight against the board. The side of the board with the bolt heads showing will be the top of the seat. You are now ready to pad and cover the seat.

Lay the piece of 1″ thick foam rubber (item 6) on the top of the seat so that it extends 2″ beyond the edge of the board on all sides. Fold the foam down over the edges of the board, and staple or tack (item 7) it in place all the way around.

Stretch the piece of vinyl upholstery material (item 8) over the top and edges of the seat. Then staple or tack the fabric to the underside of the board. The seat is now completed.

Slip the finished seat onto the seat support by inserting the protruding ends of the bolts through the slot between the pieces of angle iron. Secure the seat in place with wing nuts (item 9).

Slip the pipe end of the seat support into the top of the seat riser of the wheel and tighten in the correct position with the adjustment bolt.

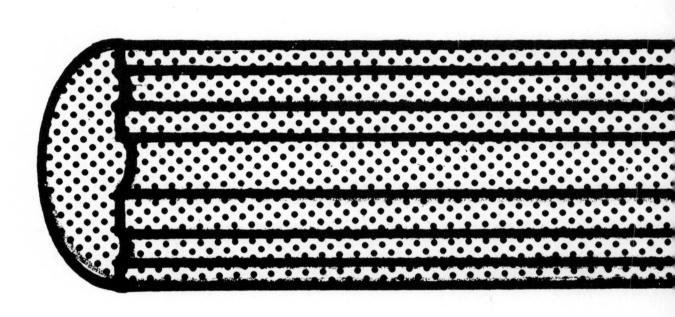

PART 3
HAND TOOLS

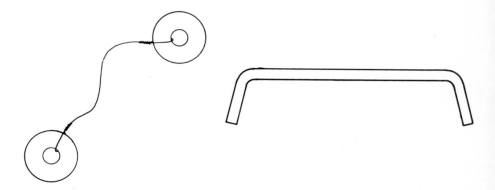

The tools suggested here are just a few of the many kinds of small, useful implements that can be made from common materials. Making hand tools is usually more economical than buying commercial ones. Another, more essential, advantage is the fact that "made" tools can be tailored to fit the exact needs of the individual potter. This individuality is important since hand tools generally play a strong role in the final design of a pot.

Sponges

The natural sponge has long been the standard type of sponge used by potters while throwing on the wheel. It is still widely preferred because most synthetic sponges do not hold enough water or are not strong enough to withstand the abrasion that occurs when they are pressed against the clay. One exception is the "Hydra Sponge," a synthetic sponge made in Greece. It is stronger and holds even more water than most natural sponges. It comes in a variety of sizes in a loaf shape that can be cut into usable slices with a band saw, an electric carving knife or a knife with a serrated edge. (See *Material Sources* in the *Appendix* for places to obtain this kind of sponge.)

Cut-off Wire

A cut-off wire for cutting clay or removing pots from bats or wheelhead can be made from two steel washers and a 16" or so length of plastic-coated, braided, stainless steel fishing-leader wire. Make sure to obtain washers that are big enough to grasp securely while working.

Thread the ends of the leader wire through the holes in the washers. Twist the ends as shown in the drawing.

Then hold the wire taut horizontally by either placing one washer under a heavy nonburnable object and holding the other end, or having a helper hold the end for you. Put a match to the plastic coating at the center. The plastic will burn with a small flame. When the flame reaches the twisted portions at the ends near the washers, the plastic will melt, bonding the wire strands together. Blow out the flame. The cut-off wire will be ready for use as soon as it cools.

Slab Cutter

To make a slab cutter, you will need a 3' length of steel rod 1/2" in diameter and about 48" of wire, either single-strand, stainless steel fishing-leader wire (80 to 100 pound test strength) or similar strength piano wire. (For suggested sources of these materials, see *Material Sources* in the *Appendix*.)

The rod must be bent to the shape shown in the drawing. An easy way to bend it is to slip one end of it into a 2' to 3' length of 1" steel pipe. About 6" of the rod should be inside the pipe. Set the rod and pipe on the floor. Stand on the rod at the point where it enters the pipe. Then, pull the pipe up to a nearly vertical position. Remove the rod. Insert the opposite end of the rod into the pipe and repeat the same bending operation.

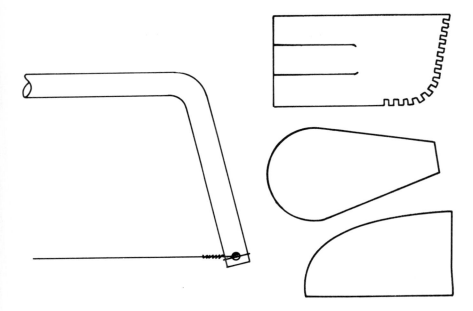

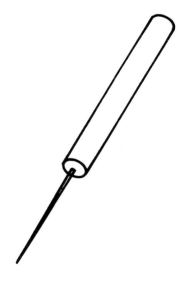

To fasten the wire to the ends of the bent rod, drill a 1/8" hole about 1/4" from each end of the rod. Thread the wire through one of these holes, wrap it around the rod, and secure it in place by twisting as shown in the drawing. Then thread the wire through the other hole, and while a helper is springing the rod so that the ends are a couple of inches closer together than normal, secure the second end of the wire. When the rod is released, it will stretch the wire taut.

The function of this cutter is to slice off a slab of clay of desired thickness. To use it, first select two strips of wood of the same thickness as the slab to be cut. Place the strips on opposite sides of a lump of clay. Press the cutter's wire against the top surface of the strips of wood and draw it toward you through the clay. Remove the detached mass of clay and put it to one side. The remaining clay will be a slab of the desired thickness.

Ribs

Ribs can be made from many materials, including wood, rubber, or plastic. Two excellent materials are translucent fiberglass-reinforced roof panels and the plastic laminates used for countertops.

Ribs of these materials can be cut to desired shapes with a jig saw, band saw, or metal-cutting shears. The edges can be sanded or filed smooth. The drawing shows some possible rib shapes.

A very good comb-type of rib can be made from the nylon blade of a kitchen spatula by cutting notches in the edges as shown.

Cut-off Needle

There are many cut-off tools on the market but some have needles which are too thick to work well. A very good tool is the biology probe that is often available inexpensively from scientific equipment supply companies.

You can make a cut-off tool by forcing the eye end of a long thin sewing needle into the end of a 4" length of 1/4" dowel. Do this by clamping the needle in a vise and pushing or pounding the dowel over the eye end of the needle.

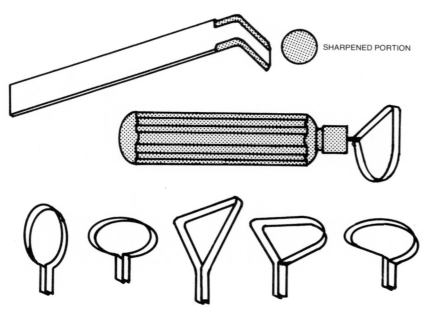

SHARPENED PORTION

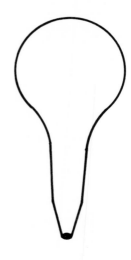

Trimming Tools

There are a number of ways to make trimming tools. A simple one can be made from a 6″ length of hacksaw blade. Grind off the sharp points of the teeth (be sure to wear safety goggles if you use a power grinder). Sharpen about 1″ of each edge of the blade at one end.

Then heat the sharpened edge to red heat with a propane or acetylene torch and bend the blade at a right angle, as shown. Reheat the sharpened part of the blade to red heat, then quickly submerge the hot end in motor oil to cool it. This last is a tempering process that hardens the blade so that it will resist abrasion in use.

More refined tools requiring more complex shaping can be made from band saw blades. These blades can often be obtained from a woodworking shop. Ask them to save a broken blade for you. These blades are often

several feet long, so one will be enough to make a number of trimming tools.

Begin by cutting off 4″ to 5″ lengths of the blade with metal shears. Next, cut off the teeth and sharpen both the edges of each piece of blade on a bench grinder or with a file.

You can bend the blades with your hands or with pliers. Some useful shapes are shown in the drawing. Note that, for all the tool shapes, the ends of the blade must be even and parallel.

The trimming tool blades can be clamped in an X-Acto knife holder. If the blade is too wide for the holder, the ends can be trimmed with metal shears.

Any trimming tool will become dull with use and will need to be sharpened occasionally. Sharpening can be done on a bench grinder or with a file if the steel is not too hard.

Glaze and Slip Syringes

To apply small amounts of glaze or to trail thin slips or glazes, use a rubber ear syringe that can be purchased in most drugstores. For applying larger amounts, there is a larger irrigating type of syringe available either at drugstores or at surgical supply houses. Some of these come with a removable tip. If you replace the tip with a larger-diameter metal tubing, this type of syringe can be especially useful for putting glaze in small openings, such as bottle necks. A cheaper alternative is the kind of syringe used to put water in automobile batteries. These are available in auto supply stores. You can also experiment with old plastic squeeze bottles from liquid soaps or hand lotions.

BANDING WHEEL

A banding wheel is handy for use during glaze application and also for turning a fragile piece during hand building. Heavy-duty banding wheels can be quite expensive; therefore directions here provide a sturdy piece of equipment at little cost that can be assembled in an hour or less.

Tools

1. Compass.
2. Saber saw, band saw, or coping saw.
3. Drill with 3/16" bit.
4. Screwdriver.
5. Lubricating oil.
6. Allen wrench to fit set screws in pulley.

Parts and Materials

Item No.

1. A sheet of 5/8" plywood, 10" × 20".
2. Round-head wood screws:
   a. One 1/2", #6.
   b. Six 1", #8.
3. Two V-belt pulleys, any diameter up to 8", 5/8" bore size.
4. One 4" length of 5/8" cold-rolled steel shaft.

Assembly. Cut two disks, 10" in diameter, out of the 5/8" plywood (item 1). Screw the 1/2" round-head wood screw (item 2a) all the way into the center of one disk. The exposed head will provide a pivot point which will rest on the end of the shaft.

Drill three holes all the way through each pulley (item 3) in the locations indicated in the drawing. Place one of the pulleys on the plywood disk that has the screw in it so that the screw head is centered in the hole of the pulley. Use three of the 1", #8 screws (item 2b) to fasten the pulley to the disk. This assembly completes the top disk of the banding wheel.

Use the remaining 1" screws (item 2b) to attach the second pulley to the center of the other plywood disk. Insert the 5/8" shaft (item 4) into this pulley and tighten the set screw.

Now oil the inside of the pulley on the top disk. Slip the pulley of the top disk over the end of the shaft. Do not tighten the set screw in this pulley.

The top disk should now turn freely on the shaft. If it does not, remove the disk and polish the end of the shaft with steel wool or fine sandpaper.

The completed banding wheel should now be ready to use.

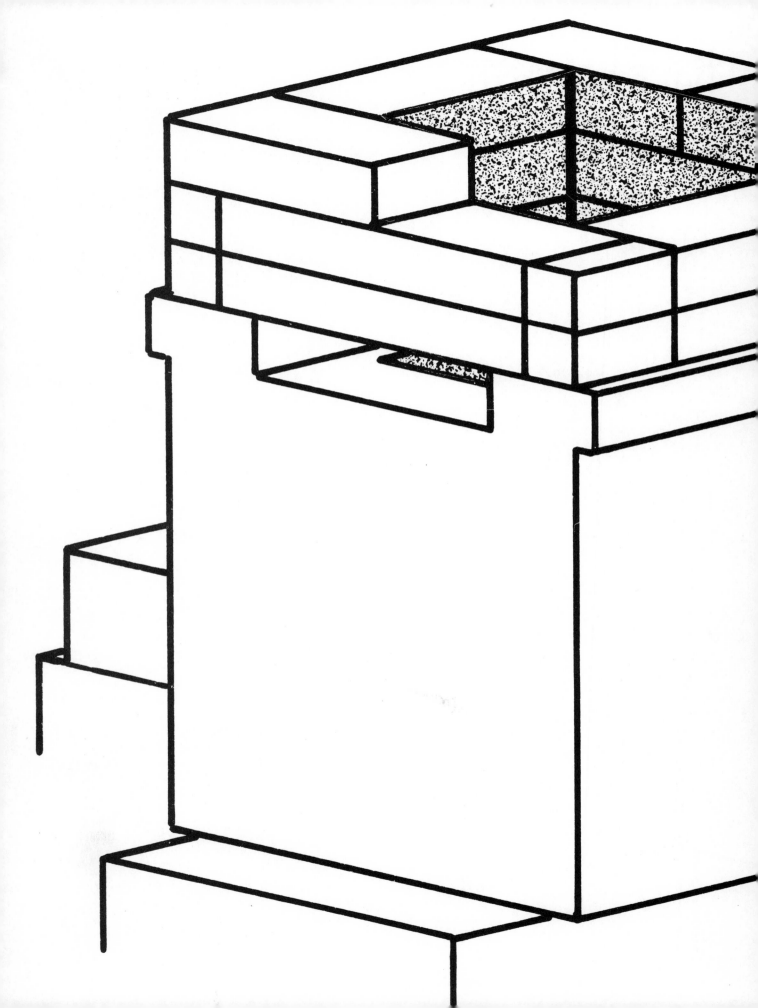

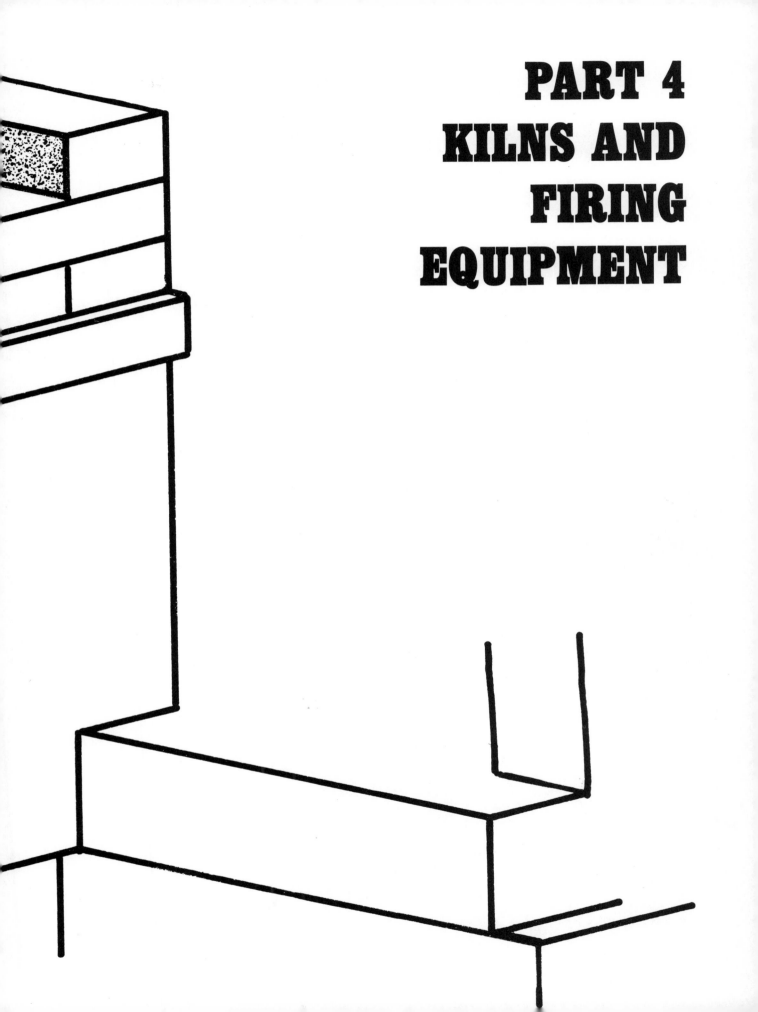

PART 4
KILNS AND
FIRING
EQUIPMENT

There are more varieties of kilns in use than would fit into a book of this size, even if no other kind of equipment were discussed. But since this book contains plans for constructing most other kinds of pottery-making equipment as well, it was necessary to limit the types of kiln designs.

The selection we offer here represents the most widely used types and most of the basic principles of kiln construction are demonstrated. We have also tried to limit our selection to kilns that are feasible for inexperienced kiln builders to construct with the minimum of assistance from specialists such as welders, plumbers, and electricians. All the designs can be constructed from materials that are available in most areas, or that can be obtained by mail order.

Instructions are given here for kilns capable of firing most kinds of ceramic ware—high and low temperature as well as raku and salt glaze—and designs for both regular and car-kiln structures.

We have not included electric kilns, because we think that inexperienced kiln builders should not attempt them, nor wood-fired kilns, because of their specialized requirements, including the problem of obtaining adequate fuel supplies.

The section on burner systems includes design and construction information for firing kilns with natural gas, LP (liquid petroleum) gas, or oil. In another section, firing practices are discussed from the standpoint of safety, production of high-quality ware and economic operation.

The construction costs of these kiln designs have been held down wherever possible. We estimate that the catenary arch car kiln described in this section can be built for a little more than a quarter of the going price for a comparable one built commercially, and, of course, such commercial prices do not include shipping or installation charges.

For many prospective kiln builders, perhaps one of the most useful sections in this part will be the one on modifying kiln designs. The kilns presented in this book are relatively small,

Sheet metal roof vent installed on the chimney of an indoor kiln.

Atmospheric burners connected to a single gas supply line.

yet they should fill the needs of those potters just beginning to build kilns. For others who want larger units, detailed suggestions are given for enlarging the designs we have provided (see *Kiln Design Modification*). Information is also included on adapting the kilns for special purposes, such as salt glazing (see the *Catenary Arch Kiln*) and indoor locations (see *Special Considerations for Indoor Kilns*).

We consider the section on kiln design modification one of the most important in this book, because we want to encourage potters to build equipment that fills their own particular needs.

The question may arise, when a potter decides to build his own kiln, of the energy it will be consuming and the pollution it will be adding to our already overburdened atmosphere. The catalog for a show at the Museum of Contemporary Crafts in New York City in 1972, entitled "Salt Glaze Ceramics," includes an article that sheds some light on this question: In firing a 30 cubic foot salt glaze kiln to cone 9, the kiln consumes 30 pounds of natural gas, 570 pounds of air, 25 pounds of salt. In the last two hours of firing, the effluents produced are 60 pounds of water vapor, 84 pounds of carbon dioxide, 456 pounds of nitrogen, one pound of sodium compounds, 13.5 pounds of chlorine (in the form of hydrochloric acid and other chlorine compounds).

The catalog concludes, "With the exception of the sodium and chlorine compounds, the firing of this kiln is comparable—in energy consumed and effluent produced—to a car running at 70 m.p.h. for one hour or a 707 aircraft at cruising speed for three seconds."

Catenary arch car kiln.

Completed all-welded car frame for catenary arch car kiln.

Sprung arch kiln, updraft type, nearing completion.

CATENARY ARCH KILN

These plans are for an 18 cubic foot outdoor kiln which provides 10 cubic feet of useful interior space. Although the basic design is also suitable for indoor use, certain changes would be necessary. (These are discussed in *Special Considerations for Indoor Kilns.*)

The first step in constructing any kiln is to select a desirable site. It is important to locate an outdoor kiln at least 10' from the nearest building or solid wall. If such existing structures are especially tall, it may be necessary to locate the kiln even farther away. Allow for an ample walkway around the entire kiln so that you can adjust the burners and kiln structure when necessary. Also leave plenty of room at the front of the kiln for loading and unloading.

Once the site is selected, it must be prepared. A space of at least 7' by 9' should be cleared of all large stones, trees, shrubs, and other obstructions. Then level the surface. Over the area where the chimney will be located, cut away overhanging branches of trees or shrubs, because the hot flue gases could kill them or set them on fire.

Tools

1. Shovel.
2. Rake.
3. Wood-cutting saw.
4. Hacksaw with regular and/or carbide-tipped blades.
5. Tape measure or folding rule, 6'.
6. Carpenter's square.
7. Carpenter's spirit level.
8. Concrete mixing box, or child's rigid plastic wading pool.
9. Wheelbarrow (optional).
10. Screed (a 7' long 2 × 4).
11. A l0' length of sash chain.
12. Can of spray paint, small amount, any color (optional).
13. Saber saw.
14. Circular saw with a blade to cut hard masonry, or a cold chisel.
15. Pliers.
16. Screwdriver.
17. Knife.
18. Drill with 1/4", 3/8", high-speed bit and 1/4" masonry bit.
19. Hammer.

Parts and Materials

1. Pieces of 2 × 6 lumber:
   a. Two 8' lengths.
   b. Two 68" lengths.
2. One-half lb. 16D common nails.
3. Wet-mix concrete, 2 cu. yds.
4. Two 48" × 67" pieces of 6" × 6" mesh wire fence.
5. Newspaper.
6. Ten 18" lengths of 2 × 2 or 2 × 4 lumber.

Note: items 1 through 6 are needed to pour a concrete slab that will provide a foundation for the kiln. If some other suitable surface is available, the slab may be omitted.

7. One 4 × 8 sheet of 1/8" thick non-tempered hardboard.
8. One 4 × 8 × 1/2" sheet of plywood (CD or plyscore grade).
9. Two 2 × 2s or 2 × 4s, 30" long.
10. Pieces of 1" × 5" board:
    a. Four 12" lengths.
    b. Four 18" lengths.
    c. Two 35" lengths.
    d. Two 24" lengths.
11. Four 3/4" thick wooden blocks.
12. Nails:
    a. Two finishing nails.
    b. 1 lb. of 1 3/8" sheet rock nails.
    c. 1/2 lb. 10D common nails.
    d. 1/2 lb. 8D common nails.
13. Four plastic shields with 1 1/2" No. 12 screws.
14. Screw hooks with nuts:
    a. Eight 1/4".
    b. Four 3/8".
15. Chain:
    a. Four 40" lengths—medium weight.
    b. One 24" length—medium weight with a hook.
    c. Two 54" lengths—heavy weight (for salt kiln only).
16. A 40' length of braided galvanized steel wire.
17. A heavy tension spring.
18. One pint of urethane finish or equivalent.
19. A piece of plastic drop cloth, 4' × 6' or larger.

20. Twenty 8″ × 8″ × 16″ concrete or cinder blocks.

21. One 3′ × 8′ sheet of 20 to 24 gauge aluminum.

22. Pieces of 1″ × 1″ × 1/8″ angle iron:
    a. Four 4′ lengths.
    b. Four 5′ lengths.

23. Two 60″ lengths of 3″ channel iron (for salt kiln only).

24. Ten lbs. of dry fireclay.

25. Five lbs. of grog.

26. Aluminum hydrate and kaolin, about 5 lbs. of each. Only if this kiln is to be used for salt glazing.

Note: brick sizes and shapes can be found in the *Table of Standard Brick Sizes* in the *Appendix.*

27. Two hundred low-duty firebricks.

28. High-duty firebricks:
    a. 270 straights.
    b. 4 13 1/2″ straights.
    c. 30 soaps.
    d. 7 splits.
    e. 35 #1 arch.
    f. 42 #2 arch.
    g. 7 #3 arch.
    h. 14 #1 wedge.
    i. 12 #2 wedge.

29. Insulating firebricks:
    a. 35 straights.
    b. 50 #1 arch.

30. An 8 1/2 cu. ft. piece of castable insulation (2400° F. quality).

Note: if the kiln is to be used for salt glazing, use a castable insulation that contains 50% or more alumina.

31. Thirty sq. ft. of 1 1/2″ thick block insulation, 1900° F.

32. One 12″ × 12″ (minimum) to 18″ × 18″ (maximum) kiln shelf or fireclay bat.

33. Four atmospheric burners, rated at about 185,000 Btu/hr. (see *Burners*).

34. Safety equipment and plumbing supplies (see *Burner Systems and Safety Controls*).

35. Four kiln flaps (see *Kiln Flaps*).

36. One damper (see *Damper*).

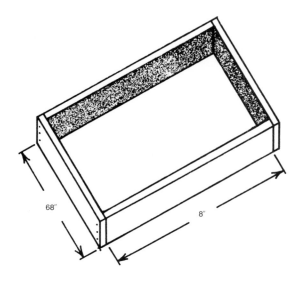

1

Making the Foundation. The foundation for this kind of kiln is a poured concrete slab. To make the wooden frame into which the concrete for the slab can be poured, nail the 2 × 6s (item 1a, 1b, 2) together, as shown in the drawing.

Next place the frame where the slab is to be poured. Make the frame level by removing dirt from underneath it wherever necessary.

Next drive the wooden stakes, made of 2 × 2s or 2 × 4s (item 6), into the ground until even with the top of the frame at about 3′ intervals around the outside of the frame. Nail the frame to the stakes so the top edge is level. Now remove, or redistribute, and tamp down the dirt inside the frame until you have a well-packed dirt floor about 4″ below the top edge of the frame.

You are now ready to pour the concrete slab. You can buy and mix the ingredients yourself (see the *Appendix* for how to mix concrete) or buy ready-mixed concrete from a local supplier. Unless you have had experience at mixing large quantities of concrete, it is probably best to order the ready-mix.

Note: it is important that you have the frame properly positioned and everything else ready to use before the ready-mix concrete truck arrives. Otherwise, you will have to pay extra for waiting time. Also, if the truck cannot be driven right up to the frame to be unloaded, be prepared to transport the wet concrete by wheelbarrow or some other means.

Soak the dirt inside the frame with water. Next pour in concrete until the surface comes about half-way up the inside of the frame. Then rake it level.

Now place the wire mesh (item 4) inside the frame and pour in the remaining concrete. As soon as possible, smooth the top surface so that it fills all parts of the frame evenly. The best way to accomplish this is to use what masons call a "screed." This is simply a straight length of 2 × 4 about 2′ longer than the width of the frame. Smooth the concrete by resting the screed on the edges of the frame and sliding it across the surface using a back-and-forth motion.

It will take three or four days before the slab will be cured and strong enough to permit laying the kiln floor. In the interval, after the slab becomes hard to the touch, keep it wet by covering it with several thicknesses of wet newspapers. Keeping the slab wet during the curing period makes it stronger.

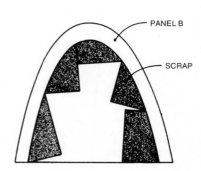

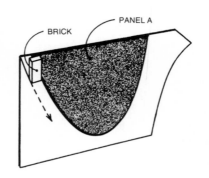

2

Making the Arch Support Form.
While waiting for the concrete slab to cure, you can make the hardboard and plywood arch support form. Cut a 31 1/2″ × 96″ piece of hardboard (item 7). To make the hardboard flexible enough to bend without breaking, lay it on a clean, flat surface and pile several thicknesses of soaked newspapers on it.

While the hardboard is soaking, prepare to cut the two arch-shaped sections out of the plywood panel (item 8) by standing the panel on one of its long edges. Use a carpenter's spirit level to make sure that the top edge of the panel is level; use wood or paper shims, if necessary, to keep it level.

To establish the correct shape of the kiln arch, drive a finishing nail (item 12a) part way into the top edge of the plywood panel near the upper left corner. From the nail, measure 37″ across the top edge and drive in another finishing nail. Now, draw a line on the panel 37″ from the top edge. This line must be parallel to the top and bottom edges of the panel.

Now hang one end of a length of sash chain from one of the nails. Loop the chain over the second nail, allowing enough of it to hang free so that the bottom of the curve it forms intersects the line drawn on the panel.

Mark the curve established by the chain with a pencil, or even better, by spraying over the chain with a can of spray paint. With the saber saw, cut out the piece outlined by the line established by the chain. This is panel A of the arch form.

3

The curve for the larger B panel is established by laying panel A on the remaining part of the plywood. Mark the shape of panel A on panel B. Then stand a firebrick on end against the edge of panel A. Mark along the outside of the brick while moving it around the periphery of panel A so that a curve is laid out 4 1/2″ from the curved edge of panel A. Cut out panel B.

4

Some of the uncut portions of the plywood panel can now be used to make pieces to duplicate the curved part of panel A. Use panel A as a template in cutting out the pieces of plywood needed, then arrange and nail (item 12b) the cutouts on panel B so that they duplicate the shape of panel A. Make sure to leave a 4 1/2″ margin all around, as shown in the drawing.

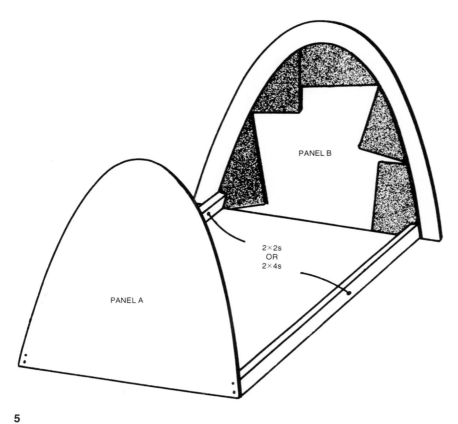

PANEL B

2×2s
OR
2×4s

PANEL A

5

Nail the ends of the 2 × 2s or 2 × 4s
(item 9) to the A and B panels with
10D nails (item 12c), as shown.

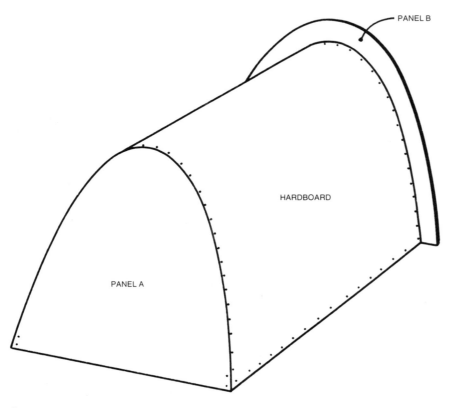

PANEL B

HARDBOARD

PANEL A

6

Now it is time to use the wet, softened
hardboard. Bend it over panel A and
the built-up A panel on the B panel
as shown, and nail it into position
with the sheet rock nails (item 12b).

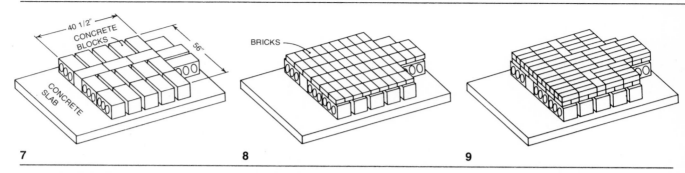

7

8

9

Laying the Kiln Floor. When the concrete base has cured, the concrete (or cinder) blocks (item 20) on which the kiln floor will be laid can be put in place. Note that the two outer side rows of blocks must be evenly spaced and positioned so that their holes are aligned from front to rear, as shown in the drawing.

Now arrange the low-duty bricks (item 27), making up the first layer of the kiln floor in the pattern indicated in the drawing. No mortar is needed.

Next, place the second layer of the kiln floor on top of the first, using the high-duty brick (item 28a). Arrange the bricks in the pattern shown in the drawing.

This overlapping alignment of the bricks has the effect of interlocking the two layers of the kiln floor thereby helping to stabilize the structure of the rest of the kiln.

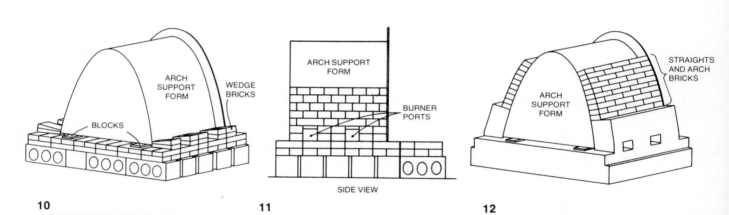

10

11

12

Building the Kiln Arch. Stand the arch form on the kiln floor with a wooden block (item 11) under each side of the front and back panels as shown.

Begin the brickwork by laying one course (or layer) of #1 and one course of #2 wedge bricks (item 28h, 28i), as shown in the drawing.

Next lay up the 9″ straight sections on both sides of the arch with high-duty straights (item 28a). The joints must be staggered, as in the drawing. The end bricks of each course, as shown in the drawing, can be straights or soaps (item 28c), depending on what is needed to complete each course so that its ends are flush with those beneath. Leave two openings for burner ports in each side of the arch, using straights to bridge the openings.

Note: do not attempt to lay up all rows of the bricks on one side of the form before starting the other side, because the weight of the bricks will move the arch form. Lay up a few courses of bricks on one side, then a few on the other side.

After you have laid about five rows of straights, their inner faces will no longer butt perfectly flat against the arch-support form. At that point, begin laying up the courses of #1 and #2 arch bricks (item 28e, 28f), and straights that will make up the rest of the arch, as shown in the drawing. From this point on the arch will be only 4 1/2″ thick. It will now be necessary to cut one brick to complete each course (see the *Appendix* for how to cut brick).

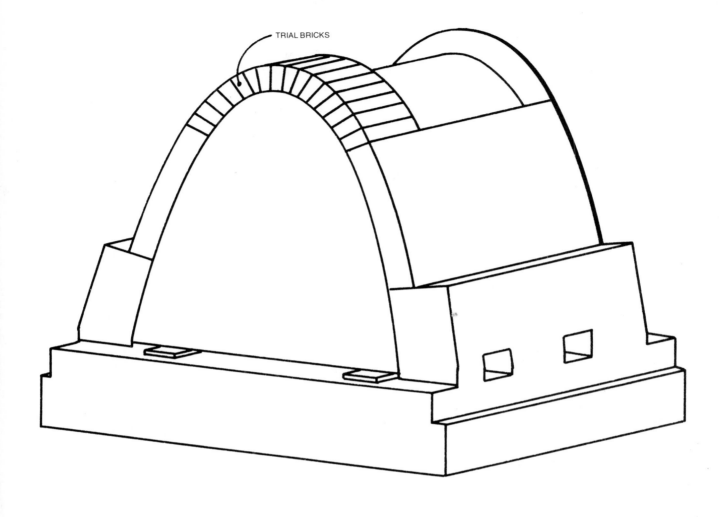

TRIAL BRICKS

13

Completing the Arch. It is important to lay up the arch bricks so that their inner faces fit flat against the arch-support form. Choose the brick shapes for each row with this in mind. A good rule of thumb is to use less tapered bricks if space occurs between the bottom edges of the bricks and the arch-support form; more tapered bricks if the space is at the top. If a course of bricks is not perfectly level, brush a thick liquid mixture of fireclay (item 24) and water over the low spots. Then set the bricks in this mixture so that no space is left between any two courses.

At the point where a gap of about 2′ remains between the two sides of the arch, it will be necessary to determine in advance which types of bricks should be used to complete the arch.

Both sides of the arch must have the same number of courses of the same types and sizes of bricks, and they must occur in the same sequence.

This order must be kept even if it results in something less than perfect fit between the courses of the bricks and the arch-support form.

Stack up one brick per course at the front of the arch, as shown in the drawing. It may be necessary to use some splits (item 28d) or #3 arch bricks (item 28g) to achieve the proper fit. If the bricks do not fit properly, it may be necessary to adjust the opening between the finished parts of the arch by slightly changing the height of the arch-support form. Try making such adjustments by sliding shims made of thin pieces of wood or metal under

both ends of the support form, or by replacing the 3/4″ blocks supporting the form with thinner ones. Keep blocks that are at least 3/8″ thick under the form.

Once the test bricks are fitted into place, mark the sequence of types of bricks on the end of the arch form, remove the test bricks, and finish laying up the arch. When it is complete, remove the blocks from under the ends of the arch-support form and slide the form out.

Inspect the arch carefully for loose or crooked bricks. Adjust problem bricks or those immediately surrounding them by tapping them with a hammer from the inside or outside, as required. This will help tighten the arch and make it more stable.

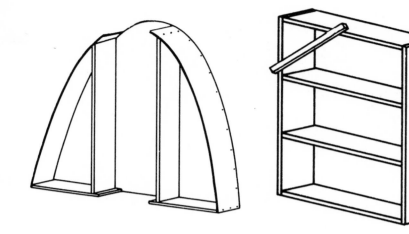

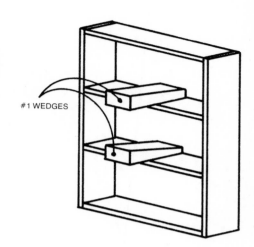

#1 WEDGES

14

15

16

Casting the Front and Back Walls.

To make the mold for the end walls, remove the larger, B panel from the arch-support form and pull off the scrap pieces making up the outline of the A panel. Cut two 5″ × 48″ pieces of hardboard (item 7) and nail them to the curved edges of panel B, as shown. Complete construction of the mold by nailing in the lengths of 1″ × 5″ board (items 10a, 10c) in place. The long boards must be parallel and 16 1/2″ apart.

Next build the box-shaped mold for the door sections, as shown in the drawing, from 1″ × 5″ lumber (items 10b, 10d, 12d). The three compartments of the mold should be equal in size.

Check the door mold with a carpenter's square and nail a strip of wood across one corner of it to keep it square. Coat all interior surfaces of the molds with urethane finish (item 18) or some other suitable sealer and allow to dry. Spread a sheet of plastic (item 19) on a smooth floor and lay the door molds on it.

Altogether, it is necessary to make four wall sections and five door sections. However, mix only enough castable insulation (item 30), following directions on the package, for two of the wall sections and three of the door sections, because that is all that can be cast at one time, using the molds you have made. Since different types of insulation produce different volumes, mix only one or two bags at first and from these you can determine how much you will need to fill all the molds. If a concrete mixer or mixing box is not available, you can mix the castable in a child's small rigid plastic wading pool.

Pour the mixed castable into the two molds, filling them completely. If necessary, remove any excess and smooth the top surfaces of the newly poured castable by sliding a screed across the molds as you did when making the slab.

Allow at least 24 hours for the castable to cure. To remove the cast parts, the molds will have to be partially disassembled.

Put the first castings aside and reassemble the molds for a second casting. Mix enough additional castable for two more door sections and two more wall sections. This time, before pouring the castable, place two water-soaked #1 wedge bricks in two of the compartments of the door mold, as shown in the drawing. As soon as the insulation in this second casting becomes firm enough so that it does not flow, remove the bricks from the door mold. The resulting holes will form the peepholes in the door.

Note: if this kiln is to be used for salt glazing, follow the instructions at the end of this section for casting the wall sections.

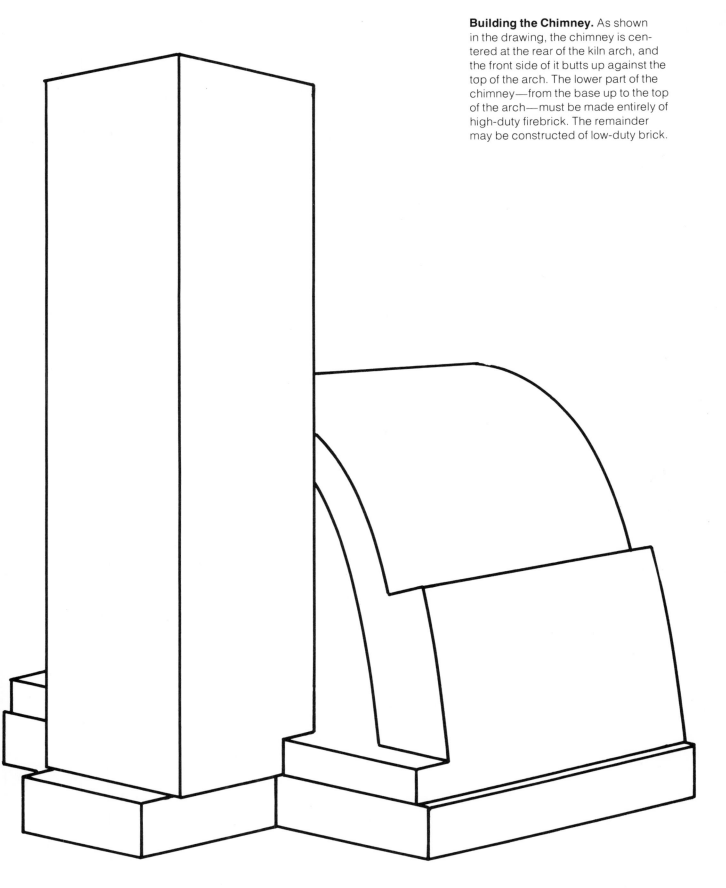

Building the Chimney. As shown in the drawing, the chimney is centered at the rear of the kiln arch, and the front side of it butts up against the top of the arch. The lower part of the chimney—from the base up to the top of the arch—must be made entirely of high-duty firebrick. The remainder may be constructed of low-duty brick.

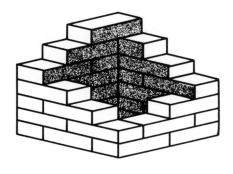

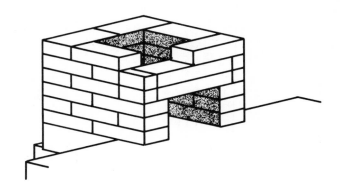

18

It is important to lay all the bricks used in the chimney so that their joints interlock, as indicated in this detail drawing, to make a more rigid, stable chimney.

19

For the base of the chimney, omit the bricks that would normally form the front center of the first three courses. This gap constitutes the flue opening. Bridge the flue opening with two 13 1/2″ straights (item 28b). Complete these two courses with regular straights, some of which will have to be cut in half and soaps cut in half to fit at the ends of the 13 1/2″ straights.

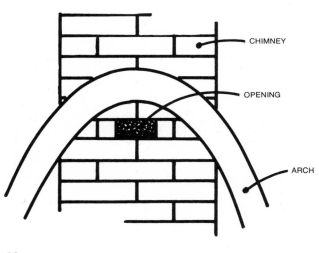

22

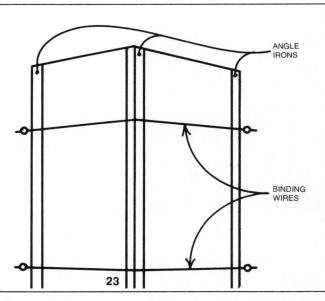

23

Continue laying up the bricks until you are one row beneath the inside edge of the arch. This row should have a half-brick opening let into the front chimney wall to provide a small, secondary flue opening.

Continue using high-duty firebrick to the top of the arch. The remainder of the chimney can be made of low-duty firebrick. The chimney must be at least 4′ higher than the top of arch—or even higher if the nearest buildings or walls are particularly tall. If, during the first few firings, frequent downdrafts occur, this will be an indication that the height of the chimney must be increased.

Place a length of angle iron (item 22a) on each corner of the portion of the chimney that extends above the top of the arch.

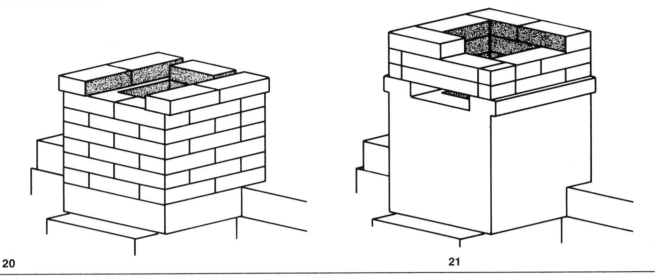

20

The damper opening must be made in the next course. To do this, place the four side bricks·so that they extend out over the sides of the chimney walls 3/4" on each side. This will leave an opening between the bricks 10 1/2" wide. Place one brick in the opening of the front wall of the chimney, centering it, as indicated in the drawing. The 3/4" wide openings on either side of this brick can be packed with clay after the chimney is completed.

The opening that remains in the rear wall of the chimney wall accommodate the 10" × 16" × 1/2" thick steel plate (item 36) that will be used as a damper. (See instructions for making the damper later in this part.) The 3/4" spaces on either side will function as tracks, permitting the damper to slide in and out.

21

The damper opening should be bridged with straights (item 28b) in the same manner as the flue opening.

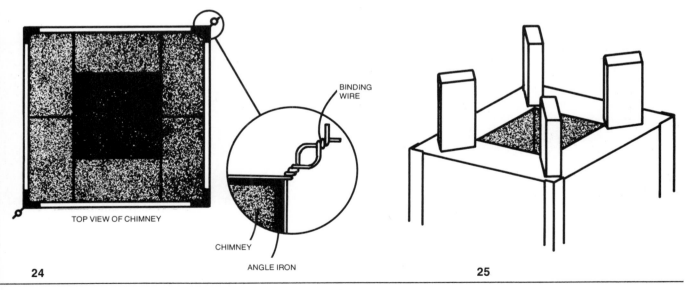

TOP VIEW OF CHIMNEY

BINDING WIRE

CHIMNEY

ANGLE IRON

24

Secure the angle irons to the chimney corners with two or more lengths of heavy wire (item 16), twisting the ends at two corners of the chimney to clamp the angle irons tightly around the bricks, as in the drawing.

25

To minimize downdrafts, place a brick at each corner of the top of the chimney, as shown, and set a kiln shelf or fireclay bat (item 32) on top of the bricks.

Insulating the Arch. The upper portion of the arch must now be insulated with 2000° F. insulating firebricks and block insulation. Start by laying a single row of the firebricks (items 29a, 29b) at the front and another at the back of the arch, as indicated in the drawing. Shape these bricks to fit as snugly as possible against the inner layer of arch bricks by rubbing them against a rough surface, such as concrete. Some cutting of the insulating firebricks will be necessary to secure a good fit where they meet the chimney. Although these firebricks can be cut with any coarse-toothed saw, they are very abrasive and will wear out the blade quickly. For best results, use an old saw or a hacksaw with a blade that has a cutting edge of silicon carbide chips.

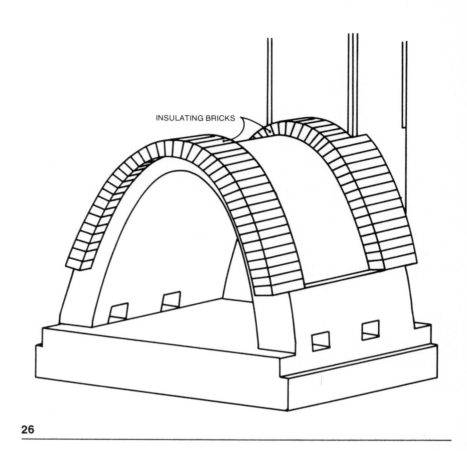

26

Apply three layers of 1 1/2″ thick block insulation (item 31) between the two rows of insulating bricks. To make the insulation fit as tightly as possible, some pieces will have to be cut half-through, lengthwise, and partially broken so that they fit the curved arch more closely, as shown in the drawing.

Note: block insulation that is 1 1/2″ thick, generally comes in a case containing 30 square feet. This may not be quite enough to fill the space in the drawing. If more is needed, substitute a few of the 2000° F. insulating firebricks. These can be placed on top of the hard firebricks forming the outer half of the 9″ thick portion of the arch. The block insulation should be used on the more curved top and sides of the arch.

Finally, cover the insulation layer with a sheet of aluminum (item 21). Run two heavy wires (item 16) over the arch and anchor them into the concrete blocks with screws in lead or plastic shields (item 13) to hold the aluminum sheet in place.

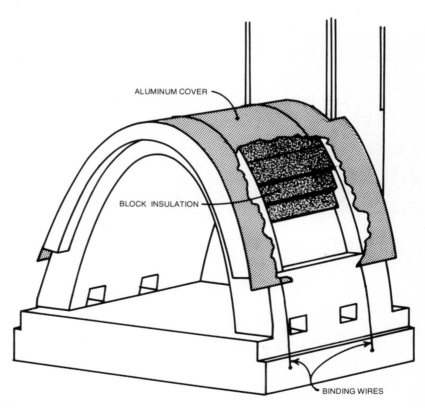

27

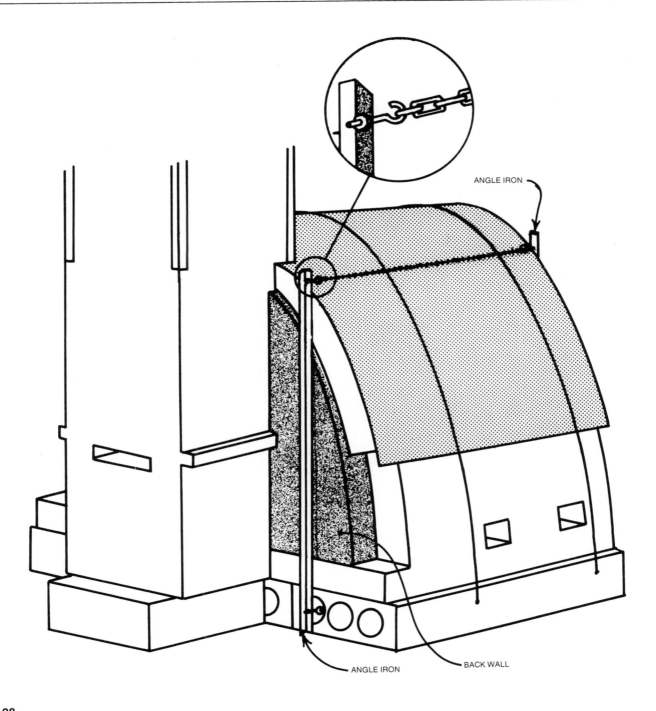

ANGLE IRON

ANGLE IRON

BACK WALL

28

Kiln Assembly. Set the four cast wall sections in place. The rear sections will have to be notched to fit around the damper track. The notches can be cut with a circular saw equipped with a masonry-cutting blade or with a cold chisel. Sawing the notches will avoid the possibility of breaking the cast pieces. Adjust the wall sections by putting clay under the low spots to level them so they fit into place.

Drill a 3/8″ hole about 2″ from each end of each of the four pieces of angle iron (item 22b). To hold the wall sections in place with the angle irons, run chains (item 15a) through the concrete blocks at the bottom and over the metal cover on the top of the kiln. Put the screw eyes (item 14a) into the holes that you drilled in the angle iron and loop

the chains over these screw eyes, as shown in the drawing. Butt the rear wall sections up against the chimney as closely as possible. Position the front wall panels in place on each side of the kiln. Do not tighten the chains completely at this time because the front wall panels will have to be moved to fit around the door section.

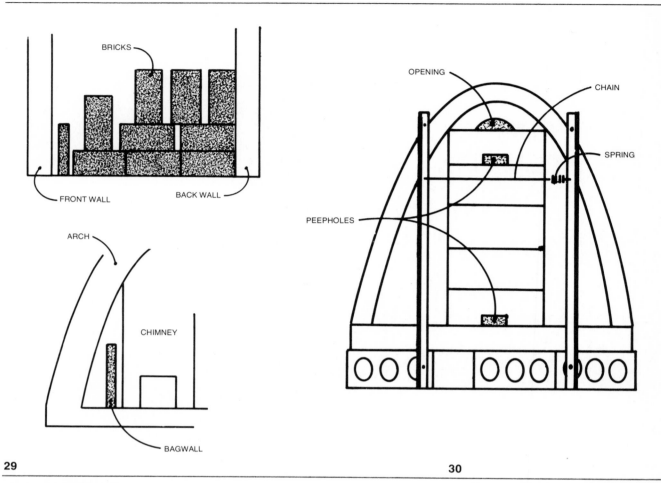

29

30

Installing the Bagwall. The bagwall is a loosely stacked arrangement of bricks used to distribute the heat evenly throughout the kiln. It consists of high-duty straights (left-over wedge and arch bricks can be used, also) arranged roughly, as shown, between the burner ports and the area where the ware to be fired will be stacked. This is only a trial arrangement of the bagwall. It may have to be adjusted after the first couple of firings. (Detailed suggestions for adjusting the bagwall can be found in *Kiln Design Modification.*)

Sealing the Kiln. To insure that the front wall sections stay in place during firing, attach a chain with a heavy tension spring (item 15b, 17) to one of the front angle irons. Fit the other end of the chain with a hook. Stretch the chain across the front of the kiln and hook it to the other angle iron during each firing.

Any large cracks, which may appear around the cast wall sections or at the ends of the brick at the front of the damper track, can be packed tightly with a mixture of 2/3 fireclay (item 24) and 1/3 grog (item 25) and just enough water to make all the ingredients stick together. Small cracks do not have to be sealed.

This kiln requires four burners (item 33) and related plumbing and safety equipment (item 34). It also requires kiln flaps (item 35) and a damper (item 36). For instructions on how to make these items, as well as on the special considerations for indoor kilns, see specific sections on these subjects later in this part.

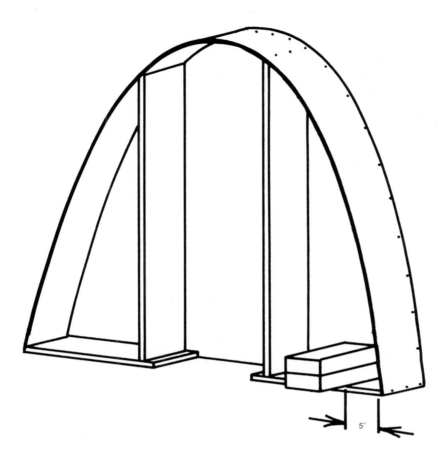

5"

31

Salt Glazing Modifications. The only kiln in this book entirely suitable for salt glazing is the regular catenary arch kiln (*not* the catenary arch car kiln), and even this kiln design must be modified before it can be used for salt.

Special holes for adding salt during firing must be provided at the bottom of the cast front wall sections. The best time to do this is when the wall sections are being cast. Position two water-soaked bricks at the bottom of each mold. (These bricks are shown in place in one mold.) Pour in the castable insulation. Remove the bricks as soon as the insulation is firm enough to support itself, so that it will not flow back into the holes left by the bricks. These holes can be plugged with bricks during firing.

All interior surfaces of the kiln must be coated with a special protective material to avoid rapid deterioration of the bricks. This coating is made of equal parts aluminum hydrate and kaolin by volume (item 26). Stir in enough water to produce a creamlike consistency. Paint this coating on all the interior kiln surfaces. After about 20 firings this coating will have to be scraped off and a new coating applied. The firebox and floor should also be protected; coat them with 1″ of castable insulation (item 30).

The bagwall in a salt glaze kiln needs to be only 9″ high. The arrangement of bricks for the bagwall should present a solid surface directly in front of each burner with open space between burners.

Do not place the pots directly on the brick floor of the kiln. The fire-brick used in the floor is a poor heat conductor and will therefore cause uneven heating of the pots that can result in severe cracking. Place the first layer of shelves directly on the floor. The silicon carbide conducts even heat to the bottoms of the pots.

Salt glazing causes the kiln floor to expand. This in turn causes the bottom of the arch to spread out on a catenary arch kiln. To counter this, run a length of 3″ channel iron (item 23) along the bottom of the arch at each side so that it covers about 1/2″ of the first row of wedge bricks. Hold these pieces of channel together with lengths of heavy chain (item 15c) at the front and back of the kiln. The chains can be tightened by attaching them to screw hooks (item 14b) in 1/2″ holes drilled in each end of the channel.

SPRUNG ARCH KILN

The 24 cubic foot sprung arch kiln presented here has 12.5 cubic feet of useful space—about the same as the catenary arch kiln in the preceding section. Plans for both are offered to demonstrate the two basic arch shapes and the different problems encountered in building each type.

With the catenary arch, the arch-support form is more difficult to make, but the kiln requires rather simple steel reinforcements to hold it together. The sprung arch design, on the other hand, uses two arch-support forms that are somewhat easier to build, but the kiln requires a rather elaborate system of steel braces to hold it together. The sprung arch kiln also entails greater structural volume than the catenary, yet it provides just about the same amount of useful interior space.

This kiln cannot be used for salt glazing because the interior is made of insulating firebricks.

Parts and Materials

Item No.

1. Pieces of 2 × 6 lumber:
   a. Two 8' lengths.
   b. Two 4' lengths.
2. One-half lb. 16D common nails.
3. Wet-mix concrete, 1 1/3 cu. yds.
4. One 45" × 94" piece of 6" × 6" mesh wire fence.
5. Newspaper or straw.
6. Ten 18" lengths of 2 × 2 or 2 × 4 lumber.

Note: items 1 through 6 are needed to pour a concrete slab that will provide a foundation for the kiln.

7. Pieces of 1 × 8 lumber:
   a. Three 34" lengths.
   b. Two 18" lengths.
8. Fourteen 1 × 3s, 31" long (often called strapping or furring strips).
9. Four 2 × 4s, 34" long.
10. One lb. 6D common nails.
11. Seventeen 8" × 8" × 16" concrete or cinder blocks.
12. Ten 3/8" washers and nuts (16 threads to the inch).

Note: brick sizes and shapes can be found in the *Table of Standard Brick Sizes* in the *Appendix*.

13. Two hundred low-duty firebricks (available at lumberyards).
14. Insulating firebricks, 2300°F.:
    a. 300 straights.
    b. 10 featheredge skews.
    c. 3 #2 arch.
    d. 46 #1 arch.
    e. 8 straights, 2" × 4 1/2" × 9".
15. High-duty firebricks:
    a. 5 straights, 2 1/2" × 4 1/2" × 13 1/2".
    b. 45 straights.

16. Seven super-duty firebrick soaps (more of these will be needed for shelf supports depending on the size and number of shelves you plan to use).
17. Eleven and one-half sq. ft. of block insulation 2" thick.
18. Seven to ten 12" × 18" kiln shelves.
19. One 12" × 12" (minimum) to 18" × 18" (maximum) kiln shelf or fireclay bat.
20. Pieces of 3/8" steel rod, threaded 1 1/4" with a 3/8"–16 thread-cutting die:
    a. Two 44" lengths, threaded at one end.
    b. Two 47" lengths, threaded at both ends.
    c. Four 48" lengths, threaded at one end.
21. Pieces of 1 1/2" × 1 1/2" × 3/16" angle iron:
    a. Two 40 1/2" lengths.
    b. Two 53" lengths.
    c. Two 45" lengths.
22. Pieces of 18 to 24 gauge sheet aluminum or galvanized sheet steel (omit b and c if the kiln is built indoors):
    a. One 40 1/2" × 58" piece.
    b. Two 40" × 40" pieces.
    c. Two 44" × 50" pieces.
23. Four atmospheric burners, rated at about 150,000 Btu/hr. (see *Burners*).
24. Safety equipment and plumbing supplies (see *Burner Systems and Safety Controls*).
25. Four kiln flaps (see *Kiln Flaps*).
26. One damper (see *Damper*).

Tools

1. Shovel.
2. Rake.
3. Concrete mixing box, or child's rigid plastic wading pool.
4. Screed (a 7' long 2 × 4).
5. Wheelbarrow.
6. Wood cutting saw.
7. Carpenter's square.
8. Tape measure or folding rule.
9. Hammer.
10. Saber saw.
11. Hacksaw with regular and carbide-tipped blades.
12. Carpenter's spirit level.
13. Drill with 7/16" metal cutting bit.
14. A 16' length of light rope.
15. A 3/8"–16 thread cutting die.
16. Thread cutting oil.
17. Two pieces of 3/8" pipe about 2' long.
18. Oxyacetylene torch (optional).
19. Knife.
20. Metal shears (optional).
21. Wrench to fit 3/8" nuts.
22. Pliers.
23. Screwdriver.
24. Circular saw with masonry bit or cold chisel.

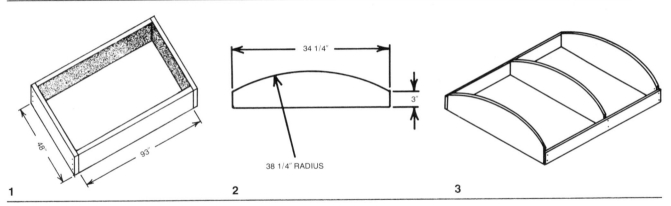

1   **2**   **3**

Making the Foundation. The site is prepared and the sprung arch kiln's foundation is built in the same manner as the catenary arch kiln's—except for dimensional and quantity changes, which are indicated in the drawing and in the list of materials. To construct the foundation, follow the instructions in "Making the Foundation", *Catenary Arch Kiln*.

Building the Arch Support Form. While the concrete slab is curing, you can build the wooden arch-support form. Begin by cutting the three pieces of 1 × 8 board (item 7a) to the shape and dimensions shown in the drawing (instructions for making the pencil compass to draw the curve can be found in the *Appendix*.) These pieces will serve as front, center, and back of the arch-support frame.

To complete the frame, position these pieces between two of the 31" long 1" × 3" wood strips (item 8), as shown in the drawing, and nail (item 10) the assembly together.

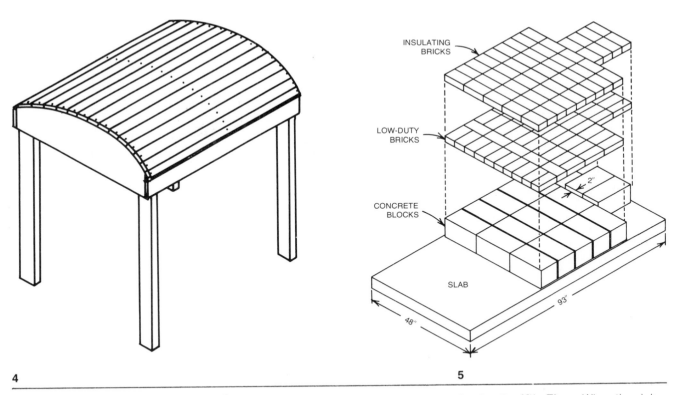

4   **5**

To make the top of the form, arrange the remaining 12 wood strips (item 8) across the curved top of the support frame. Nail (item 10) the strips in place. To complete the support structure, nail the 2 × 4 legs (item 9) inside the corners of the form, as shown.

Laying the Kiln Floor. When the slab has cured, you can install the kiln floor. Set the concrete blocks (item 11) and the two layers of firebrick (items 13 and 14a) in place, as shown in the drawing.

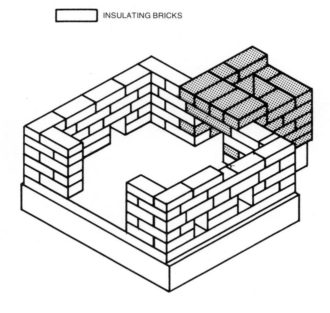

HIGH-DUTY FIREBRICKS

INSULATING BRICKS

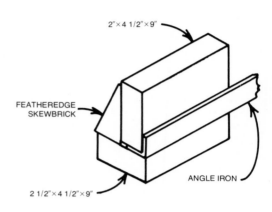

2″ × 4 1/2″ × 9″

FEATHEREDGE SKEWBRICK

ANGLE IRON

2 1/2″ × 4 1/2″ × 9″

6

7

Building the Kiln Walls. Unlike the walls of the catenary arch kiln, the walls of the sprung arch kiln are constructed entirely of insulating firebrick (item 14), except for the flue opening, which is bridged with one high-duty firebrick (item 15a), and the base of the chimney, also made of high-duty firebrick (item 15b), as shown. These walls are only one brick (4 1/2″) thick. No mortar is used in the construction. Lay the bricks for the kiln walls and the base of the chimney as indicated in the drawing, remembering to leave holes for the burner ports.

In laying the bricks, it is important, wherever possible, to position them so that the joints between those in one layer occur near the centers of those in the layer below. This staggered arrangement has an interlocking effect that helps strengthen the walls. To assure the continuity of this interlocking pattern, keep all the walls of the kiln at about the same level, as you lay up the brick. If the surfaces of the courses become slightly un-

even, smooth the high spots by rubbing them with a hard brick. Check frequently with a carpenter's square and spirit level as you build to make sure that all the walls are straight and plumb and the corners square.

You will find that some bricks will have to be cut in order to complete some of the courses evenly, and to allow space for burner ports or other necessary openings. Any coarse-toothed saw can be used for the cutting, but bear in mind that insulating firebrick is abrasive and will wear out a saw blade very quickly. For best results, use a hacksaw with a carbide-tipped blade.

When the side and back walls are 14 courses high (about 35″), slide the arch-support form into the kiln from the top. Put 3/4″ wood blocks, made from scraps, under each leg of the form. Use blocks of a thickness that will bring the upper corners of the arch-support form even with the top of the wall.

When the arch support is in place, the walls must be prepared to accept the arch. To accomplish this, use eight 2″ straight bricks (item 14e), 8 featheredge skew bricks (item 14b), and the two 40 1/2″ lengths of angle iron (item 21a) as follows.

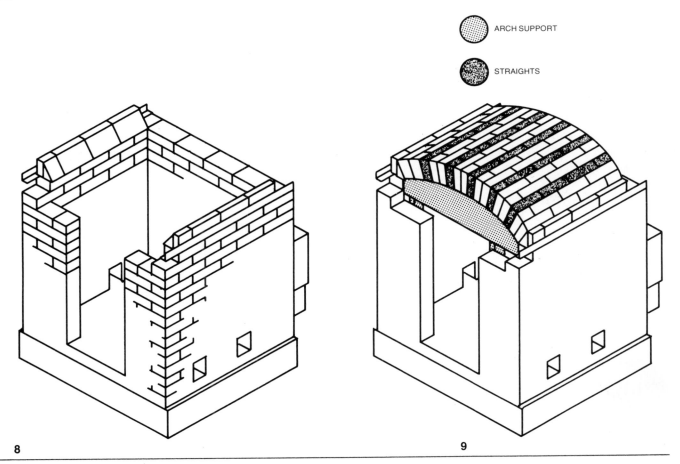

ARCH SUPPORT

STRAIGHTS

8

9

Place the two lengths of angle iron (item 21a) on top of the side walls so that the open angles face inward; the outside of the angle irons should be flush with the outer surface of the side walls. Next place the 2″ straight bricks on the angle irons, as shown. Set the skew bricks inside the rows of staights. One skew and one straight brick on each side will have to be cut. There will now be four straight bricks and four featheredge skew bricks on each side wall of the kiln; these bricks establish the angle needed for the arch.

The lengths of angle iron you placed on top of the side walls will later be incorporated into a steel reinforcing structure built around the exterior of the kiln. This steel structure must be completed before the arch-support form is removed to keep the weight of the arch from pushing the walls apart.

Building the Arch. With the skew bricks in place, you are ready to begin laying up the arch. The arch structure consists of 12 courses of #1 arch bricks (item 14d) combined with five courses of straights (item 14a). The courses of straights should be uniformly interspersed among the courses of arch brick, as shown in the drawing and all joints should be staggered.

Now, complete bricking up the back wall until it is even with the top of the arch. The bricks at the top will have to be shaped, either by rubbing or cutting, to match the curve of the arch.

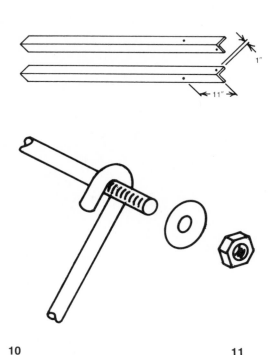

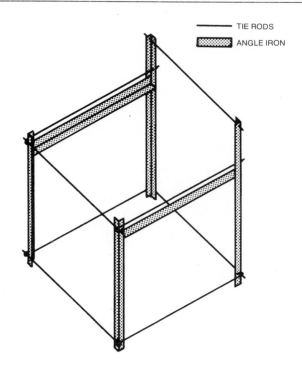

TIE RODS
ANGLE IRON

10   **11**

Installing the Steel reinforcements.

Begin by drilling two 7/16" holes in each of the two 53" long pieces of angle iron (item 21b), located as shown in the drawing.

Then take the eight lengths of 3/8" steel rod (item 20) and bend all the unthreaded ends to form U shapes, as shown. (See the *Appendix* for how to bend steel rod.)

Begin assembling the reinforcing structure by positioning the angle irons so that they fit around the outside rear corners of the walls. Make sure that the hole nearest the end is in the face of the angle iron against the side, not the back, of the kiln. Place the two 45" lengths of angle iron (item 21c) on the outside front corners, as shown in the drawing (the reinforcing structure is shown apart from the kiln in the drawing in order to indicate its framework; in practice, the kiln is positioned inside the structure). You can use lengths of lightweight rope to keep the angle irons in place while you install the remainder of the reinforcing structure.

With the frame temporarily in place, you can now begin securing it with the steel rods. Start at the bottom of the kiln. Lay two pieces of rod (item 20c) along the two side walls. The bent end of one rod should be toward the front of the kiln, and the bent end of the other toward the rear. The next step is to install a piece of rod across the front. For this connecting rod, use the shortest piece of rod (item 20b). Hook its bent end over the threaded end of the rod at one side of the kiln and secure it with a washer and nut (item 12), as shown. Then pass the threaded end of the connecting rod through the hooked

end of the rod on the opposite side of the kiln and secure this link also with a washer and nut.

Now, at the rear of the kiln, pass another of the 47" rods through the 2" space between the concrete blocks laid for the chimney base and those under the kiln floor. It may be necessary to bend this rod slightly to make it fit in place (see drawing 5). Fasten this rear rod to the long side rods on each side of the kiln in the same way that you installed the rod across the front.

The next step is to install the side reinforcing rods at the top of the kiln. For these, use the two 48" pieces of rod (item 20c). Pass their threaded ends through the holes in the angle iron at the rear corners and secure them with washers and nuts. Through their hooked ends at the front, pass one of the two remaining 44" rods (item 20a); fasten it in place with washers and nuts.

Pass the last 44" piece of tie rod through the top two holes in the rear-corner angle irons and secure it with washers and nuts. The assembled reinforcing framework of the kiln should now look like the structure in the drawing. Do not tighten the nuts at this time.

SHEET METAL COVER

BLOCK INSULATION

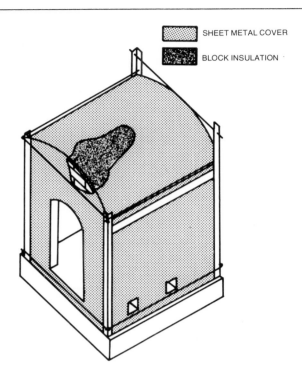

12

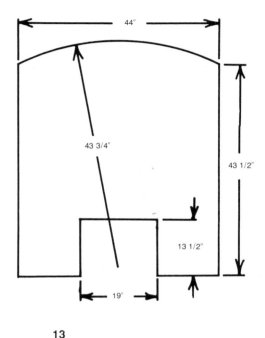

13

Insulating the Arch. Cover the top of the arch with one layer of block insulation (item 17). This insulation can be cut with a knife to fit the arch. The insulation should extend to the outer edge of the bricks that make up the front and back walls, as shown.

Covering an Indoor Kiln. If the kiln is being built in a roofed-over area, cover the top with the 40 1/2″ × 58″ piece of sheet metal (item 22a) to protect the soft block insulation and keep it in place. (Although it is possible to cut the sheet metal with metal shears, it is far easier to have it cut at a sheet metal or heating and air-conditioning shop.) Lay the metal over the arch so that it completely covers the insulation. Bend down both sides enough to come below the top tie rods. Slip the ends of the metal sheet down between the brick side walls of the kiln and the angle irons on the corners.

Covering an Outdoor Kiln. An outdoor kiln requires a more elaborate metal jacket to keep the bricks dry, since insulating bricks can absorb a tremendous amount of water.

Cut holes in the two 40″ × 40″ pieces of sheet metal (item 22b) to match the holes for the burners in the side walls of the kiln. Slide one of the sheet metal pieces down each side of the kiln between the angle iron framework and the bricks of the side walls.

Next, put the top cover (item 22a) on. Lay the metal over the arch so that it completely covers the insulation and extends down both sides enough to come below the top tie rods. The ends of the top cover should fit between the outside of the metal covers just installed on the sides of the kiln and the angle irons on the corners.

Now cut out the 44″ × 50″ metal cover (item 22c) for the rear wall, as shown in the drawing. Slip the rear cover into place between the bricks and the angle iron framework. The front cover will be added after the front of the kiln is completed.

Removing the Arch Support. Tighten the nuts that pull the corner angle irons against the sides (but not the front or back) of the kiln. Be sure to leave enough space between the angle irons and the front wall for the sheet-metal front cover that you will slip in later. If the kiln is being built indoors, tighten all the nuts to pull the angle irons tight against all four corners. Next, pull the legs off the arch support; then carefully slide the support out of the kiln through the space between the arch and the top of the front wall. Check the brickwork in the arch to make sure that it is tight and solid. Adjust the bricks which are out of line by tapping them with a hammer. This will help tighten the arch and make it more stable.

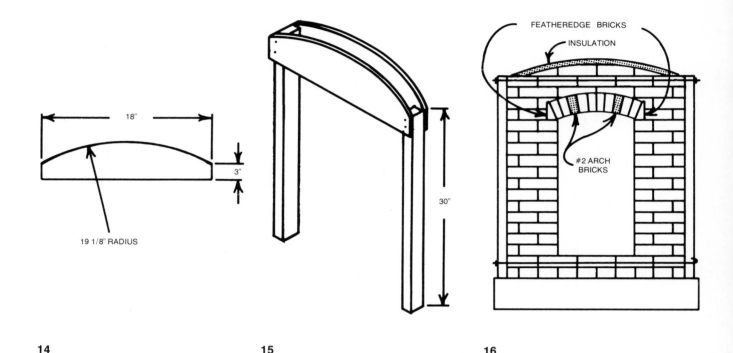

14

15

16

Completing the Front of the Kiln.
To build the support for the door arch, cut the two 18" pieces of 1 × 8 wood (item 7b) to the arched shape shown in the drawing. (Instructions for making a pencil compass to draw this curve are given in the *Appendix.*)
Cut two of the 2 × 4 legs you removed from the main arch support to 29" lengths.

Nail the two boards to the two 2 × 4 legs, as shown. Stand this arch support in the door opening and set wood blocks under the legs to bring the curved top even with the top of the twelfth row of bricks in the wall. The support is now ready to accept the arch brick.

To build the door arch, you will need to cut two featheredge bricks (item 14b), three #2 arch bricks (item 14c), and seven #1 arch bricks (item 14d) to half their length. Lay these half-bricks on the door-arch support in the arrangement indicated in the drawing.

When the arch bricks are in place, take out the blocks under the legs of the arch support; then remove the support itself. Again, check the brick-work to make sure it is tight.

Complete bricking up the front wall until it is even with the top of the kiln arch, as shown. To accomplish this, several of the bricks will have to be shaped, as the drawing indicates, to match the curve of the arch over the door as well as that of the arch of the roof.

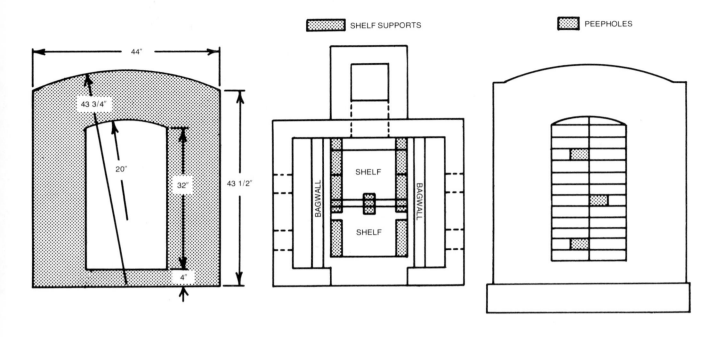

SHELF SUPPORTS · PEEPHOLES

44"

43 3/4"

20"

32"

43 1/2"

4"

SHELF

BAGWALL

SHELF

BAGWALL

17   **18**   **19**

If the kiln is to be located outdoors, cut out the 44" × 50" metal cover (item 22c) for the front wall. Slip this cover between the brick wall and the angle irons, as shown in the drawing.

Now, tighten the nuts on all the tie rods at the front and rear of the kiln.

Building the Chimney. The chimney for this kiln is built in exactly the same way as the one for the catenary arch kiln (see "Building the Chimney" in *Catenary Arch Kiln*), with a few simple differences as follows. The front wall of this chimney does not also form the back wall of the kiln; the chimney is a separate structure built against the back wall of the kiln. In addition, the one-brick opening in the chimney left just below the kiln arch is omitted in this kiln. Finally, the holes that were left at the front of the catenary arch chimney when the damper track was formed should be filled with pieces of insulating brick during the construction, since they cannot be reached after the chimney is completed.

Two kinds of brick are used for this chimney—high-duty brick (item 15) for the portion below the damper; low-duty brick (item 13) for the section above it. Put a cap (item 19) on the chimney (as on the *Catenary Arch Kiln*).

Installing the Bagwall. The bagwall for this kiln is constructed in the same way as that for the catenary arch kiln (see "Installing the Bagwall" in *Catenary Arch Kiln*), and the same methods are used to adjust it in order to change the kiln's firing characteristics. The position of the bagwall in the kiln is shown in the drawing.

Set the bottom kiln shelves (item 18) in place, as shown. Use super-duty soaps (item 16) laid on their sides as supports for the shelf.

Stacking the Door. The "door" is made of 4 1/2" thick insulating bricks (item 14a) which are stacked in place for each firing. The bricks at the top must be shaped to fit under the arch. A few bricks should be cut in half, as you can see in the drawing, so that half-brick open spaces can be left for peepholes. Use whole bricks to plug the holes. These plugs can be rubbed slightly on a rough surface, such as concrete, so that they will fit into the holes easily.

This kiln requires four burners (item 23) and related plumbing and safety equipment (item 24). It also requires kiln flaps (item 25) and a damper (item 26). For instructions on how to make and install these items, as well as on the special considerations for indoor kilns, see specific sections on these subjects later in this part.

CATENARY ARCH CAR KILN

A car kiln is more expensive to build than a regular one because the welded steel car must be very sturdily constructed. Not only must it be capable of withstanding the weight of the bricks comprising the kiln floor and the door (both of which are laid in the car itself) but also the weight of the pots to be fired, the shelves, and other kiln furniture. However, most of the potters who have used car kilns have found that the easier loading and closing, and the possibility of wheeling the cart into the glazing area, make the extra expense worthwhile.

The base for the track on which the car runs can be an existing floor, it can be made of concrete when the kiln foundation slab is poured, or it can be constructed of concrete blocks. Whatever the material, the top surface must be flush with the kiln slab. In order to make the car more mobile, the track can be extended as needed.

Most of the instructions for preparing the site, making the slab, and even constructing the arch itself are the same for this kiln as for the regular catenary arch kiln.

Note: do not use the car kiln for salt glazing. The same effects of salt that cause brick to deteriorate will eventually fuse the car to the kiln walls.

Tools

1. Shovel.
2. Rake.
3. Hammer.
4. Wood-cutting saw.
5. Six ft. folding rule.
6. Carpenter's framing square.
7. Carpenter's spirit level.
8. Welding and cutting equipment.
9. Concrete mixing box, or child's rigid plastic wading pool.
10. Wheelbarrow.
11. Screed, a 7' long 2 × 4.
12. A 14' length of sash chain.
13. Can of spray paint, small amount, any color (optional).
14. Saber saw.
15. Circular saw with blade to cut hard masonry, or a cold chisel.
16. Pliers.
17. Screwdriver.
18. Knife.
19. Drill with 1/4" high-speed bit and 1/4" masonry bit.
20. Hacksaw.
21. C clamps.
22. Four 3/4" wooden blocks; these can be made from scrap pieces of wood.

Parts and Materials

Item No.

1. Pieces of 2 × 6 lumber:
   a. Two 68" lengths.
   b. Two 74" lengths (two 144" lengths, if the slab is to be extended for a loading area).
2. One-half lb. 16D common nails.
3. Two 48" × 63" pieces of 6" × 6" mesh wire fencing (three pieces for the extended slab).
4. Wet concrete. 1 1/2 cu. yd. (2 2/3 cu. yd. for the extended slab).
5. Newspaper.
6. Ten 18" lengths of 2 × 2 or 2 × 4 lumber (16 if the slab is extended).

Note: items 1 through 6 are needed to pour a concrete slab that will provide a foundation for the kiln. If some other suitable surface is available, the slab may be omitted.

7. Pieces of angle iron:
   a. A 13 1/2' length of 3/16" × 2" × 2", cut to the dimensions shown in drawing 2.
   b. A 20' length of 1/8" × 1 1/4" × 1 1/4", cut to the dimensions shown in drawing 3.
   c. Two 10' lengths of 1" × 1" × 1/8" (more will be needed if the track is to be extended).

d. Four 4' lengths of 1" × 1" × 1/8".

8. Four casters with V-groove steel or iron wheels that can run on angle iron tracks. The wheels should be 4" in diameter.

9. A 16' length of chain (like that used for dog leads).

10. One large turnbuckle with hooked ends that will fit into the links of the chain (item 9).

11. Nails:
   a. Two finishing nails.
   b. 1/2 lb. 10D common nails.
   c. 1/2 lb. 8D common nails.
   d. 1/2 lb. sheet rock nails.

12. Twelve plastic shields with 1 1/2" long sheet metal screws (proportionately more for an extended track).

13. Eight 1/4" washers (proportionately more for an extended track).

14. A 50' length of braided galvanized steel wire.

15. One pint of urethane coating, or equivalent.

16. One 17" × 48" piece of 18 to 26 gauge galvanized sheet steel.

17. Two 3' × 8' sheets of aluminum.

18. Four 2 × 2s or 2 × 4s, 44" long.

19. A 14' length of 1 × 6 board.

20. An 8' length of 1 × 5 board.

21. Two 4' × 8' sheets of 1/2" exterior CD plywood.

22. One 4' × 8' sheet of 1/8" nontempered hardboard.

23. Two pieces of 5 1/2" wide hardboard 48" long (can be cut from arch-support form after it has been used).

24. Newspaper.

25. Dry fireclay, 10 lbs.

26. Grog, 5 lbs.

Note: brick sizes and shapes can be found in the *Table of Standard Brick Sizes* in the *Appendix.*

27. High-duty firebricks:
   a. 12 large straights.
   b. 625 straights.
   c. 4 straights, 13 1/2".
   d. 22 soaps.
   e. 70 splits.
   f. 70 #1 arch.
   g. 65 #2 arch.
   h. 5 #3 arch.
   i. 22 #1 wedge.
   j. 18 #2 wedge.

28. Two hundred low-duty straights.

29. Insulating firebricks:
   a. 100 straights (2300°F.).
   b. 25 straights (2000°F.).
   c. 50 #1 arch (2000°F.).

30. Sixty sq. ft. of 1 1/2" thick 1900°F. block insulation.

31. Four and one-half cu. ft. of castable insulation (2400°F.).

32. Wet refractory cement, 25 lbs.

33. Silicon-carbide kiln shelves (bats):
   a. Nine 12" × 24" × 1".
   b. Three 12" × 18" × 1".

34. Shelf posts as needed, see *Kiln Furniture.*

35. One 12" × 12" (minimum) to 18" × 18" (maximum) kiln shelf or fireclay bat.

36. Four atmospheric burners, rated at about 185,000 Btu/hr. (see *Burners*).

37. Safety equipment and plumbing supplies (see *Burner Systems and Safety Controls*).

38. Four kiln flaps (see *Kiln Flaps*).

39. One damper (see *Damper*).

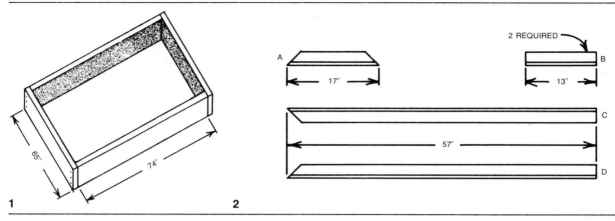

1

2

Making the Foundation. The recommendations for selecting and preparing the site for the regular catenary arch kiln, presented earlier in this part, apply to this kiln, too.

The foundation (items 1–6) is also built in the same way, using 2 × 6s for the slab form and steel mesh for reinforcement. This concrete slab, however, should be at least 65" wide by 74" long. In addition, there must be a level space extending at least 6' in front of the kiln. It is advisable to extend the slab to include this area, if the kiln car is to be loaded there.

After the slab has been poured, begin constructing the kiln car.

Building the Kiln Car. Build the car before starting the walls of the kiln because it is easier to fit the kiln to the car than to adjust the car to fit the kiln. The types of wheels recommended in the parts and materials list may not be locally available in exactly the dimensions given. A change in these dimensions will change the height of the car. In that case, it will be necessary to make minor adjustments in the height of the kiln walls

to compensate for the difference in size.

Welded construction is required for the kiln car. Although this may involve using a professional welder, this kind of construction works best for the car.

The kiln car consists mainly of two metal frames—one horizontal; the other vertical. The horizontal frame serves as the base of the car and supports the kiln floor.

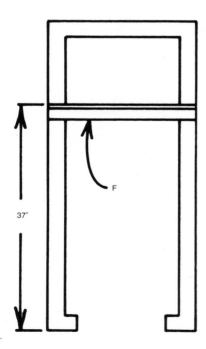

5

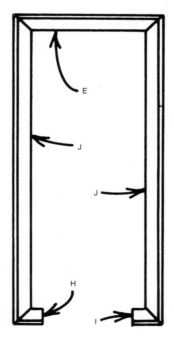

6

Welding the Door Frame. Arrange all of the parts from drawing 3 except F and G, as shown. Check the angles with a carpenter's square, then clamp and weld the pieces together.

Turn the frame over and weld part F at a point 37" from the open end of the frame, as shown in the drawing. Be sure that the two long sides of the frame are parallel before welding the cross piece into place.

Joining the Base and Door Frames. Place the base frame on a flat surface suitable for welding. Position the door frame on it in the position shown in drawing 7. Next, clamp in position the two remaining pieces of angle iron from drawing 3 that are to be used to brace the door frame. Before welding, make certain that the door frame is perpendicular to the base frame; and the front face of the door frame is 48 3/4" from the back end of the base frame, as shown.

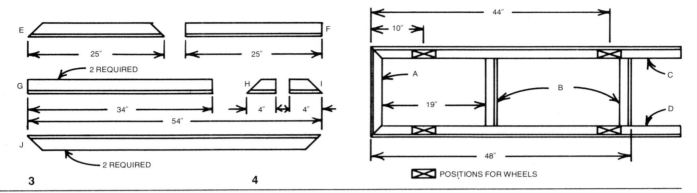

E   25″   F

2 REQUIRED

G   34″   H   4″   4″   I

54″

J

2 REQUIRED

3

4

44″

10″

A

B

C

D

19″

48″

POSITIONS FOR WHEELS

The vertical frame is attached near one end of the base and supports the door of the kiln. Both frames are made by welding lengths of angle iron together. Since it is simpler to have all the angle iron pieces ready before starting to weld, begin by cutting the required lengths for the base (item 7a), see drawing 2, and the door (item 7b), see drawing 3, with either a hacksaw or a cutting torch, to the shapes shown. All cuts are right (90°) or 45° angles.

Welding the Base Frame. If you are not experienced at welding, you should have this welding done by a professional. If you do the job yourself, choose a flat, smooth working surface that can withstand the heat of welding. Arrange the lengths of 2″ angle iron (item 7a) as shown. Check all corners with a carpenter's square to make sure they form right (90°) angles. Clamp the parts together, if necessary, and weld the joints. When

completely welded, the top surface of the frame should be flat and free of weld beads.

Attaching the Wheel Mounts. Weld the wheel mounts (item 8) at the positions indicated in the drawing. Before welding, make certain that the distance between the two front wheels is exactly the same as the distance between the two rear wheels. This is necessary for the car to run freely on the tracks.

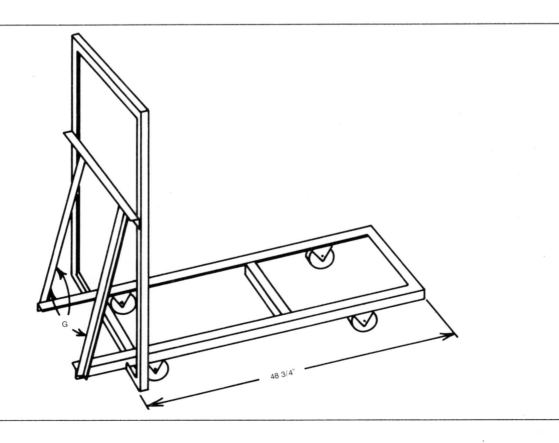

G

48 3/4″

7

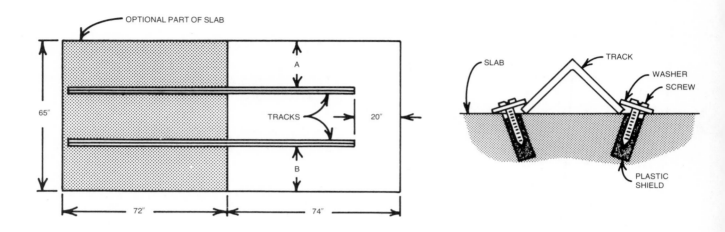

8

Laying the Kiln Car's Tracks. The tracks on which the kiln car will ride in and out of the kiln are two lengths of angle iron (item 7c). To extend the tracks, add as many lengths of angle iron as needed.

Arrange two tracks on the concrete slab in the positions indicated in the drawing. Note that both angle-iron pieces are set in an upside-down V position, with the corner formed by their sides on top. The tracks should be the same distance apart as the wheels welded to the car bed. Dimension A must equal dimension B shown in the drawing.

Now, carefully place the kiln car on the tracks. Roll the car back and forth a few times to make sure the tracks are parallel and that the wheels can roll freely. Adjust the position of the tracks, if necessary, but make certain that both the tracks and the kiln car remain centered on the slab.

9

The next step is to drill holes of a size that will accept the plastic shields (item 12) for the screws which will hold the tracks in place. Locate these holes at both sides of both ends of each track; drill them so that they angle under the track a few inches from each end of each track, as shown. Use a masonry bit to drill the holes. Put the shields in the holes and anchor the tracks in place with washers and screws (items 12, 13), as shown.

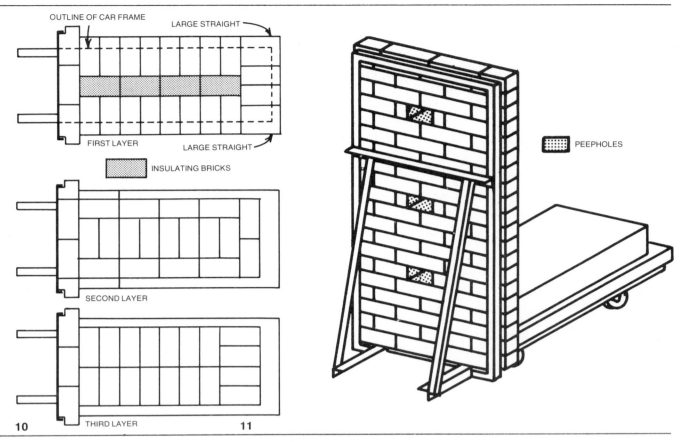

OUTLINE OF CAR FRAME   LARGE STRAIGHT

FIRST LAYER   LARGE STRAIGHT

▨ INSULATING BRICKS

SECOND LAYER

THIRD LAYER

10   11

▦ PEEPHOLES

Installing the Kiln Car's Floor and Door.

The car should be on its tracks while you are installing the floor and the door.

To start installing the floor, lay the 17" × 48" piece of galvanized sheet metal (item 16) on the car bed so that its edges are flush with the sides and rear edges of the bed. The floor itself consists of three layers of bricks. Place the first layer on the car bed, as shown. The rear corner bricks are large straights (item 27a). All the other edge bricks are low-duty straights (item 28). The center bricks are insulating straights (item 29b). (See the *Appendix* for instructions on how to cut bricks.) The edge bricks should overhang the car bed equally on both sides. The back edge of this layer of bricks should overhang the frame about 1 5/8".

The second layer is made entirely of insulating bricks (item 29a), arranged as shown.

The third layer is also made of insulating bricks (item 29a) with the same overall dimensions as the second layer. The arrangement of this layer is indicated in the drawing.

Laying Up the Door Frame.

The door consists of one 4 1/2" thickness of insulating bricks (item 29a), laid up in the door frame. Note that the end bricks of each course must be notched to fit inside the angle-iron frame, as shown. Leave three half-brick holes in the door for peepholes. The peepholes should be spaced so that one is near the bottom of the door, one in the center, and the third near the top, as shown. Plugs for the peepholes can be made of insulating bricks inserted endwise.

Cut the top front corners out of the top course of bricks so that they fit inside the frame.

Cement all courses of brick in the door with refractory cement (item 32), according to manufacturer's instructions.

Note: refractory cements are fast-setting compounds; the bricks to which they are applied cannot be moved or adjusted after they have been in position for even a few seconds. Therefore, take care to place the bricks properly the first time, and check frequently to be sure that you are keeping the door plumb and the sides straight as you put the bricks in place.

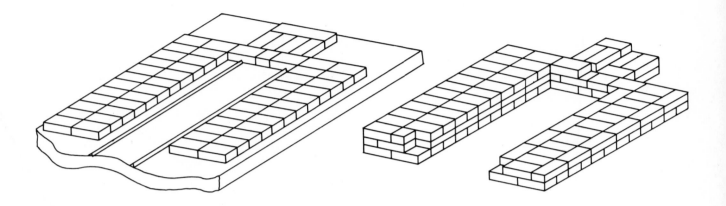

12

Building the Kiln Base. The walls forming the base of the kiln are laid up according to the patterns shown in drawings 16, 17, 18, 19. High-duty firebrick is used throughout.

13

The fourth course is made of splits (item 27e); all the other courses are made of 2 1/2" thick straights (item 27b). Note that the first course of bricks laid down for the back wall of the kiln should butt up against the ends of the car tracks.

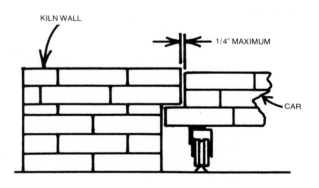

14

Roll the car into position and lay the third and fourth courses so that a space of 1/4" or less exists between them and the first course of bricks in the car floor, as shown. The car should roll in and out without touching these courses. The top of the fourth course should be about 1/4" higher than the top of the first course of the car floor, as shown.

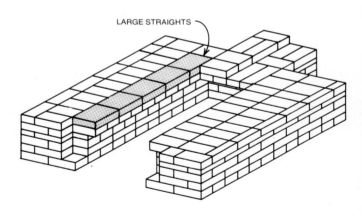

15

The fifth and sixth courses should also be precisely placed so that their inner edges come within 1/4" of the top two courses of the car floor, as shown in drawing 14. The car should roll out of the kiln without touching the side walls. The fifth row uses some soaps (item 27d) and the sixth some large straights (item 27a).

When the car is in the kiln, its back end should fit tightly against the back wall of the kiln.

Making the Arch Support Form.

The arch form for this kiln is made the same way as the one for the regular catenary arch kiln (see "Making the Arch Support Form" in *Catenary Arch Kiln*). However, this arch form must be larger. Use the following dimensions for the panels making up the arch for this car kiln: (1) panel A (item 21) is 41" wide and 43 1/2" high at the top of the curve; (2) panel B (item 21), the largest panel, performs the same function here as its counterpart in the regular catenary arch kiln. It measures 50" wide by 48" high at the top of the curve; (3) cut the hardboard (item 22) so that it is 45" × 96". This is too short to fit around the entire plywood arch; therefore, before nailing it in place, position the hardboard carefully over the arched curve so that the gaps at the bottom on both sides are approximately the same, and most important, so that both ends of the hardboard are parallel with the kiln base. This placement is critical, because if the gap is not exactly the same on both the front and back plywood panels, the arch form will twist and will not sit flat on the kiln base. Two 2 × 2s or 2 × 4s (item 18) will have to be used under the lower portion of the hardboard on each side of the support to strengthen it. They should fit tightly against the hardboard on the inside of the support at the bottom edge and about a foot up from it. Nail them to the hardboard and the end panels.

Building the Kiln Arch. Place the assembled arch form on the kiln base. Put 3/4" wooden blocks under all four corners of the form. Position the form so that it is 4 1/2" from the front and back edges of the kiln base and 9" from each side.

The first course of brick in the arch is made of #2 wedge brick (item 27i), arranged as shown in the drawing. Otherwise, except for dimensional changes, the arch and chimney for this kiln are built in the same way as the regular catenary arch kiln (refer to these sections in the *Catenary Arch Kiln*). Because of the greater height and depth of this kiln, more courses are required, and each course is 45" long, instead of 31 1/2". The quantities and types of materials (items 7d, 9, 11, 15, 19, 20, 23, 25, 26, 27, 29, 31, 34, 35) required are included in *Parts and Materials* for this kiln.

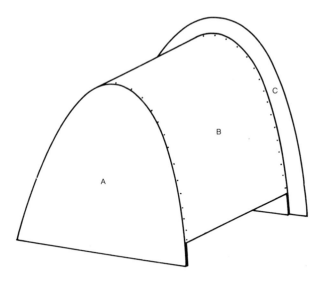

16

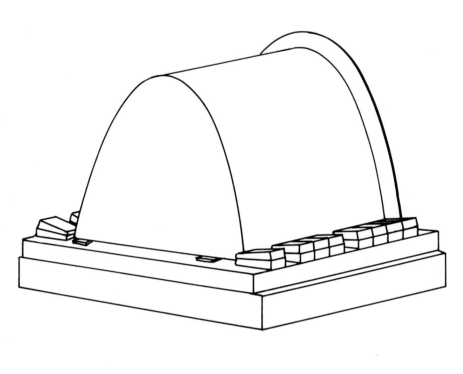

17

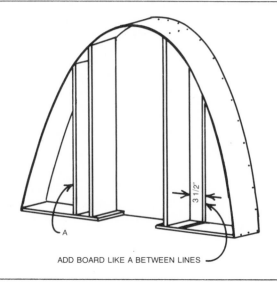

ADD BOARD LIKE A BETWEEN LINES

18

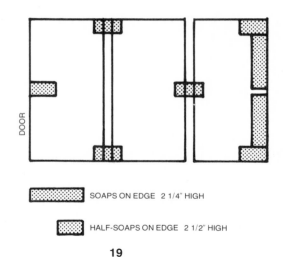

DOOR

▨▨▨ SOAPS ON EDGE 2 1/4" HIGH

▨▨ HALF-SOAPS ON EDGE 2 1/2" HIGH

19

Casting the Walls. The back wall molds are made like those for the regular catenary arch kiln. However, the cast sections required for the front wall are not as wide as those for the back wall. The reason for this difference is that the door on the kiln car requires a wider space than the chimney. However, the mold used for the back wall can also be used for the front by adding the board (item 23), as indicated in the drawing. The board will have to be measured to fit your particular mold. To get this measure-ment, draw a line parallel to and 3 1/2" from the long straight board of the mold. Measure the length of the line to determine the length of the added board. Cut the board to this length and nail it into the mold making sure that it is parallel to the long straight side of the original mold.

For each firing, bricks for a small section at the top of the door will have to be stacked in place. These can be insulating bricks (item 29a) cut to fit the arch curve and set in place on top of the kiln door after loading.

Insulating the Arch. This kiln is in-sulated in the same way as the regular catenary arch kiln, using block insula-tion (item 30) and a metal cover (item 17) for protection. The wires (item 14) that hold the cover in place are slightly different on this kiln, see drawing 21. (See "Insulating the Arch," *Catenary Arch Kiln* for instructions.) The ends of the wires can be attached to nails (item 11b) driven into the cracks between bricks in the kiln base.

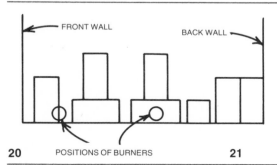

FRONT WALL   BACK WALL

20   POSITIONS OF BURNERS

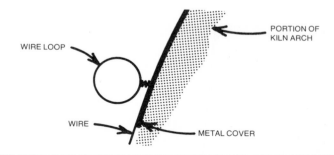

WIRE LOOP   PORTION OF KILN ARCH

WIRE   METAL COVER

21

Arranging the Bottom Shelf and Bagwall. Arrange the soaps (item 27d) on the car floor, as shown. Three kiln shelves (item 33b) can be placed on top of these. Nine additional shelves (item 33a)   will fit the kiln.

Arrange the bagwall, as shown using high-duty soaps. This arrangement may have to be modified to achieve good firing results (see *Firing In-structions*).

There is no opening under this kiln, as there is under the regular catenary arch kiln, through which to pass chains to hold the angle irons in place at the front and back of the kiln. How-ever, there is another simple way to hold the cast front and back walls of this kiln in place while it is being fired. This method uses a chain (item 9) that is run all the way around the kiln and pulled tight during firing by a turnbuckle (item 10) at the front of the kiln. The chain can be held in place by passing it through loops in the two wires (item 14) that hold the kiln's

metal cover in place. When the wires are installed, twist a loop about 1" in diameter in each of the front wires near the bottom of the cover on each side of the kiln, as shown.

This kiln requires four burners (item 36) and related plumbing and safety equipment (item 37). It also requires kiln flaps (item 38) and a damper (item 39). For instructions on how to make and install all these items, as well as on the special considerations for indoor kilns, see the specific sec-tions on these subjects in this part.

RAKU CAR KILN

This 8 cubic foot kiln, which provides 7 cubic feet of useful interior space, is particularly designed for ease in loading and unloading. The basic design feature is a wheeled cart, or "car," as it is most often called, that rolls in and out of the kiln. Loaded outside, it carries the pots into the kiln to be fired; afterwards it rolls out of the kiln for unloading. Besides convenience, the car method of loading and unloading may also help hold down breakage, especially of large pieces.

The car functions as part of the basic structure of the kiln. When the car is inside the kiln, the "front" of it becomes the door of the kiln; its base becomes the kiln floor.

This kiln will reach operating temperature in about half an hour and has a very fast recovery time between loads.

Tools

1. Shovel.
2. Rake.
3. Hoe.
4. Tape measure or folding rule.
5. Hammer.
6. Wood-cutting saw.
7. Carpenter's framing square.
8. A 4' length of 2 × 4 lumber.
9. Hacksaw.
10. Cutting torch (optional).
11. Welding equipment (optional).
12. Four C clamps.
13. Drill with 1/16", 3/8", 1/4", and 7/16" bits.
14. Masonry drill bit (size as required for shields, item 13).
15. Screwdriver.
16. Pliers or wrenches.
17. Allen wrench to fit wheel set screws.
18. Circular saw with masonry blade or a cold chisel.
19. Saber saw, band saw, or jig saw.
20. A 3' length of lightweight wire.
21. Scissors or metal shears.

Parts and Materials

Item No.

1. Pieces of 2 × 6 lumber:
   a. Two 45" lengths.
   b. Two 84" lengths.
2. One-half lb. 16D common nails.
3. Wet-mix concrete, 8 1/4 cu. ft.
4. Newspaper.
5. One 40" × 80" piece of 6" × 6" mesh wire fence.
6. Eight 2 × 2s or 2 × 4s, 18" long.

Note: items 1 through 6 are needed to pour a concrete slab that will provide a foundation for the kiln. If some other suitable surface is available, the slab may be omitted.

7. A 24' piece of 1 1/4" × 1 1/2" × 1/8" angle iron.
8. Pieces of 1" × 1" × 1/8" angle iron:
   a. Two 74" lengths.
   b. Two 27" lengths.
   c. Four 39" lengths.
9. Four cast-iron V-belt sheaves (pulleys) 2 1/2" outside dia. with 3/4" bore.
10. Four 3/4" rigid-mount pillow blocks (sleeve or ball bearing).
11. Two 24" lengths of 3/4" cold-rolled steel shaft.
12. Eight 3/8" × 1" round-head machine screws with nuts and lock washers.
13. Four lead or plastic shields with 2" long screws for mounting in concrete.
14. A 13' length of galvanized steel clothesline cable.
15. Pieces of 5/16" threaded steel rod:
   a. Two 11" lengths.
   b. Four 36" lengths.
   c. Four 2" lengths.
16. Twelve 5/16" nuts.
17. Two heavy compression springs (1" to 2" long) to slip over the 5/16" rod.
18. Ten 5/16" washers.
19. One 16" × 16" × 1" silicon carbide kiln shelf (see *Kiln Furniture*).

Note: brick sizes and shapes can be found the *Table of Standard Brick Sizes* in the *Appendix.*

20. Low-duty firebricks:
   a. 195 straights.
   b. 10 splits.
   c. Sixteen 2" straights.
   d. 6 featheredge skew bricks.
   e. Thirty-nine #1 arch bricks.
21. Twenty-four 2000°F. insulating firebricks.
22. Four high-duty firebrick straights.
23. A 30 sq. ft. piece of 3/4" or 1" thick ceramic fiber insulation with glue to attach it to brick.
24. Two 27" pieces of 1 × 8 board.
25. Two 12' lengths of 1 × 3 low-grade lumber (often called strapping or furring strips) cut into 27" lengths (9" will be wasted on each length).
26. Four 19 1/2" lengths of 2 × 4 lumber.
27. One lb. 8D common nails.
28. Pieces of 2 × 6 lumber:
   a. Two 84" lengths.
   b. Two 45" lengths.
29. One forced-air blower rated at about 150,000 Btu/hr. (see *Burners*).
30. Safety equipment and piping to connect the forced-air burner (item 29) to the gas source (see *Burner Systems and Safety Controls*).

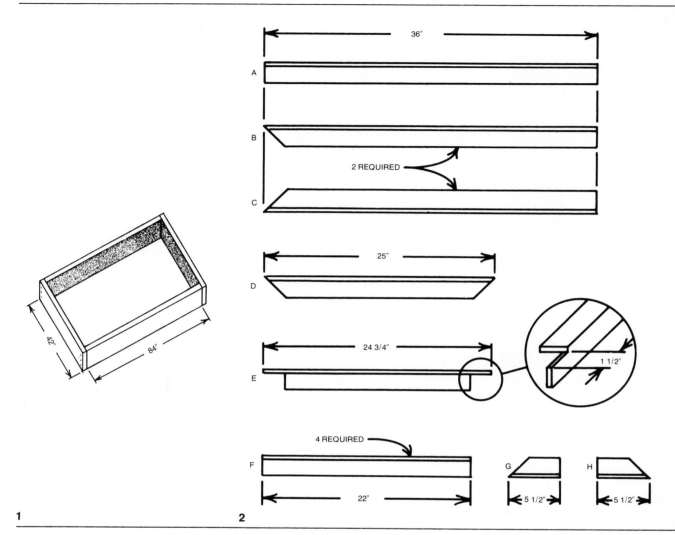

1

2

Making the Concrete Foundation.
Directions for selecting and preparing
the site and for pouring the concrete
foundation (item 3) can be found in
"Making the Foundation," *Catenary
Arch Kiln.* The slab for this kiln should
be 42" wide and 84" long. Use 2 × 6s
(items 1a, 1b) for the form and wire
mesh (item 5) for the reinforcement.

While the slab is curing, begin constructing the kiln car.

Building the Kiln Car. Build the kiln
car before laying up the walls of the
kiln to allow for fit adjustments.
For example, the specific types of
pillow blocks and wheels recommended in the parts and materials·
list may not be available in your area.
A change in these dimensions will
change the height of the car, neces-
sitating minor adjustments in the
height of the kiln walls to compensate
for the difference in size.

The main structure of the kiln car
consists of two metal frames—one

horizontal, the other vertical. The
horizontal frame serves as the base
of the car and as the kiln floor support.
Attached near one end of the base
is the vertical frame which will hold
the door of the kiln. Both frames are
made by welding lengths of angle
iron together.

Begin by cutting the angle iron (item
7), with either a hacksaw or a cutting
torch, to the shapes shown in the
drawing. All angles are either 45°
or 90°.

LOCATION
OF PILLOW
BLOCKS
FOR MOUNTING
WHEELS

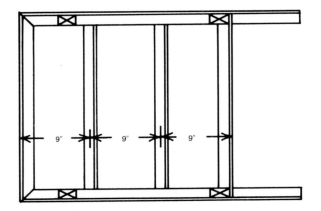

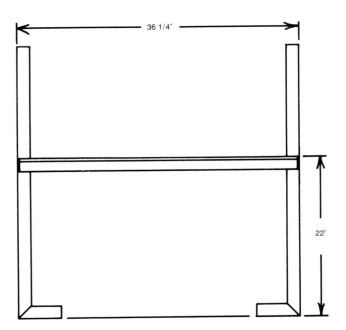

36 1/4"

22"

9" 9" 9"

3

Welding the Base Frame. If you are
not experienced at welding, you should
have the welding done by a professional. If you do the job yourself,
choose a flat, smooth working surface
that can withstand the heat of welding.
Arrange one each of parts B, C, D, E,
and two Fs from drawing 2 as shown
in the drawing above. Check all corners with a carpenter's square to
make sure they form right (90°) angles. Then clamp them in position
and weld the joints. The top surface
of the frame should be flat and free
of weld beads.

4

Welding the Door Frame. The door
frame is made of five lengths of angle
iron from drawing 2. Arrange parts
B and G on a flat, heat-resistant surface so that the ends with the 45° angles join to form a right angle. Check
the angles with a carpenter's square;
clamp the pieces together and weld
the two joints. Repeat the process
with parts C and H. Now turn these
two assemblies over and weld part A
in the position shown so that the outer
sides of the frame are 36 1/4" apart.
This will allow the 36" wide brick door
to fit between the sides of the frame.

Joining the Base and Door Frames.
Begin by placing the base frame on a flat surface, suitable for welding. Then position the door frame on it so that it forms a right (90°) angle with the base, as shown. Set the two diagonal braces (parts F from drawing 2) in the positions indicated. Clamp the joints and weld the parts together.

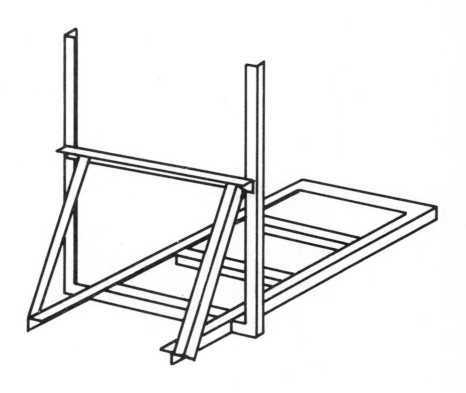

5

Attaching the Wheels and Axles.
If possible, the cast iron V-belt pulleys (item 9) that serve as car wheels and the pillow blocks (item 10) in which they will be mounted should have the specified dimensions. If these sizes are not available, choose alternatives according to the following guidelines: (1) the distance between the top surface of the angle-iron base of the car and the bottom of the track should be as close as possible to 3 1/2"; (2) the rims of the wheels should not extend above the top mounting surface of the pillow blocks—if they do, they will rub aginst the lower surface of the bricks in the base of the car.

Drill 7/16" holes in the base to mount the pillow blocks (item 10) at the points shown in the drawing. Use round-head machine screws (item 12) to mount the four pillow blocks. Then install the axles and the wheels (items 11, 9) in the pillow blocks in the manner shown in the drawing. Make sure that the axles are positioned so that they do not protrude beyond the outer face of the pillow blocks. Then tighten the set screws in the wheels.

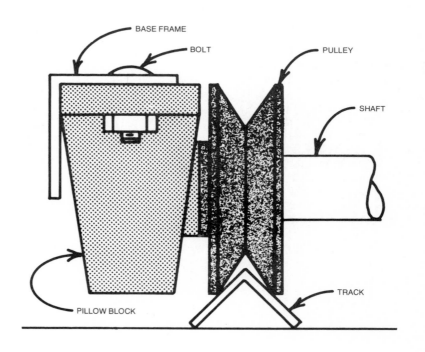

BASE FRAME

BOLT

PULLEY

SHAFT

PILLOW BLOCK

TRACK

6

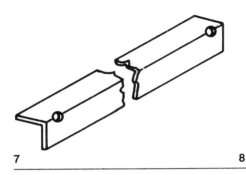

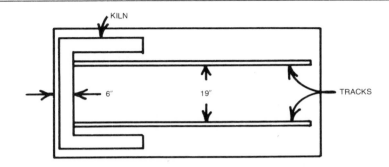

7

8

Laying the Tracks for the Kiln Car.

The tracks on which the car will ride are two 74" lengths of angle iron (item 8a). To attach them to the concrete slab, it is necessary first to drill a 1/4" hole near each end of both of them, as shown.

Next, arrange the two drilled angle-iron lengths on the concrete slab in the positions indicated for the tracks in the drawing. Set both the angle-iron pieces in an upside-down V position, with the corner formed by their sides on top. The tracks should be about 19" apart; this dimension should equal the distance between the grooves in the wheels on opposite sides of the car.

Now, carefully place the kiln car on these tracks. Roll the car back and forth a few times to make sure the tracks are parallel and the wheels can roll freely. Adjust the position of the tracks, if necessary.

Then, before removing the kiln car, mark on the slab the location of the holes previously drilled in the angle-iron tracks. Remove the kiln car and tracks, and at the marked points drill holes of a size that will accept the lead or plastic shields (item 13) in the slab, using a masonry bit. Put the shields in the holes and anchor the tracks in place with the 2" long screws.

If after the tracks are bolted in place further adjustments are required in order for the kiln car to ride easily, it is possible to alter the positions of the wheels on the axles by loosening their set screws and moving them in or out, as needed.

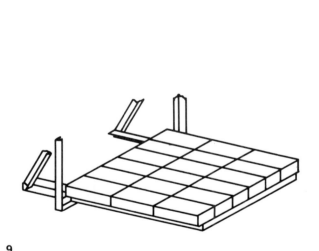

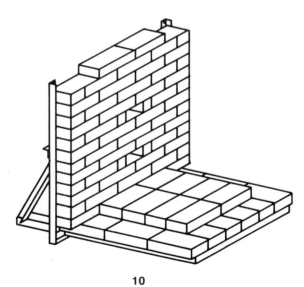

9

10

Installing the Kiln Floor and the Car Door.

Place the car on the tracks while you are installing the floor in its base. The floor is composed of two courses of bricks laid without mortar.

To make the bottom layer, arrange the low-duty bricks (item 20a) in the base frame of the car, as shown. The

bricks should be flush with the inner surface of the angle irons of the door frame. Use insulating (item 21) bricks with depressions gouged out to fit flat over the heads of the bolts used to mount the pillow blocks.

For the top layer, use more low-duty brick, arranged as shown.

For the kiln door, stack more bricks (item 20a) inside the door frame of the car, using the pattern indicated in the drawing. Leave two half-brick openings part way up in the door to serve as peepholes. (See the *Appendix* for how to cut bricks.)

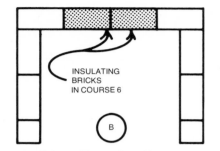

INSULATING
BRICK
IN COURSE 5

(A)

BRICK PLACEMENT–ODD COURSES

11

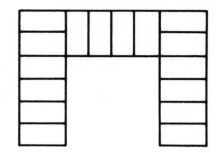

INSULATING
BRICKS
IN COURSE 6

(B)

BRICK PLACEMENT–EVEN COURSES

Building the Kiln Walls. The walls of the kiln are also made of low-duty brick laid in two alternating patterns, as shown in the drawing.

Using 1 1/4″ thick splits (item 20b), lay the first course according to the pattern shown in drawing A. Make sure that the back wall butts flush against the ends of the kiln-car tracks, and remember to keep the tracks centered in the kiln. Use the brick patterns in drawing A for all of the odd-numbered courses. Use the pattern shown in drawing B for all the even-numbered courses, except the fourth one.

In the second course lay 2″ straights (item 20c). For all other courses, both odd and even, use 2 1/2″ straights (item 20a).

If you alternate the course patterns according to the drawings, the joints between the bricks of one layer will occur in the middle of the bricks in the course above. This staggered arrangement helps strengthen the walls. No mortar is used. However, it will be necessary to end both sides

of each even-numbered course with half-bricks.

After the third layer is completed, stop and check dimensions. Try rolling the car into the kiln on its tracks. The sides of the car should clear the inner surfaces of the walls by 1/8″ to 1/4″.

If there is not enough space between the walls and the car floor, nudge the side walls out a little. Small gaps that appear as a consequence between bricks in the back wall are not a matter for concern.

After the width is adjusted, and while the kiln car is on the tracks inside the kiln, also check the height of the kiln walls. The top surface of the bricks making up the third layer of the walls should be 1/8″ to 1/4″ above the top surface of the bottom layer of the bricks in the floor of the car. If the walls are too high, remove one layer and replace it with insulating bricks (item 21); the thickness of these bricks can be reduced by cutting them or rubbing them on a rough surface, such as concrete. If the walls are

too low, replace the 2″ thick row with another course of firebricks or insulating bricks of the required thickness.

With the kiln car still in place, lay the fourth course of bricks on the walls, positioning these bricks crosswise on the third layer, as shown in the drawing. When completed, this fourth layer will overhang the inner edges of the third course. Make sure to maintain 1/8″ to 1/4″ clearance between these inner edges and the second layer of the floor of the kiln car.

Now, lay the fifth course according to the pattern given to odd-numbered layers. This course, together with those that follow, will hold the bricks in the fourth course firmly in place.

With the fifth layer in place, try rolling the kiln car in and out of the kiln again. It should ride in and out without touching the walls.

Lay the remaining courses. Note that insulating bricks are to be used in the back wall of courses five and six, as indicated.

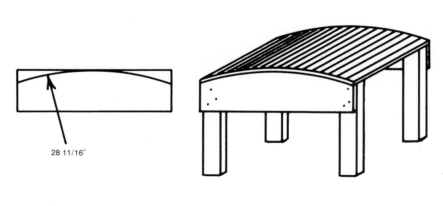

28 11/16″

Making the Arch Support Form. Cut the two 27″ long pieces of 1 × 8 board (item 24) to the curved line shown in the drawing. To draw the curve that will become the top edge on each of these boards, use a pencil compass. (Instructions for making this compass are given in the *Appendix.*)

When the curves have been drawn on both boards, cut along the pencil lines with a saber saw, jig saw, or band saw. Then nail the 27″ long 1 × 3 wood strips (item 25) together to make the arch-support form shown in the drawing. Next, nail (item 27) the form's four legs, made of 2 × 4s (item 26), into place, as indicated.

Stand the arch-support form in position within the walls of the kiln, as shown, and put a small wooden block under each of the four legs to bring the lower edge of the curve of the arch-support form even with the upper surface of the top course of the bricks of the walls, as shown in the drawing.

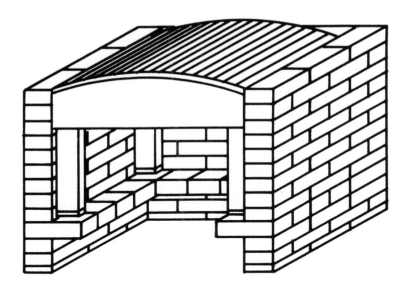

13

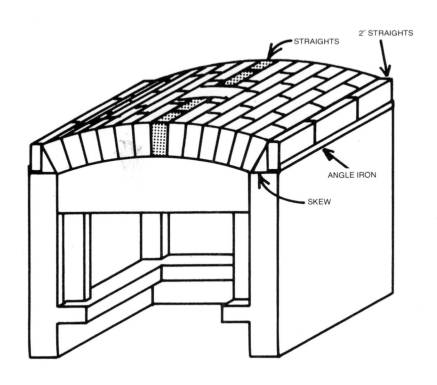

STRAIGHTS

2" STRAIGHTS

ANGLE IRON

SKEW

14

Building the Arch. The side walls must be prepared for the arch by adding skew bricks to establish the proper transition from the vertical wall to the nearly horizontal arch. Use three featheredge skew bricks (item 20d), three 2" thick straights (item 20c), and a 27" long piece of angle iron (item 8b) on each side of the kiln, as shown.

When the skew bricks and arch support are in place, begin laying up the arch from each side. The completed arch consists of twelve courses of #1 arch bricks (item 20e) and one course of straights (item 20a). The row of straights should be in the center of the arch. Lay the bricks in one course so that the joints between them occur at or near the centers of the bricks in the adjacent courses. Staggering the bricks like this will necessitate ending alternate courses with half-bricks.

Leave the opening for the chimney in the center of the arch. It should be three brick courses wide and 4 1/2" deep, as in the drawing. It will be necessary to cut some of the arch bricks to make the opening.

To complete the back wall, cut insulating bricks (item 21) to fit the opening between the top of the back wall and the underside of the arch.

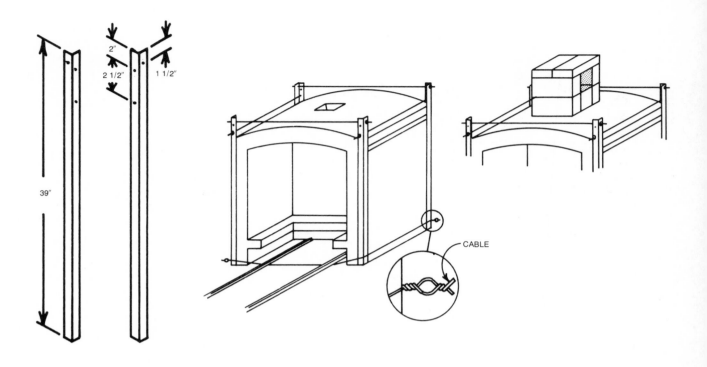

CABLE

15

Installing the Reinforcing Framework. The reinforcing frame for this kiln consists of six pieces of angle iron which are bolted or wired together. This frame must be assembled and secured in place before the arch-support form is removed, or the arch will collapse. Drill 3/8″ holes in the four 39″ lengths of angle iron (item 8c), as shown.

16

Now stand one of these pieces of angle iron at each corner of the kiln in the positions indicated in the drawing. Note that the upper ends of the four vertical angle-iron pieces enclose the ends of the horizontal pieces at the skew bricks. Weld together the 2″ and 36″ lengths of threaded rod (items 15b, 15c) to make four 38″ threaded rods. Now bolt the entire reinforcing structure together by sliding the four threaded steel rods through the holes drilled in the angle iron as shown. Secure the rods in place with washers and nuts (items 16 and 18).

To hold the bottom ends of the corner angle-iron pieces in place, run galvanized steel cable (item 14) around the outside of the kiln about 2″ above the slab. The cable must pass under the car tracks at the front of the kiln. Twist the ends of the cable tightly together at two diagonal corners of the kiln, as shown in the drawing.

With the corner angle irons firmly in place, remove the blocks from under the legs of the support form. Then remove the form from the arch. If any bricks move out of position, use a hammer to tap them gently back into place.

17

Applying the Insulating Blankets. The inside of the door and all other surfaces of the interior of the kiln (above the fourth course of bricks) must be covered with a layer of insulating blanket (item 23). Any one of a number of commercially available materials can be used for this purpose; simply follow the manufacturer's instructions.

Installing the Chimney. A small chimney will help offset the effects of wind when this kiln is fired. Make it from bricks (item 20a) arranged around the chimney opening, as illustrated in the drawing.

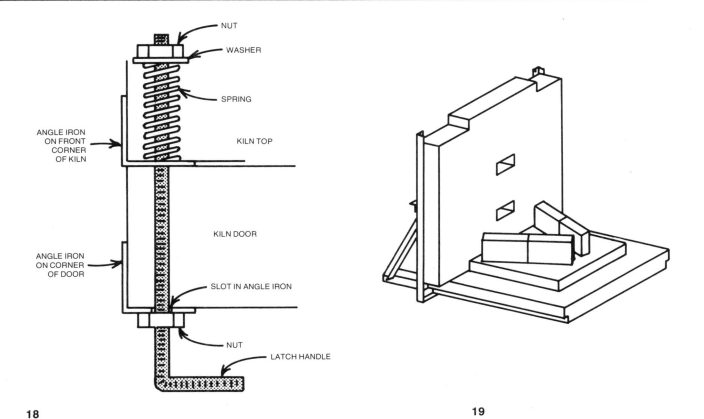

18

19

Making and Installing the Door Latches. You will need door latches if the door does not close tightly when the car is in the kiln. To prepare for the latches, cut a slot 3/4″ deep by 3/8″ wide into the top edge of the front face of the vertical angle irons on each side of the door frame by drilling a 3/8″ hole at the bottom of the location for the slot. Then hacksaw out the metal to continue the slot to the top of the angle iron.

Make the latches from two 11″ lengths of 5/16″ threaded rod (item 15a). Bend 2″ at one end of each piece of rod into a right (90°) angle in order to form latch handles (see Method 2 in "How to Bend Steel Rod" in the *Appendix*).

Install the rods, together with the washers, nuts, and compression springs (items 16, 17, 18), in the re-maining holes in the front face of the two front corner angle irons, as shown in the drawing.

To operate the latch mechanism, roll the car into the kiln and pull the latch handle to compress the spring until the rod can slip into the slot cut in the door frame. Adjust the nut on the threaded rod as much as necessary to achieve a tight fit between door and arch.

Cutting the Burner Hole. To provide an opening for the burner, cut a hole through the insulating bricks in the back wall with a saber saw or even with a knife. This hole should be only large enough to let the burner tip pass through.

Use a burner (item 28) with a blower that can supply about 150,000 Btu /hr. (For more information, see *Burners.*)

Installing the Flame Deflector.
The flame deflector consists of high-duty firebricks (item 22) placed on edge on the kiln floor, as shown. The flame will strike the point of the V and spread to both sides of the kiln, as-suring even heating. The small open-ing at the point of the V allows some flame to pass under the shelf and up the front wall. The width of the open-ing between the ends of the bricks can be adjusted to regulate the flame, and thus the amount of heat in the front and back of the kiln.

Lay a kiln shelf (item 19) on top of the deflector; this is the surface on which the ware to be fired will be placed. The front edge of the shelf should be about 2″ from the door.

This kiln will also require safety equip-ment (item 29) and piping necessary to connect it to the gas source.

To remove ware from the kiln, turn the burner down and pull the latch handles forward and upward to re-lease the door. Roll the car out as far as necessary to remove the ware with tongs. Wear asbestos gloves. Reload the car and push it back into the kiln.

CATENARY ARCH VERMICULITE KILN

Vermiculite, mixed with clay and water, provides an inexpensive material which can be used to build low-temperature kilns for firing pottery such as earthenware or raku. Vermiculite is widely available, since it is used as an insulating material in the building trades and as a soil conditioner in gardening. Vermiculite is easy to cast in the mold shapes used for kilns, and wood-working tools or a knife can be used to cut holes for burners, flues, and peepholes.

Although vermiculite kilns are relatively easy to make, they have some disadvantages that must be taken into consideration. Each cast piece must be pre-fired in order to make it hard enough to use. And even after this first firing, the vermiculite is still comparatively soft and corners tend to break off easily. Vermiculite is also highly moisture-absorbent and becomes extremely heavy when wet. Therefore, these kilns should not be situated outdoors unless they are well protected by waterproof covers. Also, low-temperature vermiculite kilns can be fired to a maximum of cone 2. When fired higher than this, the interior surface of the kiln fuses and develops deep cracks that destroy much of the vermiculite's insulating properties. Nevertheless, for low-temperature ware, vermiculite offers a functional, low-cost, easy-to-construct kiln.

The simplest design for this kind of kiln consists of a brick floor on which square or rectangular cast wall-sections are arranged in a box-like structure. The roof is made of another large, or several smaller, blocks laid across the top of the "box."

A better design uses the catenary arch. The curved arch is more difficult to build but it provides a stronger roof than the flat roof of the square kiln. A support form similar to the one used for the high-temperature catenary arch kiln described earlier in this part can be used as a mold for the arch of the vermiculite kiln. Instructions for building both the square and the arch-form kilns are provided here.

Tools

1. Shovel.
2. Hoe.
3. Hammer.
4. Wood-cutting saw.
5. Concrete-mixing box, or child's rigid plastic wading pool.
6. Circular saw with a blade to cut brick, or a cold chisel.
7. Carpenter's spirit level.
8. A 10' length of sash chain.
9. Can of spray paint, small amount, any color (optional).
10. Saber saw with blades for cutting wood and metal.
11. Kiln to pre-fire pieces that measure about 20" × 28" × 5 1/2".
12. A 12' length of light rope.
13. Drill with 1/2" wood-cutting and 1/8" metal-cutting bits.
14. Marker that will write on metal.
15. Metal shears.
16. Wire cutter.
17. Pliers.
18. C clamps.
19. Four or five people to help in building the arch.
20. Pop rivet tool.

Parts and Materials

Item No.

1. Pieces of 2 × 6 lumber:
   a. Two 48" lengths.
   b. Two 72" lengths.
2. One 46" × 70" piece of 6" × 6" mesh wire fence.
3. Wet-mix concrete, 1/3 cu. yd.
4. One-half lb. 16D common nails.
5. Newspaper.
6. Six 2 × 2s or 2 × 4s, 18" long.

Note: items 1 through 6 are needed to pour a concrete slab that will provide a foundation for the kiln. If some other suitable surface is available, the slab may be omitted.

7. Thirty-six 8" × 8" × 16" concrete or cinder blocks.

Note: brick sizes and shapes can be found in the *Chart of Standard Brick Sizes* in the *Appendix*.

8. One hundred and twenty low-duty firebricks.
9. Eighty-four 2000°F. insulating firebricks.
10. Fifteen high-duty soaps.
11. Eight clay or silicon carbide kiln shelves, 1" × 12" × 18" (see *Kiln Furniture*).
12. Sticky fireclay, 200 lbs. (A.P. Green's PBX works very well).
13. Vermiculite, 55 cu. ft.
14. One 4 × 8 sheet of 1/8" non-

tempered hardboard cut into the following pieces:
   a. One 30″ × 96″.
   b. One 6″ × 96″.
   c. Five 5 1/2″ × 29″.
15. One 4 × 8 sheet of 1/2″ exterior plywood (CD or plyscore grade).
16. One 12′ length of 1 × 6 lumber.
17. Two 24″ lengths of 1 × 4 lumber.
18. Four 30″ lengths of 2 × 2s or 2 × 4s.
19. Fifty 1/8″ × 1/8″ aluminum pop rivets.
20. Nails:
   a. 2 finishing nails.
   b. 1/2 lb. sheet rock nails.
21. A 30′ length of braided galvanized steel wire.
22. Galvanized sheet metal, steel or aluminum:
   a. One 3′ × 8′ sheet.
   b. One 4′ × 4′ sheet.
23. One forced-air burner, rated at about 160,000 Btu/hr., with necessary safety equipment (see *Burners* and *Burner Systems and Safety Controls*).
24. Hood-exhaust system, if the kiln is located indoors (see *Special Considerations for Indoor Kilns*).

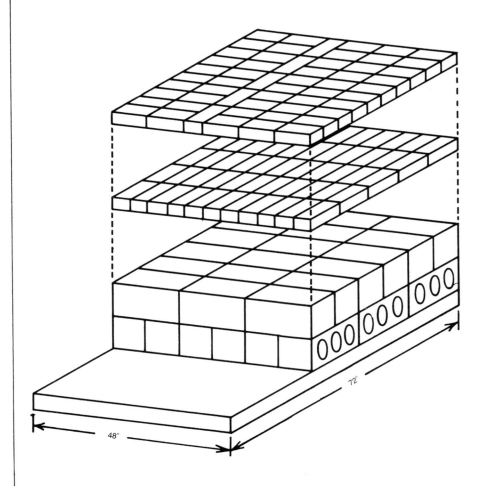

1

Making the Foundation. Like other kilns, the vermiculite catenary requires a concrete slab base (items 1 through 6). (For directions for selecting a site and making the slab see "Making the Foundation," *Catenary Arch Kiln*.) The method for preparing the base for this kiln is the same, but the slab should be 48″ × 72″. To raise the floor to a comfortable loading height, stack concrete blocks (item 7) on the slab in the manner shown in the drawing. The floor of the kiln is made of two layers of low-duty firebricks (item 8), arranged as shown.

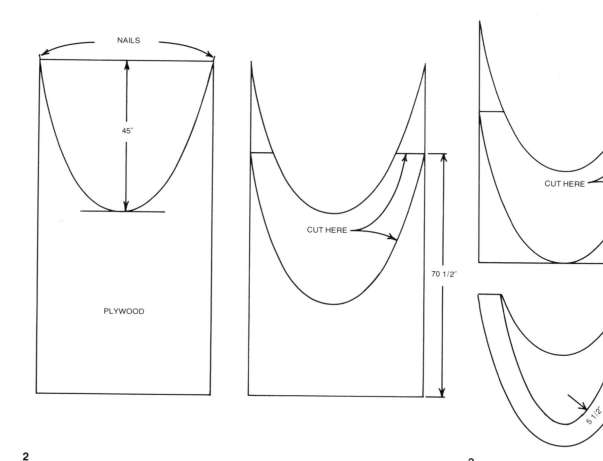

2

3

Building the Molds for the Arch.

To make this type of kiln, you will have to build an arch-shaped mold. If an arch support is available from another kiln, it can be modified to make this mold, but the castings for the arch sections are done inside the form rather than outside, so the resulting vermiculite kiln will be smaller.

To build the arch-shaped mold from scratch, lay two pieces of hardboard (item 14a, 14b) on a flat surface and cover them with several thicknesses of water-soaked newspaper. Let them soak for a few hours until the hardboard is flexible enough to bend without breaking.

Meanwhile, prepare to cut the sheet of plywood (item 15) to make the three arch-shaped sections. First, draw a line across the panel 45″ from one of the shorter (48″) ends. On the same end, drive a finishing nail (item 20a) partly into the edge at each of the two corners. Stand the plywood sheet on end on a flat surface, with the corners into which you have driv-

en the nails at the top. Use a carpenter's level to make sure that the 96″ edges of the panel are plumb; use wood or paper shims underneath the bottom end, if necessary, to make them plumb.

Hang one end of a length of sash chain from one of the nails; then loop the chain over the second nail, allowing enough of it to hang free so that the bottom of the curve it forms intersects the line drawn across the plywood. Trace the curve established by the chain with a pencil or by spraying over the chain with a can of spray paint. Cut out the arch-shaped panel with a saber saw.

From the other end of the same plywood sheet, measure off and mark 70 1/2″ along each of the long sides. Now place the arch shape you just cut on the plywood, positioning its base along the 70 1/2″ marks. The base will partially overhang the opening from which it was just cut. Trace around the arch shape on the plywood panel and cut it out, as shown.

Again, from the uncut end of the plywood panel, measure off and mark 45″ along each of the sides. Place the base of the *first* arch-shaped panel at the 45″ marks in the same manner as before. Trace around the arch shape and cut out the third panel.

Next, take the *last* two panels you cut out (these will be the ones with the shallow arched sections already cut out of them) and clamp them together so that their edges are flush on all sides. Now draw a line on the top panel 5 1/2″ inside the curved edge, as shown. With the two panels still clamped together, cut along this line with a saber or band saw. This will give you two plywood arch shapes, 5 1/2″ wide.

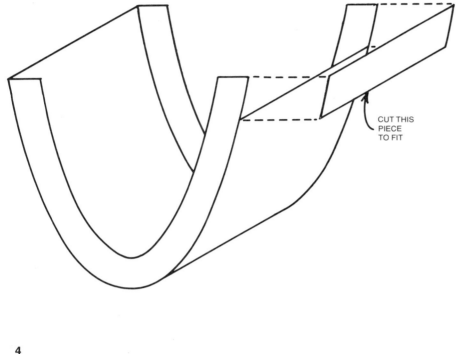

CUT THIS
PIECE
TO FIT

When the 30″ × 96″ piece of hardboard is soft enough, bend it over the two arch-shaped panels just cut out, as shown, and nail (item 20b) through the edges of the hardboard into the plywood arch shapes. You will note that the hardboard is *not long enough* to reach from one side of the arch shape to the other. To complete the mold, cut another piece of hardboard (item 14), 30″ wide and long enough to extend to the base, as shown. Also nail in place the reinforcing block, made of a 2 × 2 or 2 × 4 (item 18), that will overlap and reinforce the outside of the joint between the two pieces of hardboard.

4

VERMICULITE MIXTURE

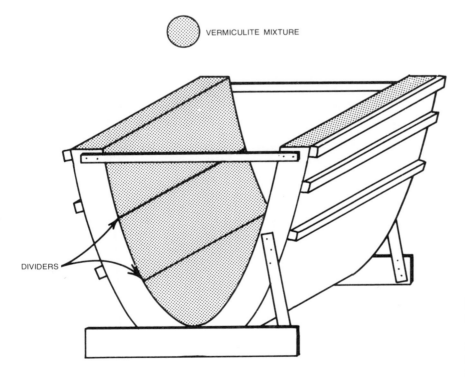

DIVIDERS

Next, for additional reinforcement, nail the 30″ long 2 × 2s or 2 × 4s (item 18) to the outside of the plywood arch molds, as shown in the drawing. Also nail in place the lengths of wood (items 16, 17) that constitute the base and braces of the mold, as shown. The mold for the arch is now complete.

5

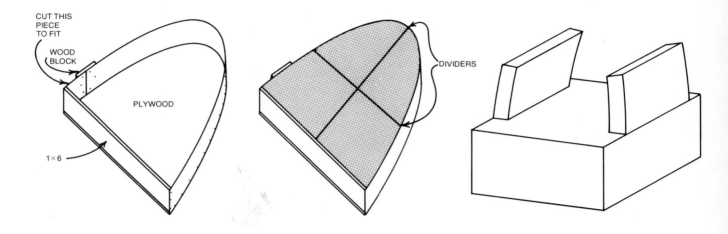

6

7

Building the Mold for the Back Wall.
Nail the piece of 1 × 6 (item 16) to the
bottom edge of the first plywood arch
shape you cut, as shown. Now bend
the 6″ × 96″ piece of softened hardboard (item 14b) around the curved
edge of the plywood. Nail (item 20b)
one end of it to the 1 × 6, and continue
nailing it around the plywood arch. You
will notice that the hardboard strip is *not
long enough* to go all the way around
the arch. Just as you did with the arch
mold, cut out and nail in place a 6″
wide piece of hardboard (item 14)
long enough to extend to the base.
Reinforce the joint between the two
pieces of hardboard with a block cut
from a 1 × 6, as shown.

Finally, cut three 5″ wide hardboard
dividers (item 14) to fit into the back-
wall mold, approximately as shown.
One piece extends from the 1 × 6 to
the top of the mold.

Mixing the Vermiculite and Clay. You
can mix as much vermiculite and clay
as is practical, because this mixture
has a very long working life. For a mixing tub, you can use a concrete-mixing box, or a child's rigid plastic wading pool. Pour in about six parts, by
volume not weight, vermiculite (item
13) to one part clay (item 12), and mix
together with a hoe. Add enough
water so that the mixture pushes out
between your fingers when squeezed
in your fist.

Filling the Molds. Before filling the
molds with the vermiculite-clay mix-

ture, position them on a flat surface
that is protected from rain. Shovel
the mixture into the arch mold, packing
it into the corners. When a loosely
packed layer about 2″ thick covers all
the interior surfaces of the mold, position and insert the dividers (item 14c)
by pushing them down in the vermiculite until their top edges are flush with
the edges of the arch mold (see drawing 7). Arrange the dividers in the arch
so that it is divided into six sections
approximately equal in size.

Complete filling the molds to a uniform 5 1/2″ thickness, making sure
that the mixture is packed into all sections of the molds right up to the top
edges. The best way to do this is to
shovel a little too much of the mixture into the mold, pack it down very
firmly, and then scrape the top surface level with a straight board long
enough to reach across from one side
of the mold to the other.

Now shovel the vermiculite into the
back-wall mold to a depth of about 2″.
Then position and insert the hardboard dividers so that the back wall
is sectioned into four parts, as shown
above.

When all the sections are dry (this
will take several days), carefully remove them from the molds; they are
fragile at this point. Load the sections
into a kiln for pre-firing, leaving
spaces between them so that the heat
can circulate around all sides of all the
sections. Fire to cone 04.

Building the Arch. It will take four
or five people to assemble the arch
since there is no arch support. Begin
by arranging the bottom sections of
the two sides so that about 7″ of the
kiln floor is exposed at the back and
about 10″ to 11″ in front, as shown.

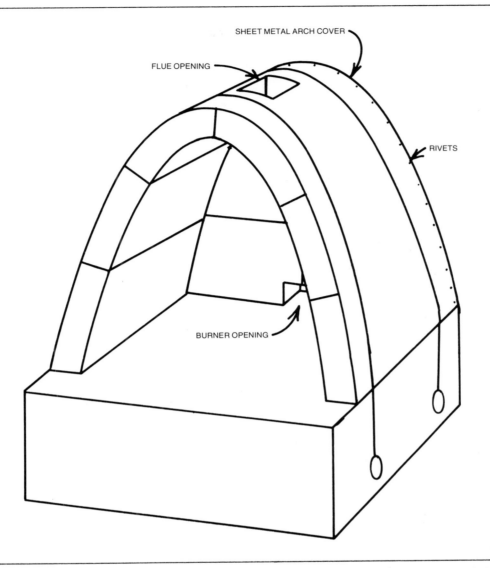

FLUE OPENING

SHEET METAL ARCH COVER

RIVETS

BURNER OPENING

8

Have one person sit inside the kiln with his back up against one of these bottom sections of the arch. Set the third and fourth sections of the arch in place on each side and let the person inside the kiln support these two sections with his hands and back. Put the fifth section in place, as shown in the drawing, and position one person outside of the kiln at the front and another person at the back to hold this section in place. Now have two more people slide the sixth and final section into place.

The arch should be self-supporting now but may need some adjustment to be really stable. If there are spaces at the joints between the arch sections at their inside edges (inside the kiln), the bottom sections of the kiln walls should be moved closer together.

If the spaces are in the joints at the outside edges of the sections, move the bottom sections apart slightly. These adjustments must be made gently to prevent any crumbling of the cast parts.

Building the Back Wall. When the arch is completed put the back-wall sections in position. Tie them in place with rope temporarily, if necessary.

Cut a 4" × 5" burner opening in the center of the back wall at floor level, as in the drawing. Also, cut a 6 1/2" square flue opening in the center of the top of the arch as shown. The best way to cut these holes is to drill starter holes first. Then cut them out with a saber saw, using a wood-cutting blade.

Installing the Sheet-Metal Jacket.

The kiln requires a sheet-metal jacket, consisting of an arch cover and a back cover, to help hold all the arch and back-wall sections together. If the kiln is located outdoors, the jacket is necessary also to keep the highly absorbent vermiculite dry.

Lay one 3' × 8' sheet of aluminum or galvanized sheet steel (item 22a; the aluminum is much easier to cut) on top of the arch. It will cover all or nearly all of the arch. Next, mark the sheet metal (item 22b) for the back wall for cutting by holding it against the back wall (with the arch cover in place) and tracing the outer edge of the metal arch cover on it. Then, draw another line, 1" outside of the first on this piece of sheet metal. Now cut out the arch-shaped piece of sheet metal along the outside line.

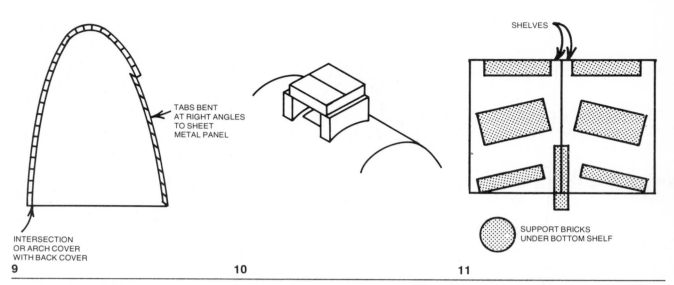

9

TABS BENT
AT RIGHT ANGLES
TO SHEET
METAL PANEL

INTERSECTION
OR ARCH COVER
WITH BACK COVER

10

11

SHELVES

SUPPORT BRICKS
UNDER BOTTOM SHELF

In order to fasten the back cover to the arch cover, mark off the 1″ wide marginal area into segments about 2″ wide, as shown. With a pair of metal shears, cut along each of the lines separating the segments down to the line representing the kiln arch. Bend all the segments to form right angles with the rest of the sheet metal. The tabs are now completed.

Place the back cover, with the tabs up, on a flat surface. Stand the arch cover on its long edge so that it follows and fits the curve of the back cover, as shown. Beginning at one end, drill a 1/8″ hole through each tab and through the cover. Pop rivet each tab to the cover. To assure a good fit, drill only a few holes and install only a few rivets (item 19) at a time. Proceed until all the tabs are riveted to the arch.

Place the completed jacket over the kiln and mark on it the location of the holes for the flue and burner openings. Remove the jacket and cut out these openings with metal shears or a saber saw with a metal-cutting blade. Reinstall the jacket.

The jacket must now be secure with heavy wire (item 21) anchored to concrete blocks in the foundation of the kiln. To install this wire, pass one end of a 15′ length through the holes in the concrete blocks under the front of the kiln. Run the wire up and over the arch and back down to its starting point. Grip both ends of the wire and pull it tight. Twist the two ends of the wire together near the base of the kiln. Then install another wire in the same way, at the back of the kiln.

If the kiln is outdoors, the flue opening should be covered to help prevent downdrafts and to keep rain out. This can be accomplished with a simple arrangement of bricks. Shape one side of a pair of insulating bricks (item 9) to match the curve at the top of the arch so that they sit solidly on top of it. Place one of these bricks on each side of the flue opening and set two firebricks (item 8) crosswise on top of them, covering the flue opening, as in the drawing.

Arranging the Kiln Shelves. The bottom shelf (item 11) can rest on firebricks (items 8, 10) (straights and soaps) laid in the pattern shown.

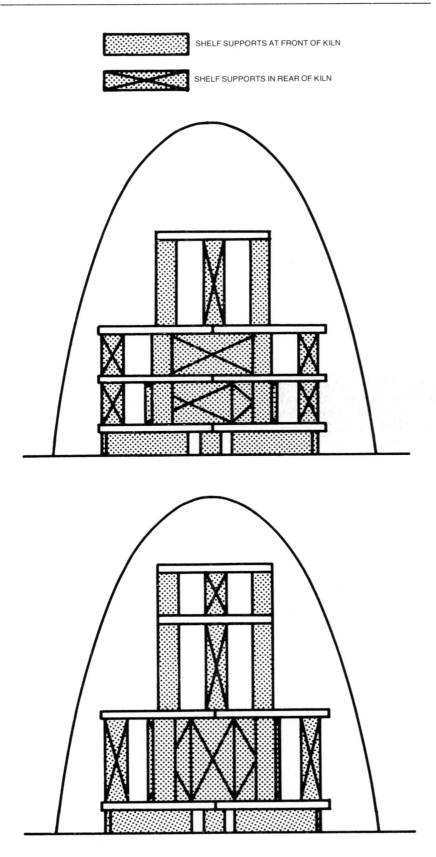

SHELF SUPPORTS AT FRONT OF KILN

SHELF SUPPORTS IN REAR OF KILN

The posts to support the upper shelves can also be made of firebrick straights and soaps. Since some of the posts in the back of the kiln also serve as a bagwall, they can be arranged, in either of the patterns shown, to fulfill the additional function of protecting the pots from direct flame.

The kiln door is stacked in place against the front of the arch for each firing. It is composed of insulating bricks (item 9) one brick (4 1/2″) thick. Provide for peepholes, as needed, by inserting a brick endwise and allowing half of it to protrude outside the door. This brick can be rubbed on a rough surface, such as concrete, to make it slightly thinner so that it will slip in and out easiy.

The burner (item 23) to use with this kiln is the forced-air unit discussed in *Burners*; it should produce about 160,000 Btu/hr.

In operation, the flame from the burner enters the burner port and strikes the bottom shelf and the bagwall so that about half of it goes under the shelf and the other half goes up the back of the kiln. If, during firing, the front of the kiln is cooler than the back, tilt the burner so that more flame goes under the shelf. Conversely, if the back of the kiln is cooler, tilt the burner so that less flame goes under the shelf. (For additional information, see *Burners* and *Burner Systems and Safety Controls.*)

If this kiln is indoors, it should have the hood-exhaust system (item 24) (see *Special Considerations for Indoor Kilns*).

SQUARE VERMICULITE KILN

A simpler kiln can be made from the cast vermiculite-clay mixture if the unit can be built and fired indoors. This is a kiln composed of four square cast slabs of the same dimensions, and a bricked-up door.

This kiln is designed solely for use indoors or in a dry, sheltered location where it will not get wet. Unlike the catenary arch which is self-supporting even when weakened by water, the flat top of this kiln could collapse if it became saturated with water. Even a metal jacket would not insure that the kiln would stay dry enough for outdoor use.

Tools

1. Hacksaw.
2. Shovel.
3. Hammer.
4. Hoe.
5. Wood-cutting saw.
6. Concrete-mixing box, or child's rigid plastic wading pool.
7. Circular saw with blade to cut brick; or a cold chisel.
8. Saber saw.
9. Kiln to fire pieces measuring 28″ × 28″ × 5 1/2″.
10. Drill with 1/2″ wood-cutting bit.

Parts and Materials

Item No.

1. Pieces of 2 × 6 lumber:
   a. Two 48″ lengths.
   b. Two 72″ lengths.
2. One 46″ × 70″ piece of 6″ × 6″ mesh wire fence.
3. Wet-mix concrete, 1/3 cu. yd.
4. One-half lb. 16D common nails.
5. Newspaper.
6. Six 2 × 2s or 2 × 4s, 18″ long.

Note: items 1 through 6 are needed to pour a concrete slab that will provide a foundation for the kiln. If some other suitable surface is available, the slab may be omitted.

7. Thirty concrete or cinder blocks, 8″ × 8″ × 16″.

Note: brick sizes and shapes can be found in the *Table of Standard Brick Sizes* in the *Appendix*.

8. Ninety low-duty firebricks.
9. Eighty-five 2000°F. insulating firebricks.
10. Fifteen high-duty soaps.
11. Eight clay or silicon carbide kiln shelves, 1″ × 12″ × 18″ (see *Kiln Furniture*).
12. Sticky fireclay, 100 lbs. (A. P. Green's PBX works very well).
13. Vermiculite, 54 cu. ft.
14. Four 1 × 6s, 40″ long (for each mold).
15. One 1 × 2, 18″ long.
16. One piece of sheet plastic or plywood, 44″ × 44″ × 1/2″ (for each mold,) optional, see text.
17. Eight 9″ lengths of 3/16″ steel rod or welding rod.
18. One forced-air burner, rated at about 160,000 Btu/hr., with necessary safety equipment (see *Burners* and *Burner Systems and Safety Controls*).
19. One hood-exhaust system (see *Special Considerations for Indoor Kilns*).

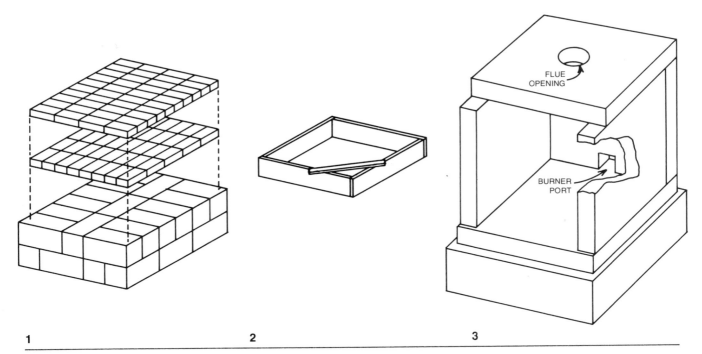

1

2

3

Making the Foundation. The base for this kiln is the same as that for the catenary arch kiln except that fewer blocks (item 7) and bricks (item 8) are used, as shown in the drawing (see "Making the Foundation." *Catenary Arch Kiln*).

The two side walls, the back wall, and the top are all made of blocks cast from the same vermiculite-clay mixture as the catenary kiln. Since all of these blocks are the same size, all four pieces can be cast in the same mold; but using two or more molds will considerably shorten the casting and drying time.

Make each mold from four 40" lengths of 1 × 6 (item 14). If a flat concrete floor is available, simply lay the form directly on it. If a concrete floor is not available, make a bottom for the mold from a sheet of plywood or lay a sheet of plastic under it (item 16). To keep the form square, nail a strip of wood (item 15) across one corner, as shown.

Mix the vermiculite, clay (items 12, 13), and water (See "Mixing the Vermiculite and Clay" in the previous section for instructions) and pack it into the molds, making sure to fill all corners. Use a flat board to scrape the top surface smooth. When the pieces are thoroughly dry (this may take several days), remove them carefully from the molds. Arrange them in a kiln so that there are spaces between the blocks on all sides to permit heat circulation. Then pre-fire them to cone 04.

Assembling the Kiln. Position the three wall pieces on the base and set the top in place, as shown. Fasten the pieces together by pushing 9" long pieces of steel rod or welding rod (item 17) into the sections, as if the rods were nails.

Cut a 4" × 4" hole for the burner at the center of the back wall. Cut a round, 6" diameter flue hole in the center of the top. These holes can be easily cut with a wood-cutting blade or even with a knife.

The bottom shelf and supports (items 8, 10, 11) are the same as those specified for the catenary kiln, and the shelf-support-bagwall (items 8 and 10) at the back is also the same (see "Arranging the Kiln Shelves" in the previous section). In this kiln, two shelves can be used on each layer since the kiln does not become narrower at the top like the catenary arch.

The 4 1/2" thick door can best be made by stacking insulating bricks (item 9) in the opening.

The burner installation (item 18) and adjustments are the same for this kiln as for the catenary in the previous section. This kiln should have a hood-exhaust system (item 19) to remove heat and waste gases during firing. (See *Special Consideration for Indoor Kilns* for instructions for making and installing this system.)

KILN DESIGN MODIFICATION

Designing kilns is both an art and a science. While most variables are known, it is nearly impossible to change one characteristic of a kiln without altering others. It is this interaction that makes kiln design complicated.

This section explains how to enlarge or otherwise modify the kiln plans presented in this book. However, all such modifications should retain the following basic considerations of economy and efficiency:

1. Easy loading and unloading.
2. Efficient use of heat. This is directly related to kiln proportions—depth, width, and height should always be approximately equal. However, in a catenary arch kiln, you can make the arch dimension *slightly* higher than the width to provide more useful firing space. If the kiln is of the updraft type, with a flue in the roof, the height of the firing chamber should not be too great.
3. Efficient use of interior kiln space.

To retain the firing characteristics, basic construction procedures and techniques should remain the same, regardless of modifications, for the kilns in this book. However, the quantities of materials will need to be altered if the size of the kiln is changed.

Both the size and the design of a kiln should be based on the kiln-shelf size to be used. Therefore, the first step in determining a kiln design is to select the kiln-shelf size that will be standard in your workshop (for suggestions, see *Kiln Furniture*). It is advisable to make your choice from those that are readily available.

Once you have decided on the kiln-shelf size, the next step is to determine the best arrangement of shelves and other kiln furniture to achieve the firing area and capacity you need. Begin by sketching various arrangements, keeping in mind the considerations of economy and efficiency just listed. Arrange kiln furniture so that a path as long as possible is provided for the heat to travel in and around the ware before leaving the kiln. The longer the path, the less heat will be lost out the flue. Small spaces between adjoining shelves improve heat circulation. They also have the effect of providing increased firing space with fewer shelves; the fewer shelf posts you use, the more room for pots.

Laying Out the Shelves and Posts.

To demonstrate these principles of efficient kiln furniture arrangement, a plan using three 12″ × 18″ kiln shelves that minimizes the number of shelf posts which must be used is shown in drawing 1. This arrangement would be suitable for the catenary arch kiln, described in this book, with two bagwalls.

This shelf plan should fit into the kiln as in drawing 2. The fireboxes are the spaces between the bagwall and the kiln wall where the flames from the burners should be concentrated.

The key near the drawing presents an acceptable range of sizes for each of the dimensions in this shelf arrangement. These dimensions are variable, within the range shown. However, before deciding on the dimensions that you want, it is advisable to read through the plans for the catenary arch kiln in this part to become familiar with this type of kiln and its construction features.

How to Alter Kiln Dimensions.

For the purpose of demonstrating the dimensional relationships suggested in the drawing, let us assume that a moderate-size kiln, about 30 cubic feet, is to be built. This is about 50% more cubic volume than that of the catenary arch kiln in this book. Here are the trial values that can be assigned to this kiln:

A = 5″
B = 2 1/2″
C = 2″
D = 3″
E = 2″
F = 9″
G = 5″ (4 1/2″)
H = 5″ (4 1/2″)
I = 1″

Note: the catenary arch kilns in this book are designed so that the front and back walls will protrude slightly beyond the floor. This insures that the angle irons holding the kilns together will press tightly against the walls rather than against the floor or base of the kiln. However, for the purpose of this discussion, it is easier to figure the sizes for the kiln by assuming that the front and back walls are flush with the edges of the floor, and then casting them just a little thicker. This is the reason for using the value of 4 1/2″ for this trial kiln. The actual walls should be 5″ thick.

Let us begin determining the overall dimensions of this kiln by referring again to the drawing of the floor plan. Obviously, the outside width of the kiln will equal the sum of the widths of the components involved.

Taking the alphabetical symbols for these widths, we see that the overall width of the kiln can be expressed: 2A + 2B + 2C + shelf width + 2F Substituting the numerical values for these alphabetical symbols, we see that the overall width would be equal to: 2(5) + 2(2 1/2) + 2(2) + 18 (shelf length) + 2(9). Simple addition now gives us the actual width of the kiln: 10 + 5 + 4 + 18 + 18 = 55″.

To minimize the number of bricks that must be cut, the width of the floor should be a multiple of 4 1/2″ (the width of a half-brick). Changing the overall width of 55″, obtained from the dimensional values assumed, to 54″ provides a multiple of 4 1/2″. To achieve this modification, the best dimension to change is C; change C to 1 1/2″.

The outside depth of the kiln can be established in the same way: 2D + 2E + 2I + G + H + 3(12″,) shelf width), or 2(3) + 2(2) + 2(1) + 4 1/2 + 4 1/2 + 3(12), or 6 + 4 + 2 + 4 1/2 + 4 1/2 + 36 = 57″. However, our result (57″) should also be a multiple of 4 1/2″,

therefore, it must be changed to either 54 or 58 1/2″. A depth of 54″ would be a little tight, so 58 1/2″ is a better choice. For this value, change I to 1 /2″ and E to 2 1/2″.

Applied to the floor plan, these dimensions of 54″ and 58 1/2″ require that one layer of the floor be made up of six bricks (9″ long) by 13 bricks (4 1/2″ wide). The second layer can then be of six and a half bricks (9″ long) by 12 bricks (4 1/2″ wide).

To provide enough floor space for the chimney, an additional area 13 1/2″ × 18″ will be needed. (Actually, the chimney measures 18″ × 18″, but its front wall is part of the back wall of the kiln.)

The two layers of bricks must be laid on a base made up of concrete blocks in order to raise the level of the floor enough to facilitate loading and unloading. Therefore, the number of blocks and the way they are arranged must also be adjusted to fit the patterns of floor brick.

In figuring how to lay out the blocks and how many are needed, bear in mind that the holes in the blocks should be lined up from front to back. This must be done so that the cable or chain used to hold the catenary arch kiln's front and back walls together can pass through them.

Concrete blocks are normally 7 1/2″ × 15 1/2″. The 54″ floor width requires three rows of full blocks and one of half-blocks (see drawing 7 in *Catenary Arch Kiln*). The half row can be made of full blocks laid perpendicular to the three full rows. This half row should be placed in the center of the kiln where no cables or chains need to pass. One block will have to be cut with a hammer and chisel (see the *Appendix* for how to cut concrete block). For the depth of 58 1/2″, seven rows of blocks will be required, with equal spaces left between each of the rows. When building the form in which to make the concrete slab for a larger kiln, remember that it should be about 4″ to 6″ wider than the kiln and 3′ to 4′ longer than the depth of the kiln plus the portion of the chimney that extends beyond the back wall. Be sure always to position the kiln on its slab so that there will be as much free space in front of it as possible, in order to expedite unloading.

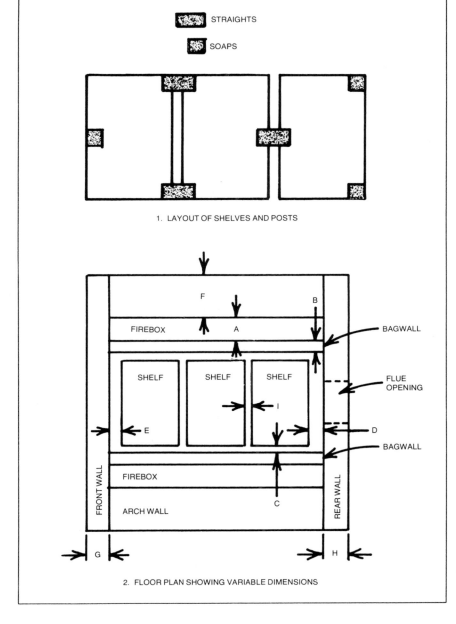

STRAIGHTS

SOAPS

1. LAYOUT OF SHELVES AND POSTS

2. FLOOR PLAN SHOWING VARIABLE DIMENSIONS

The slab, base, and floor for this larger, 30 cubic foot kiln should look as they do in drawing 9 (*Catenary Arch Kiln*) except that more blocks and bricks are used.

The arch form, as built for the catenary arch kiln, will be 1/2″ narrower than the inside width of this kiln, or about 35 1/2″. The form should be made so that it is 1″ lower than the overall height selected for the kiln. This will allow room for the hardboard used to make the form and for the wooden blocks that prop it up while the bricks are being laid up.

Therefore, the depth of the arch form should be 9″ less than that of the floor. This allows space on the kiln floor for the front and back walls. Since the form will be made from a hardboard sheet measuring only 48″, the arch bricks for this kiln can extend 1 1/2″ beyond the back edge of the form during construction. If a larger kiln is to be constructed, it will be necessary to use a second sheet of hardboard in order to build a form wide enough to support the added rows of bricks in the arch.

A 30 cubic foot kiln could be successfully fired with only two large burners; however, the main advantage to using more burners is not only to increase the heat flow into the kiln, but also to assure a more even heat distribution throughout, which in turn assures more uniform results. A larger kiln would require six burners. Remember, too, that it is always best to locate heat sources slightly nearer the front than the back of a downdraft kiln, since the heat is naturally pulled toward the flue opening in the back.

A chimney of 9″ × 9″ is adequate for kilns up to about 70 cubic feet. Larger kilns will need a 9″ × 13 1/2″ opening.

Whenever you are in doubt about a kiln dimension, it is wiser to make it bigger rather than smaller. This applies to the number of burners installed, to the burner orifices, the size of the opening into the chimney, as well as the chimney area and height. Any of these dimensions that prove to be too large in operation can be easily corrected—an over-sized opening can be partially blocked up, or the damper can be used more; a burner's orifices can be changed, or the burners just not turned on all the way.

Estimating Brick Quantities. To determine how many bricks will be required for a particular size kiln, the best way is to figure each part of the kiln, such as the floor, arch, chimney or other section, separately. Then add together the totals for each to establish overall quantities.

The arch of a catenary kiln represents a special problem in estimating the bricks needed, because there are no formulas that you can use. The surest way to determine the number of each kind of brick needed is to take with you to the brick supplier the smaller end panel you cut out of plywood for the arch form (see drawing 4 in *Catenary Arch Kiln*). Lay the end panel on the floor or ground and place the different kinds of bricks around the form. Try out different combinations using the same kind of brick at the same point on both sides of the arch (in order to attain symmetry and stability in the finished arch), until you arrive at the assortment that fits properly. When everything fits, count the total of each shape of bricks you used to determine the number of courses of each shape. Get an extra course or two of each shape since actual construction usually requires a slightly different combination of bricks.

The volume of castable can be figured from the formulas provided in the *Appendix*. For the two back-wall sections, figure the volume of the entire wall of the kiln as a whole. Then subtract the volume of the portion of the back wall that will be occupied by the chimney. The supplier of the castable can tell you the weight of this material per cubic foot, so that you can then figure out how much to order.

The amount of block insulation needed for a catenary arch kiln can be determined by counting the number of courses of brick making up the 4 1/2″ thick portion of the arch. Each course is the equivalent of 2 1/2″ of the outside curve of the arch. Simply multiply the number of courses by 2 1/2″ to determine the length of the outside curve and then multiply this by the depth of the arch. Multiply the result by the thickness of the layer of insulation that is to be applied to the arch. This will give you the required volume of block insulation in cubic inches. Tell your supplier what this

figure is and specify the thickness of the insulation you are going to apply (three layers, 1 1/2″ thick for this kiln), and he will be able to tell you how many cases of material you will need.

When ordering bricks, insulation, or castable, always get a little more than your figures indicate you need. Then you won't run out if changes must be made or if there is some breakage in the course of construction.

Heat Input Requirements. The amount of heat that will be required to obtain successful firings depends on a number of factors, such as the size of the kiln, the type and amount of insulation applied, the efficiency with which heat is utilized within the kiln. Here is an approximate comparison: for a 20 cubic foot kiln, 600,000 Btu/hr.; for a 50 cubic foot kiln, 1,000,000 Btu/hr. These figures are based on the kiln designs provided in this book. Other sizes can be approximated from these figures.

Note on updraft kilns: some small kilns, particularly of the updraft type, have the firebox located under the floor. The interior dimensions of such a kiln can be determined by taking the shelf dimensions and adding 1 1/2″ to 3″ on all sides, to allow for the space required to permit the heat to rise around the load.

A problem frequently encountered with this type of kiln is that the first shelf gets too hot. This can often be overcome by putting firebricks or bats 2″ or more thick, underneath the bottom layer of kiln shelves.

Altering the Bagwall. The height and spacing of the bricks in a bagwall control the amount and distribution of heat that passes from the firebox to the pots. The initial arrangement of bricks is largely a matter of guesswork and often has to be changed after each of the first few firings to get proper heat distribution. If in the first firing the top of the kiln is too hot, increase the size and/or number of openings in the lower part of the bagwall and/or lower its height. If the bottom is too hot, make the wall tighter and/or higher. The part of the wall just in front of each burner should be nearly solid to keep the flame from directly hitting the wall.

KILN DAMPER

This damper can be used in any of the kilns in this book that require dampers. It is made from a piece of 1/2" thick steel plate and an 18" length of 3/4" steel pipe welded together.

The design of this damper makes it impossible to close off the chimney completely. This is an important safety feature, because it assures that there will always be some draft through the kiln, especially when the kiln is first ignited for a firing. In the event of a flame failure, it can prevent unburned gas from filling the kiln. If gas continues to enter a kiln in which the chimney is completely closed, a major explosion can occur.

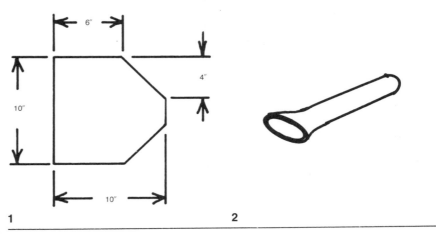

1

Making the Damper. Cut a 10" × 10" piece of 1/2" thick steel plate to the shape shown in the drawing. Use a metal-cutting torch.

2

Next, hammer one end of an 18" length of 3/4" diameter pipe so that it is partially flattened. The outside height of the oval shape of the pipe end, after hammering, must be about 1/2".

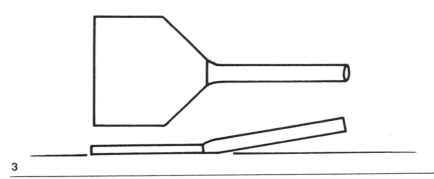

3

Weld the pipe to the damper plate in the position shown in the drawing.

The bottom of the damper plate must still be flat after the welding is completed.

KILN FLAPS

It is often necessary to close off all the openings around a kiln's burners to keep drafts from blowing out burner flames, especially when firing is getting under way, or to keep the kiln from cooling too fast after firing. The flaps described here can be made from either sheet steel or aluminum. Two pieces of metal, about 4″ × 6″, are required for each flap.

Making the Flaps. Make a paper template for each half of the flap (the two sides of some burners are not identical). You may also have to make separate templates for each burner. Use stiff paper, about 4″ × 6″. Make the first cutouts smaller than the burner/ignitor/thermocouple outline for which it is intended. Then, by trial and error, enlarge and shape the openings to make the paper fit as tightly as possible around each burner. The flaps should overlap by about 1/4″ at all points.

When the templates are finished, trace their outlines on the two pieces of sheet metal. Cut out the burner flaps with metal shears.

Before riveting the halves together, try them out around the burner and trim, as required. Then rivet them together, as shown.

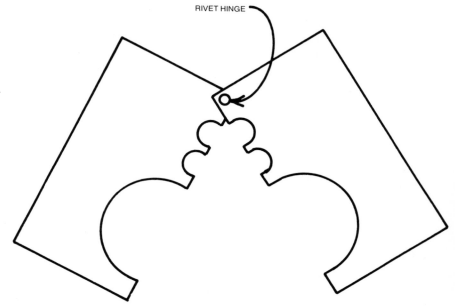

RIVET HINGE

ATMOSPHERIC WELDED BURNER

The two types of gas burners generally used on potter's kilns are atmospheric and forced air. Either type can be made from common materials and both can be purchased commercially. Commercial burners are expensive, and, for the potter's purposes, are no better than properly designed ones you can build yourself.

There are many ways to build burners. We present here only those we have found to be reliable. The pipe and welded burners that follow are interchangeable; they differ mainly in construction.

Tools

1. Hacksaw.
2. Cutting torch.
3. Pipe cutter (optional).
4. Welding equipment.
5. Drill with bit to fit orifice (see text).

Parts and Materials

Item No.

1. One 12″ length of 2″ black pipe (16″ length for burners using LP, liquid petroleum, gas).
2. Pipe couplings:
   a. One 3/4″.
   b. One 1″.
3. Pipe nipples:
   a. One 3/4″ × 3″.
   b. One 1/4″ × 4″.
4. One 1/4″ pipe cap.
5. One 4″ length of 2 1/2″ square steel tubing.
6. One 1/4″ × 5″ threaded rod.
7. Two 1/4″ wing nuts.
8. One washer with a hole 1″ in diameter.
9. Two electrical connection-box covers, 3″ in diameter.
10. Pipe-joint compound or Teflon joint tape.

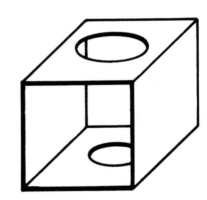

Burner Assembly. Begin by cutting a 12″ length of 2″ pipe (item 1). (If LP gas will be used for the burner, it will be better if this pipe is 16″ long.) The best way to cut pipe is to use a pipe cutter which cuts ends that are square and flat. A hacksaw or cutting torch can be used if you take care to make a straight cut.

You will also need a 4″ length of 2 1/2″ square tubing (item 5). Since these ends must be cut square, it may be best to have the cutting done by the supplier on a power hacksaw.

With a cutting torch, cut holes in the center of facing sides of the square tubing, as shown. One hole should be about 2″ in diameter and the other about 1″ in diameter.

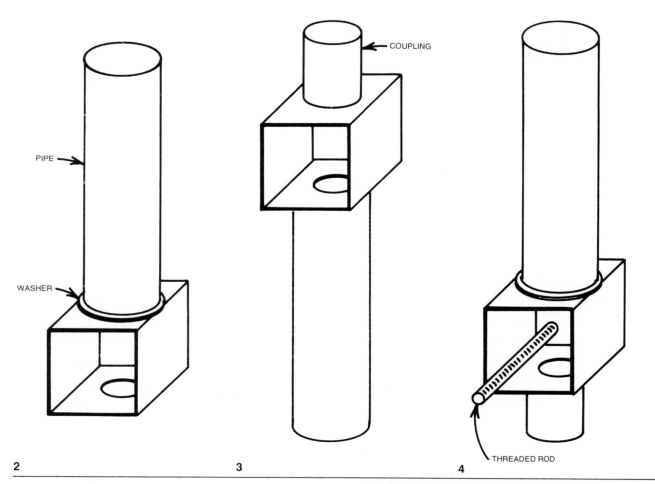

2

3

4

Lay the square tube with the 2″ hole on top on a surface suitable for welding. Place the 1″ washer (item 8) over the hole so that it is centered on the top of the square tube. Now stand the 2″ pipe (item 1) on end so it is centered on the washer. Weld the three pieces together in this position, as shown. If the washer is galvanized, be sure to weld in a well ventilated area, because the fumes that welding releases from galvanized metal are poisonous.

Reverse this assembly so that it stands up on the end of the 2″ pipe and weld the 3/4″ coupling (item 2a) over the 1″ hole. The coupling should be centered over the opening of the 2″ pipe and should be perpendicular to the surface of the square tube, as shown.

Weld the 1/4″ threaded rod (item 6) inside the back corner of the square tube, as shown. Equal lengths of the ends of the threaded rod should extend from the two ends of the square tube. The welding should be done inside the square tube so that the threads are not damaged on the parts of the rod outside the tube.

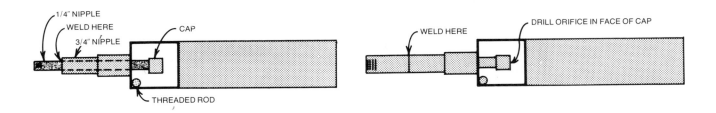

5

Cut the 3/4″ pipe nipple (item 3a) in half with a pipe cutter or hacksaw. Screw one of the cut pieces into the coupling on the welded assembly until it is finger tight. Screw the pipe cap (item 4) on the end of the 1/4″ × 4″ nipple (item 3b) until finger tight. Then slip the nipple and cap inside the half nipple (already screwed into the burner) so the cap is inside the burner. Slide the nipple and cap in so that the end of the cap is 1″ from the face of the washer in the burner. When in this position, the 1/4″ nipple should protrude from the cut end of the 3/4″ nipple. Weld the two nipples together. The weld should be at the cut end of the 3/4″ nipple, as shown.

6

Slide the remaining part of the 3/4″ nipple onto the protruding end of the 1/4″ nipple and weld in place, as shown. No gas should be able to leak through the weld.

Remove the cap-and-two-nipple assembly. Also remove the cap from the nipple. Drill the orifice (hole) in the end of the cap. The drill size you use can be determined by the Btu rating and the gas pressure which will be supplied to the kiln. Use the gas flow chart in the *Appendix*.

Coat all threads with pipe joint compound (item 10) and reassemble the burner.

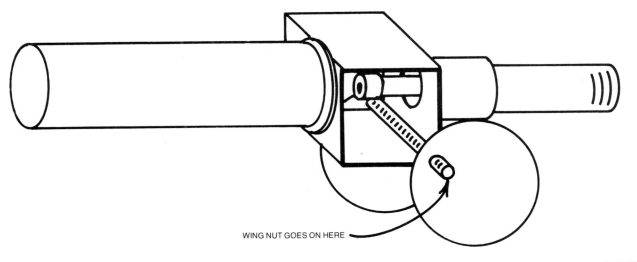

WING NUT GOES ON HERE

7

Place an electrical connection-box cover (item 9) on each end of the 1/4″ rod that protrudes from the ends of the square tube and fasten them in place with the wing nuts (item 7), as shown. The covers can be rotated to any position desired to regulate the volume of air entering the burner.

The burner is now ready to be connected to the gas line. (This procedure is described in *Burner Systems and Safety Controls*).

ATMOSPHERIC PIPE BURNER

The pipe for this burner will probably have to be cut and threaded by a plumber since it is not possible to thread pipe this large without using expensive equipment.

Tools

1. Pipe wrench.
2. Hacksaw.
3. Pipe cutter (optional).
4. Drill with No. 7 or 7/32″ bit and bit for orifice (see text).
5. Tap, 1/4″.
6. Bench grinder.

Parts and Materials

Item No.

1. One 12″ length of 2″ pipe (16″ length for LP, liquid petroleum, gas), threaded on one end.
2. One 2″ cross pipe fitting.
3. One 2″ × 3/4″ bushing.
4. One 1/4″ pipe cap.
5. Pipe nipples:
   a. One 1/4″ × 4″.
   b. One 3/4″ × 3″.
6. One 2″ plug.
7. One electrical connection box cover, 3″ in diameter.
8. One 1″ piece of 1/4″ threaded rod.
9. One 1/4″ wing nut.
10. One washer with a hole 1″ in diameter.
11. Pipe-joint compound or Teflon joint tape.

Burner Assembly. Screw the 2″ × 12″ pipe (item 1) into one opening of the cross pipe fitting (item 2). Do not tighten this joint with a wrench because the pipe will have to be replaced every few years and that job is much easier if the joint is loose.

Screw the 2″ × 3/4″ bushing (item 3) in the opening of the cross-pipe fitting opposite the opening for the 2″ × 12″ pipe above. This joint can be tightened with a wrench. You will need to use only one wrench if you put a piece of pipe or metal bar through the cross pipe fitting to keep it from turning.

Cut the pipe nipple (item 5b) in half with a pipe cutter or hacksaw being careful not to damage the threads. Screw one half into the 2″ × 3/4″ bushing (item 3) until finger tight. Screw the cap (item 4) on the nipple (item 5a). Slip the nipple-cap assembly inside the half nipple of the burner so that the cap is inside the burner. Position the nipple-cap assembly so that the end of the cap extends 2/3 of the way through the holes in the cross pipe fitting when viewed from the side of the burner. In this position the 1/4″ pipe should protrude from the cut end of the 3/4″ nipple. Weld the two nipples together at the cut end of the 3/4″ nipple, as in drawing 1. If the welding is to be done by a professional, simply mark the positions of the parts.

Slide the remaining part of the 3/4″ nipple on the protruding end of the 1/4″ nipple and weld it in place, as in drawing 2. Remove the cap and two-

nipple assembly. Also remove the cap from the nipple. Drill the orifice (hole) in the end of the cap. The drill size you use can be determined by the Btu rating and the gas pressure which will be supplied to the kiln. Use the gas flow chart in the *Appendix*.

Coat all threads with pipe joint compound (item 11) and reassemble the burner.

Drill a No. 7 or 7/32″ hole about 3/4″ deep at the top edge of one of the side holes in the cross pipe fitting. Tap this hole and insert the 1/4″ threaded rod (item 8), as shown.

Put the electrical box cover (item 7) on the protruding end of the 1/4″ threaded rod and fasten it there with the wing nut (item 9). The remaining hole in the cross pipe fitting can be plugged with the pipe plug (item 6).

The burner will work now, but adding the 1″ washer (item 10) will make it burn better at low gas volumes. First saw or grind off two sides of the washer, as in drawing 4, so it will slip through a hole in the cross pipe fitting.

Then, grind off enough of the remaining unground edges so the washer can be forced into the front hole of the cross pipe fitting and will lie flat against the end of the 2″ pipe, as in drawing 5. The washer should fit tightly enough so that it will not fall out.

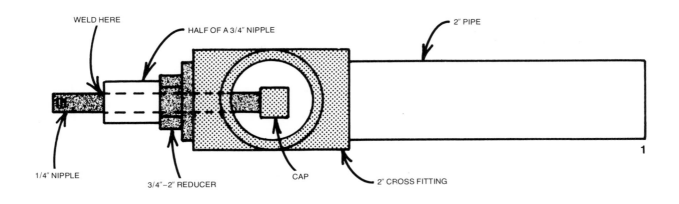

WELD HERE

HALF OF A 3/4" NIPPLE

2" PIPE

1/4" NIPPLE

3/4"–2" REDUCER

CAP

2" CROSS FITTING

1

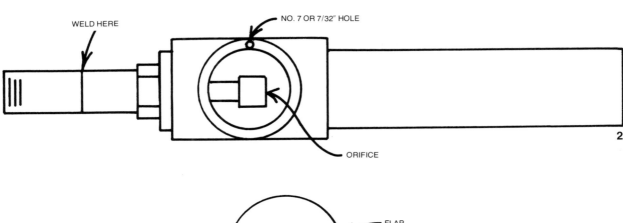

WELD HERE

NO. 7 OR 7/32" HOLE

ORIFICE

2

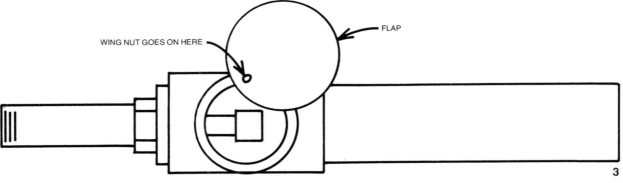

WING NUT GOES ON HERE

FLAP

3

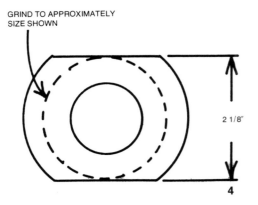

GRIND TO APPROXIMATELY
SIZE SHOWN

2 1/8"

4

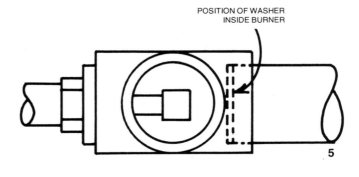

POSITION OF WASHER
INSIDE BURNER

5

FORCED–AIR PIPE BURNERS

Forced-air burners are useful in a situation where there is not enough natural draft to draw sufficient air through the kiln for proper combustion (or for a firing, like raku, that requires a very rapid heat rise). This is usually the case for updraft kilns which have no chimney but only a flue opening in the top of the arch.

Tools

1. Hacksaw.
2. Pipe cutter (optional).
3. Welding equipment.
4. Drill with 1/8" bit and bit to drill orifice (see text).
5. Screwdriver.
6. Knife.

Parts and Materials

Item No.

1. One 2" × 6" pipe nipple.
2. One 3/4" × 2" tee (2" end openings with a 3/4" side opening).
3. Black iron pipe nipples:
   a. One 3/4" × 3".
   b. One 1/4" × 4".
   c. One 1/4" × 3".
4. One 1/4" elbow.
5. One 1/4" pipe cap.
6. Pipe joint compound.
7. One three-prong plug.
8. Pipe-joint compound or Teflon joint tape.
9. One squirrel cage blower with an outlet 2 1/8" in diameter (Dayton 1C939 or equivalent).
10. One electrical connection-box cover, 3" in diameter.
11. Two 1/4" self-tapping sheet metal screws.
12. An 8' length of three-wire electrical cord.
13. Electrical tape or two wire nuts.

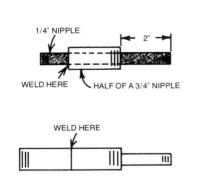

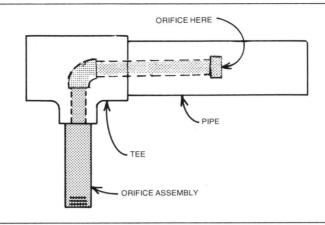

1

Burner Assembly. Begin by screwing the pipe nipple (item 1) into the tee (item 2). Cut the 3/4″ nipple (item 3a) in half with a hacksaw or pipe cutter. Insert the 1/4″ nipple (item 3b) in one half of the 3/4″ nipple so that 2″ of the 1/4″ nipple protrude from the 3/4″ one. Weld these two pieces together at the cut end of the 3/4″ nipple, as shown.

Slip the remaining half of the 3/4″ nipple over the 1/4″ nipple and weld.

Screw the elbow (item 4) onto the

end of the 1/4″ nipple until finger tight. Screw the nipple (item 3c) into the end of the elbow. Screw the cap (item 5) onto the nipple.

Drill the orifice (hole) in the end of the cap. The drill size you use can be determined by the Btu rating and the gas pressure that will be supplied to the kiln. Use the gas flow chart in the *Appendix*.

Disassemble the parts and coat the threads with pipe joint compound (item

6). Reassemble the burner, as shown. The orifice should point toward the 6″ nipple. Slip the 1/4″ nipple of the welded assembly through the 3/4″ hole in the tee and screw the elbow on the end. Tighten the joint. Screw the welded assembly into the tee so the opening of the elbow points toward the 2″ × 6″ pipe. Remove the 2″ × 6″ pipe and screw the 1/4″ × 3″ nipple into the elbow. Add the cap and tighten the joints. Replace the 2″ × 6″ pipe.

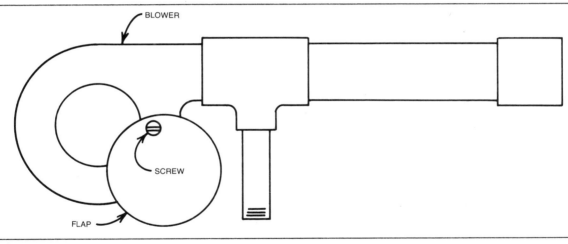

2

The blower (item 9) will slip snugly into the remaining hole of the tee. To regulate the output of the blower, mount the electrical connection-box cover (item 10) over the opening in the side of the blower. Secure the cover in place with a sheet metal screw (item 11); drill a guide hole for this screw through the side of the blower housing. The cover can then be positioned over any part of the intake opening to regulate the air flow through the blower. The finished burner will look like the one in the drawing.

Wiring the Blower. Remove the outer insulation from about 2″ of one end of the electrical cord (item 12). Then remove the insulation from 3/4″ of the end of each wire in the cord. Twist together the end of the negative, white wire and the end of one of the motor lead wires and either tape the joint or install a wire nut (item 7). Join the positive, black cord wire and the other motor lead wire in the same way. Next, fasten the ground, green wire to the blower housing. This is best done by drilling a guide hole in the housing around the fan (not the mo-

tor part of the blower) and then attaching the wire with a self-tapping sheet metal screw (item 11). (British readers can refer to the *Electrical Wire Color Coding Chart* in the *Appendix* for wire color coding equivalents.)

Attach the three-pronged plug (item 8) to the other end of the electrical cord. The white wire should be joined to the silver-colored screw, the black wire to the copper-colored screw, and the green wire to the hex-head screw.

KEROSENE AND OIL BURNER

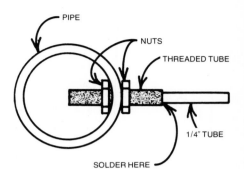

PIPE

NUTS

THREADED TUBE

1/4" TUBE

SOLDER HERE

Kerosene is generally used to start up an oil-fired kiln because it is easier to ignite and does not smoke at low temperatures as much as oil. Once red heat is reached in the fire box, oil can be substituted for the kerosene. The oil is not only cheaper, but also provides higher Btu output. Almost any kind of oil that will flow through the fuel line can be used. Some examples are fuel oil, diesel fuel, or even used crank-case oil. Among other advantages, oil usually presents no inspection or approval problem; it provides intense heat; it permits a kiln to be portable (because it requires no tie-in with fuel mains); it requires simple construction.

Its disadvantages are smoky operation, especially at low temperatures, and a clinging unpleasant odor. After firing a kerosene and oil-burning kiln, you will smell as though you have taken a bath in kerosene.

Tools

1. Soldering equipment.
2. Drill with 1/2" metal-cutting bit.
3. Two pairs of pliers.
4. Center punch.
5. Hammer.

Parts and Materials

Item No.

Note: this oil burner can be built from parts that you have on hand. These parts can vary depending on whether the unit is intended to be portable or permanently installed.

1. A powerful industrial or vacuum cleaner blower, rated at 60 to 100 CFM (cubic feet per minute) at a static pressure of approximately 80" water.
2. A 10" length of 1 1/2" pipe.
3. One electrical connection-box cover, 3" in diameter, or equivalent.
4. A 2" to 3" length of 1/2" threaded brass tubing (the kind normally used in lamps) with 2 nuts.
5. Two 18" or more lengths of 1/4" copper tubing.
6. A valve for 1/4" copper tubing, see text.
7. Miscellaneous fittings or connectors, see text.
8. Rubber hose, 1/4" inside diameter (if burner is to be portable).
9. Covered, metal 5 gal. can.
10. Stand about 1' high for the can.
11. One 1/4" sheet-metal screw.

Burner Assembly. Since the designs of the blowers (item 1) vary greatly, only general instructions can be given for connecting a blower to a burner.

Using pipe fittings or connectors made from sheet metal, attach the blower to a 10" length of 1 1/2" pipe (item 2). The air flow through the burner can be controlled by screwing (item 11) a regulator (item 3) over the air-intake opening as on the forced air burners, described earlier.

Drill a 1/2" hole in the pipe half way along its length. Insert a length of the threaded brass tubing (item 4) with a nut on the inside and outside. The threaded tube should extend half way into the burner pipe. Next, solder a length of copper tubing (item 5) into the outer end of the threaded brass tube, as shown. For a portable burner, one 18" copper tube will be long enough. If the installation is to be permanent, the entire fuel line should be made of copper tubing.

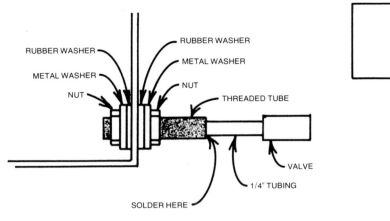

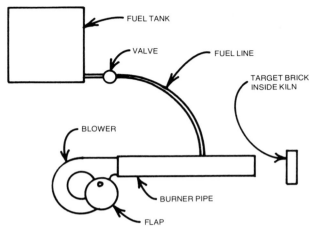

2   3

Connecting the Fuel Tank. A metal can (item 9) will serve as a fuel tank. An air vent must be made in the top so that the fuel will not create a vacuum in the can and stop flowing. The simplest air vent is just a loose cap. The fuel tank must also have an outlet and valve (item 6) at one side near the bottom. There are special fittings (item 7) for attaching 1/4" copper tubing to tap into a tank like this which would make it very easy to connect a valve, but these fittings are not always easy to find. If you cannot get the proper fittings, you can make them as follows.

Slip a 1" long piece of threaded brass tubing, like that used in lamps, over the end of a 3" length of 1/4" copper tubing and solder the two together.

Drill a 1/2" hole in the side of the tank about 1" above the bottom. Then put the threaded brass tubing in the hole. Now on the end of the tubing inside the tank, place a rubber washer, a metal washer, and a nut. On the part of the threaded tubing outside the wall, slip another rubber washer, a metal washer, and finally a nut. All the washers must fit tightly over the threaded tubing to prevent leaks. Tighten the nuts to squeeze the rubber washers against the can. Now install a valve (item 6) on the end of the 1/4" copper tubing that protrudes outside the tank, as shown.

The tank should be placed on a stand (item 10) that lifts the bottom a foot or two above the burner so that gravity will cause the fuel to flow to the burner.

There are two ways to connect the tank to the burner. You can add a short length of 1/4" copper tubing to the valve and connect this tube to the copper tubing coming from the burner with a piece of rubber hose (item 8), or you can make a more lasting connection entirely of copper tubing. A typical set-up is shown above.

How the Oil Burner Operates. The air from the blower passes through the burner and picks up fuel from the end of the fuel line. The air blasts the fuel against a target brick in the firebox. The brick gets hot and causes the fuel to vaporize and burn.

Start the kiln by stuffing paper in the firebox and lighting the paper. Begin with a low volume of air and a small flow of kerosene. As the flame becomes better established and the kiln becomes hotter, increase both the air and fuel supply as needed. This flame is extremely hot, so be very careful not to fire too fast. Switch from kerosene to oil when the firebox reaches red heat. Most of the kerosene will burn away and you can add oil directly into the same tank.

BURNER SYSTEMS AND SAFETY CONTROLS FOR GAS KILNS

An incredible number of kilns are operating today with no safety equipment at all. It is a wonder that there have been so few serious injuries because some kilns have blown apart, and a few potteries have burned down.

At least part of the reason for this situation is that, while some areas have strong regulatory codes for gas-fired equipment, others have none or do not enforce those they have. The more stringent codes may sometimes be difficult to satisfy. It may cost time, money, and effort, but compliance with them can help prevent serious accidents. The problem with almost all of these codes is that they are seldom written specifically for kilns. As a result, local inspectors often do not have the authority (or the expertise) to pass on a kiln and must call in higher officials to approve the installation. Another problem is that sometimes licensed plumbers must do the work, and this almost always means added expense.

In a gas burning system, safe operation depends on a number of factors. The first is getting the gas safely to the kiln. Use only standard fittings. Requirements for these vary from area to area. For example, some places allow the use of either black iron or galvanized pipe, while others specify the use of one or the other exclusively. Copper tubing is often used for LP (liquid petroleum) gas, which is stored in tanks. Never use garden hose or rubber tubing, because these materials can melt, burn, or be accidentally cut causing fires, explosions, or even asphyxiation.

Most accidents occur when burners are being ignited. Some potters insist on lighting burners with burning rags or rolled paper, even though this practice invites singed hair or more serious burns.

If a burner must be ignited manually, the safest way is to use a propane torch, with the flame directed at the tip of the burner. *Never* turn on the gas before applying the flame to the burner, because gas will collect rapidly in the area around the burner, and will flash or explode when the flame touches it.

Among the most frequent causes of fires and explosions are flame failures caused by such things as an interruption in the gas supply, a temporary power failure when electrically operated valves are used, or a sudden draft blowing out the flame. If there is no device to shut off the gas supply when this happens, the gas will continue to flow, and a spark or flame anywhere in the area can cause a fire or explosion.

Such accidents can be prevented by installing an automatic device to sense flame failures and shut off the gas supply to the kiln. This is generally accomplished with a thermocouple-controlled valve. This valve is normally closed and off. Therefore, in order to ignite the burner, a button must be depressed for the gas to begin flowing. The burner ignites and heats the thermocouple. A hot thermocouple generates a small electrical current that keeps the valve open when the button is released. If the flame fails, the thermocouple cools and the valve closes and shuts off the gas supply.

The problem with this system is that the intense heat of a kiln burner will burn out the thermocouple. In order to protect it, the thermocouple must be positioned away from the direct flame of the burner and heated by a small pilot flame. The pilot flame will relight the burner if the flame fails.

This is a safe system insofar as preventing fires and explosions, but there is one disadvantage, particularly when the kiln is located outdoors or in a drafty building. Should there be a flame failure during a firing and the gas is safely shut off, the potter might not be aware of it until the kiln has cooled considerably. To overcome this problem without sacrificing safety, install an ignitor on the pilot or burner.

There are two types of ignitors that can be used. One is approved by the AGA (American Gas Association), the other is not. The approved unit depends on an intermittent electrical sparking system to reignite the burner. The other utilizes a continuous electrical arc.

The approved type of ignitor produces sparks only when there is no flame. The problem with this unit is that the spark is not always strong enough and it requires very delicate adjustment. The ignitor for the oil burner is not approved by the AGA. It produces a continuous electrical arc which is very hot and is therefore a dependable reigniting device. Adjustments are easily made and are not critical to the successful functioning of the unit. There are many brands of this type of ignitor on the market, but the only one we have found to be reliable, and which produces a hot enough arc, is the Baso Multilite Series Y83. (See the *Material Sources* list in the *Appendix* for places to get this ignitor.)

The cost of both the approved and unapproved types of ignitors is about the same. If the continuous arc device is permitted in the area where your kiln is located, it is definitely the best choice.

There is one situation where the safety devices just discussed can be partially eliminated. If the kiln is located outdoors, is fired with natural gas, and has an electrically operated main gas valve, only an ignitor is necessary. In this case, the only risk is an ignitor failure. Such a failure should not be hazardous because natural gas, which is lighter than air, does not settle to the ground and collect in potentially explosive pockets. However, if the electricity goes off and then comes back on after a considerable delay, the ignitor will automatically light the burners at the settings at which they went out, thereby possibly causing the kiln to re-heat too fast and damage the ware.

All gas-burning kilns should have individual control valves on each burner. In addition, there should be a main valve controlling the entire supply of gas to the kiln. This valve should be located some distance from the kiln, so that it can be turned off in emergencies with minimum hazard to the potter.

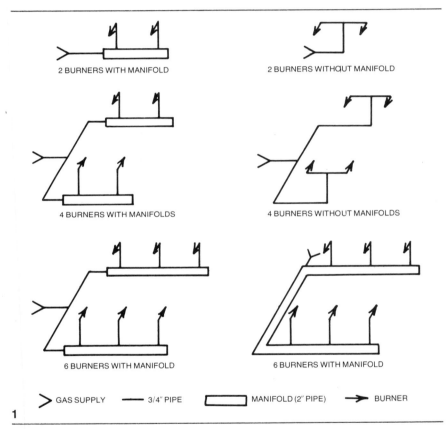

2 BURNERS WITH MANIFOLD

2 BURNERS WITHOUT MANIFOLD

4 BURNERS WITH MANIFOLDS

4 BURNERS WITHOUT MANIFOLDS

6 BURNERS WITH MANIFOLD

6 BURNERS WITH MANIFOLD

GAS SUPPLY   3/4" PIPE   MANIFOLD (2" PIPE)   BURNER

1

Selecting and Constructing Burner Systems. When designing the piping to the kiln, make sure that all burners will receive equal amounts of gas. The reason for this is simple: if a kiln has six burners and all are connected to a single 3/4" pipe, the last one in the series would probably get less gas than the first, because the pressure would be reduced at that point. If, instead, the 3/4" pipe feeds into a 2" pipe to which all the burners are connected directly, the 2" pipe will act as a manifold to equalize pressure and all burners will get equal amounts of gas. This arrangement is used on most kilns with more than four burners, and even on some with as few as two.

Typical piping and burner layouts for kilns having from two to six burners are illustrated in the drawing. There is at least one acceptable kind of multiple burner arrangement that does not use a manifold. As shown, it substitutes a riser pipe for the manifold. The riser pipe branches to connect two burners.

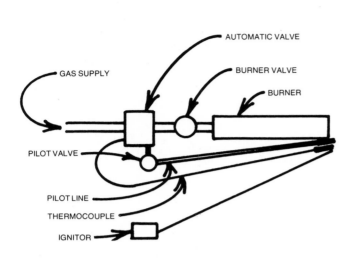

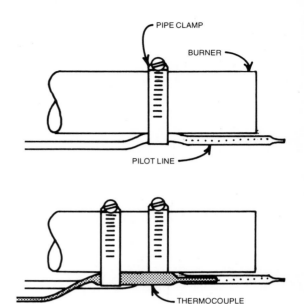

2

3

Constructing a Burner System with Safety Controls. A typical burner system with an automatic shutoff valve and an ignitor, is shown in the drawing. To assemble such a unit, first connect the automatic shutoff valve to the supply line. The arrow shows the direction of the gas flow through the valve. Connect the outlet of this valve to the burner valve with a nipple. Then screw the burner directly into the other end of the adjustment valve. If a pressure gauge is desired, it should be connected between the valve and the burner.

Be sure to use pipe joint compound on all threaded joints in the gas line and burner assembly. If copper tubing is used (for LP gas, for example),

flared or compression fittings are required.

Note: such tubing fittings require special tools and experience in using them. Either have someone teach you how to use them or have someone do this part of the job for you.

Automatic shutoff valves generally have one or two pilot line outlets, with plugs screwed into them. Remove one of the plugs and connect a 1/8" gas valve. This is the valve to which the pilot line will be attached. Pilot lines are generally made of 1/8" copper tubing and require a compression fitting. As shown in the drawing, the 1/8" tubing should be long enough to reach to the burner tip.

Before joining the pilot line to the 1/8" valve, hammer the end that will be next to the burner tip until it is flat, as shown. Beginning at this flattened or closed end, drill 1/32" holes (if possible, otherwise, 1/16") in the tubing at about 1/4" intervals. The holes should extend along about 3" of the end of the tubing. Fasten the end of the pilot line with the holes to the burner with a stainless steel pipe clamp, as shown. Connect the other end to the 1/8" valve with a compression fitting.

The fitting on the thermocouple can be screwed into the hole provided for it in the automatic shutoff valve. Attach the heat-sensing tip to the burner with a pipe clamp and position it as shown so that the pilot flame will immerse it and keep it hot.

149

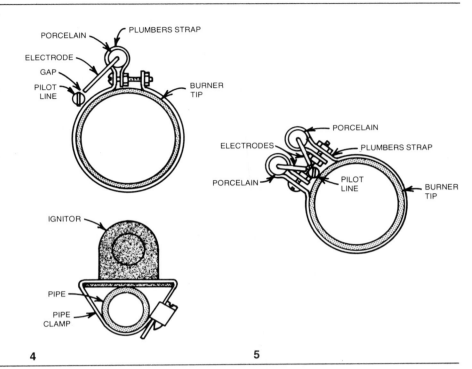

4   **5**

The wire and tip of the Baso ignitor must be replaced with parts that can withstand the heat of the burner. The principal replacement part for the tip is a porcelain-insulated electrode of the type used on oil burners. Be sure to get the longest electrode of this type available, and make certain that it is equipped with a snap-on spark-plug type of terminal.

The wire connecting the porcelain-covered electrode to the ignitor can be of the type used with oil burners, spark-plug wire, or, preferably, fiberglass-insulated high-voltage wire. Spark-plug terminals can be used to connect the wire to the electrode and to the ignitor. The electrode can be fastened to the burner with a length of plumber's strap, as shown. Use a pipe clamp to secure the base of the ignitor to the gas line, as shown.

Connect the two short wires that come out of the ignitor to an electrical cord equipped with a plug. Be sure that the connections you make between the ignitor wires and the cord are well insulated. Fill the hole where the electric wires come out of the ignitor with silicone bathtub caulking to keep the moisture out.

Adjust the gap between the electrode tip and the pilot line so it is the same as that recommended for the original tip furnished with the Baso unit.

If, instead of the Baso unit, you plan to use a continuous spark ignitor, it must be the kind that uses a high-voltage transformer and two porcelain-insulated electrodes. Connect the electrodes to the transformer with two separate wires as shown in the drawing. The gap between the electrodes should be about 1/8″. The arc that will jump this gap should be 1/4″ to 3/8″ from the pilot line at the center of the perforated end. This arc will ignite the pilot.

The burner control and safety system is now complete. Test all joints for leaks by turning off all burners and pilot valves and turning on the main valve. Paint a solution of equal parts of liquid detergent and water on all joints. A leaking joint will blow bubbles. When testing joints between the automatic valve and the manual valves, you must hold the button down on the automatic valve.

Safety Equipment for Multiple Burner Installations. When more than one burner runs off the same gas line or manifold, one automatic shutoff placed on the main supply line can often be used to control all the burners. In such an arrangement, only one of the burners is equipped with a thermocouple, ignitor, and pilot. If this burner's flame goes out, all the burners on the same line or manifold will also be shut down.

The danger of this system is that if the flame of any burner other than the one equipped with the safety equipment fails, the system will not turn off completely. Gas will continue to escape from the burner where the flame-failure occurred. This will not be a problem if the burners are close enough together so that the burner that goes out can be relit automatically by the one next to it.

In a kiln with burners on opposite sides, at least one burner on each side must be equipped with an automatic shutoff. This safety system can be used with either atmospheric or forced air burners.

However, a forced air burner should have an additional safety device. The sail switch used with some forced air units is not satisfactory for use with many kilns because an insufficient volume of air moves through the burner during the first few hours of firing to actuate a sail switch.

A better device is an electrically controlled valve (based on a solenoid), installed in the main gas line. This valve will automatically turn off the gas if there is a power failure. If this valve is not used, the blowers will stop during the failure and cause the ware to be extremely reduced.

Of course, an electrically operated switch of this type will not turn off the gas if a blower breaks down. However, this happens very rarely, and would soon be detected because of the smoke and other obvious signs of reduction. With a multiple burner kiln this occurrence would present a minor problem since reduction from only one burner is not dangerous and will seldom harm the ware.

KILN FURNITURE

Kiln shelves (called bats by the manufacturers) come in a variety of sizes and materials. The size and shape you use will depend on the kiln you want to build, your strength, and the size of the ware you expect to produce. In general you should use the largest size that you can easily handle, because small shelves require more supporting posts. A good size and weight for general use would contain about 300 cubic inches of material.

Shelves should be at least 3/4″ thick; for durability, a 1″ minimum is even better.

When buying shelves, be certain to get standard sizes (or sizes varying only slightly from standard) so they can be replaced as required. Odd sizes are often cheaper, but are usually available only because they are extras made for large orders of nonstandard sizes.

Shelves are made of a number of different materials. Clay shelves are the cheapest, but they warp at high temperatures and are therefore often impractical. Most shelves are made of silicon carbide. There are differences in the exact composition of these from one make to another, and even one company may offer different types for different uses. Check with the manufacturer's representative to determine the proper shelf for your requirements.

There are also a number of shelves made for special uses. One type is a high alumina shelf made to be used in salt glazing. While this type of shelf resists the effects of salt, it is a poor choice for conventional glazing. Any glaze that runs onto these shelves will adhere permanently, even if shelf wash is used. Alumina shelves also tend to warp much more easily than those made of silicon carbide. Silicon carbide shelves (at least Norton Company's Crystilon 63 Series) work better for salt glazing, especially when conventional glazes are used on salted ware. Any salt buildup, or dripped glazes on these shelves can be scraped off easily with a grinding stone or a piece of broken kiln shelf. After long use these shelves do get some hard glassy buildup on the underside but this is not a great problem. They also tend to crack after 30 to 60 firings. The cracking is a progressive process that starts at the edges several firings before it becomes a problem; so there is generally ample warning before a shelf fails.

Shelf Washes. A wash that keeps glaze drips from sticking to the tops of shelves can be made from equal parts (by volume) of kaolin and silica. Another mixture that allows pots to move more easily on the shelf as they shrink is made from equal parts of fine grog and Edgar plastic kaolin. If you use a wash for salt glazing, mix two parts of aluminum hydrate and one part of kaolin.

Add water to all wash mixtures and brush them on the tops (not the bottoms or edges) of the shelves. Two thin coats are better than a thick one.

Shelf Posts. Commercial posts made of silicon carbide are excellent but expensive. Very good posts can be made from super-duty firebricks. Use soaps or straights for 9″ posts. Cut straights to get 4 1/2″ posts and soaps to get 2 1/2″ or 2 1/4″ ones. Pieces of broken kiln shelves or posts can be used for minor height adjustments.

How to Use Shelf Posts. Shelves are best supported at three points; three posts will always provide sturdy support and put the least amount of stress on kiln shelves.

When a kiln is being loaded, posts should always be placed one above the other on successive shelves. This arrangement transfers the weight properly to the floor and keeps extra stress off lower shelves. If the posts overlap the spaces between the shelves, the load will be well tied together and less shaky than if adjoining shelves are stacked independently.

If there are 1″ to 2 1/2″ spaces between shelves, use straights instead of soaps for 9″ posts. Such spaces are desirable since they allow better heat circulation; they also make it possible for pots to extend a little over the shelf edges which increases the useful area of the kiln without increasing the number of shelves.

Cone Pats. Cones are usually pressed into pieces of clay to support them. Cone pats are generally made in advance and allowed to dry before firing. If cones are needed, and there is not enough time to dry the clay, make the pats in the usual manner and punch the clay full of holes with a pencil. This will keep the clay from exploding during firing.

FIRING INSTRUCTIONS

It is better to fire too slowly than too fast. Firing slowly uses more fuel, but the ware is more likely to come through in good shape. Firing too fast can cause pots to explode. When this happens during a glaze firing, chips of exploded ware can lodge in the glaze of other pieces, ruining much of the load. You should also bear in mind that pots can explode when they are too damp. Be sure the pots you use to establish the best firing rate are thoroughly dry.

The firing procedures recommended here will probably be too slow, but it will be wise to follow them until you can establish your own best firing rate.

Procedure for Firing a Four-Burner Kiln

1. Close all burner valves.
2. Turn on ignitors.
3. Turn on the main gas supply valve.
4. Close all burner flaps. Push the damper 3/4 closed.
5. Depress the button on one automatic gas valve and hold it down until the pilot stays lit when the button is released.
6. Open the valve on this burner until you hear gas escaping. Ignition should take place within a few seconds. If the burner does not light, turn the valve off and make sure that the pilot flame extends slightly beyond the burner tip. Adjust the pilot as required. Turn the burner valve on again. Ignition should now occur without difficulty. When it does, adjust the burner so that the flame is about 8" long.

7. If wind or drafts are a problem, causing the flame to blow out, install kiln flaps, described previously.
8. Repeat steps 5, 6, and 7 for the front burner on the other side. The length of time that you should continue firing with only these two burners going will vary. The time can be affected by prevailing conditions such as the kind of clay being used, or the dryness of the ware being fired. For pots that are thoroughly dry, one hour may be adequate. But, if the humidity is high or the pots are very large and there is doubt as to how dry they are, this stage of the firing may need to last overnight.
9. When the first heating period is completed, turn up the front burners. Note that a gas valve makes only a quarter turn from full off to full on. Therefore, each time you turn a burner up, turn it only about 15° or 1/6th of the total distance possible.
10. After 45 minutes, turn on one rear burner. The rear burners on the kilns in this book will ignite from the flame of the front burners. For easy ignition, turn the rear burner half on until it ignites and then adjust it until the flame is about 8" long. If the rear burner fails to ignite within 10 seconds, wait 30 seconds before attempting to light it again.

Note: when lighting the rear burners, be sure to stay at arm's length from the kiln, because in some wind conditions, flame may flash out from around the burner on ignition.

11. Repeat step 10 for the other rear burner.
12. After 45 minutes, turn both the rear burners up as in step 9.

13. After 45 minutes, turn up the front burners, as in step 9. Open one burner flap slightly until you get a blue flame. If a blower is used, turn it on with its flap closed.
14. Turn up the rear burners after 45 minutes, as you did the front ones in step 13.
15. Every 45 minutes, alternate turning up the front and rear burners until all are on full. Adjust the burner, or blower, flaps each time, making sure that the flame from all burners is blue. The burner but not necessarily the blower flaps should all be completely open by the time the kiln is full on.
16. Remove the kiln flaps as soon as the wind or draft ceases to be a problem or when necessary to keep the kiln from reducing.

Damper Adjustment. Begin with the damper 3/4 closed. At some point in turning up the kiln, there will be insufficient draft and reduction will begin. Reduction can be recognized in its early stages by a smoky smell or by deposits of black carbon around cracks in the upper part of the kiln (particularly over the door and where the chimney meets the kiln). At this stage, open the damper slightly until reduction stops. This process will have to be repeated as the burners are turned up. The damper is being used most efficiently when it is in as far as possible without causing reduction. The further out the damper is positioned, the more heat is lost up the chimney.

Turning the Kiln Off.

1. Turn off the burners.
2. Turn off the ignitors.

3. Close the main valve.
4. Push the damper all the way in.
5. Put the kiln flaps back in place.

Bisque Firing. Fire the kiln, according to the directions given above, until the proper bisque temperature for the type of ware being produced is reached. Then turn off the kiln as directed.

Oxidation Firing (Firing with a Clean-Burning Flame). Again, use the procedure given above to reach the temperature desired. In this type of firing it is particularly important to make sure that a clean-burning blue flame is maintained throughout and that no reduction takes place.

Reduction Firing (Firing with Insufficient Air to Obtain Complete Combustion). Reduction firing differs in degree and timing with different potters. You can begin experimenting by reducing 1/2 hour at cone 04 to give the clay good color. Reduce again during the last two cones, to induce glaze reduction.

To get a reduction atmosphere, push the damper in until a flame about 6″ long flares out of the top peephole when the plug is removed. Some flames should also be licking through the cracks around the door. There should be a very light gray smoke and a definite smoky odor. If the smoke is black, you are reducing too much, and the temperature in the kiln will fall.

Keeping the temperature even throughout the kiln during firing can be a problem. If the bottom of the kiln becomes hotter than the top when the firing is about five cones from maturity, partially close the damper. This will cause light reduction, the flame will rise to the top of the kiln before complete combustion occurs, and the top will heat faster than the bottom.

If there is still a difference of much more than one cone between the bottom and top when the kiln is within two cones of maturity, partially close the burner flaps to increase reduction even more. If this fails to produce even temperature, it will be necessary to adjust the bagwall alignment before the next firing.

If the opposite situation develops during a firing—the top getting hotter than the bottom—you will have to wait until the load is finished. Then, try opening up the bagwall and reducing its height before the next firing. If the top of the kiln is extremely hot compared with the bottom, avoid overreducing.

Sample Reduction Firing. Here is an example of how a reduction firing to cone 9 using cones 04, 4, 7, and 9 in the stoneware kilns described in this book is likely to progress, given optimum conditions. The procedure is described in terms of actions that you should take as each cone begins to bend:

Cone 04: Begin body reduction. Reduce for about 1/2 hour.

Cone 4: Early warning. If the bottom temperature is hotter than the top, reduce to even out the difference.

Cone 7: Check top and bottom temperatures again. Time to begin glaze reduction.

Cone 9: The firing is completed. When cone 9's tip touches, the kiln has reached about cone 10; the temperature has reached cone 11 when cone 9 is flat.

Firing a Salt Glaze Kiln. The procedure is the same as that given above for reduction firing, except that the cone 04 reduction stage can be eliminated. If firing to cone 9, begin introducing salt at cone 4. Use plastic sandwich bags to hold the salt (either table salt or rock salt). You will need about 21 pounds divided into 14 bags, each containing about 1 1/2 pounds.

Throw two bags (about 3 pounds) into each firebox and adjust the kiln for very light reduction. After about 15 minutes throw in four more bags. Repeat every 15 minutes until six more bags have been added. At this point, cone 7 should be starting to bend.

If cone 7 starts going down too fast, turn the gas down slightly and readjust for reduction. When cone 7 does go down, put in the final two bags of salt and wait until cone 9 goes down and the tip touches. Then turn off the kiln according to the procedure given above.

The first few firings will require extra salt, perhaps as much as 50 pounds for the first firing. To determine how much salt to add, position about five draw rings in the kiln so that they can be removed with a steel rod through the upper peephole.

Note: draw rings are coils of clay. 1/4″ to 3/8″ thick, made into doughnut-shaped rings. Make them from the clay body you are firing. Flatten one side to make them stand up so that they can be hooked and withdrawn through a peephole with a steel rod.

In the first firing, remove a ring when about 20 pounds of salt have been added. Allow the ring to cool and note the salt texture. If more texture is desired, continue to add salt. The color of the ring has no significance, because the rapid cooling will make it much lighter than it would be if cooled in the kiln normally.

Continue to add salt and to remove rings at intervals, until the desired texture is obtained. If cone 9 is reached and more salt is still needed, turn the gas down at the main valve and continue to add salt. Maintain the reduction atmosphere and try to keep the temperature constant through the kiln.

The amount of salt needed will decrease with each firing until a point is reached when it will become stable for all firings.

You will probably want to experiment with other methods of salt firing. Some potters fire to temperature and then hold the temperature constant for an hour or two while adding salt. Some potters use strong reduction, some little or none.

Uneven temperature in a salt kiln is not as objectionable as in most others because the salt will work well over a rather wide thermal range. The color of salt-glazed ware varies with temperature. It becomes darker at higher temperatures. Fast cooling, on the other hand, makes the color lighter.

Important: once a kiln is used for salt glazing it cannot be used for other glazes, since some salt remains in the kiln and revaporizes with every firing. Also, it is important to know that the life of a kiln is greatly shortened if used for salt glazing. *Never* salt glaze in a kiln made of insulating firebricks or lined with ceramic fiber blanket materials.

SPECIAL CONSIDERATIONS FOR INDOOR KILNS

Very few changes are required in the kilns presented in this book to adapt them for indoor use. There are, however, special requirements for the building that houses a kiln.

The Effects of Kiln Weight. The plans for all kilns in this book specify a concrete slab for the kiln to rest on. If the building you plan to use has a concrete floor, a slab will not be required, unless you intend to build a large, heavy kiln, or a kiln with a tall chimney. For such a kiln, a reinforced concrete pad should be poured directly on top of the existing slab.

If the kiln is to be built on a floor that is elevated above the ground floor, you may need to install special bracing under the floor. If you have any doubt about the strength of the floor, calculate the total expected weight of the kiln (a firebrick weights about nine pounds and an insulating brick about three to four pounds), plus the weight of a load of pots. Also calculate the area (square feet) the kiln will occupy. If you are planning on a chimney, pay special attention to the area directly under it, because an 18″ × 18″ chimney, made of hard firebrick, weighs

about 275 pounds per foot of height.

After you have worked out the probable weight and space requirements of your kiln, have your local building inspector, or someone else qualified to determine the effects of heavy weights on floors and building structures, check the load-bearing capabilities of your building.

In general, a large kiln on any but the ground level presents a major problem in obtaining approval because of the structural requirements needed to support such a heavy weight.

The use of the lighter weight insulating bricks can often help solve the weight problem. Also, it is sometimes possible to locate the chimney outside the building, and so remove much of the weight from the building floor.

The Effects of Kiln Heat. Even a well-insulated kiln generates a considerable amount of heat in the area immediately around it. If the kiln is to be near a wall, certain safety precautions must be taken. To lessen the possible fire hazards, locate the kiln at least three feet from any wall made of flammable mate-

rial. Use asbestos board to cover the walls in any area near the kiln, especially an area within a few feet of a burner opening; a severe downdraft, which might occur with certain wind conditions, can cause flame to flash out of the kiln around the burners.

Since heat rises, the ceiling over the kiln is of special importance. A ceiling made of flammable material should be well covered with fiberglass insulation or asbestos board, especially if it is within four or five feet of the kiln.

A good exhaust fan should be located in or close to the ceiling near the kiln to exhaust any fumes from firing and as much of the heat as possible to the outside of the building. It is particularly important to have an exhaust fan operating during periods of reduction firing.

Causes of Fires. The primary cause of fires in pottery studios is the failure to take certain precautions at the point where the chimney passes through the roof. A hot chimney in contact with, or close to, wood can start a fire.

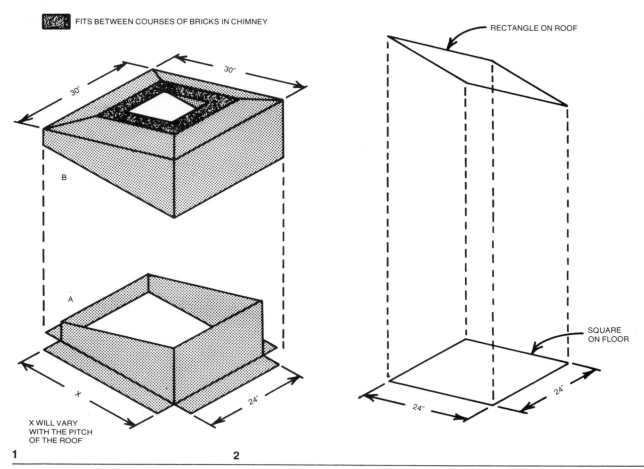

░░░ FITS BETWEEN COURSES OF BRICKS IN CHIMNEY

30"

30"

B

A

X

X WILL VARY
WITH THE PITCH
OF THE ROOF

24"

1

RECTANGLE ON ROOF

SQUARE
ON FLOOR

24"

24"

24"

2

Venting the Chimney Area for Downdraft Kilns. To prevent fires around the chimney, leave an air space in the roof around it; the air rising around the chimney will keep the area cool. A special metal hood, shown in the drawing, must be installed to allow the air to move out around the chimney and at the same time prevent rain or snow from coming in. Part A fits on the outside of the roof and part B attaches to the chimney.

It would probably be wise to have this hood made by a professional, since the construction is difficult without special tools. It is also difficult to install the hood so that there are no water leaks.

Installing a Chimney. A chimney for an indoor kiln requires a 24″ square hole in the roof. Since the rafters in most buildings are only 16″ apart, a portion of the rafter and possibly a ceiling joist will have to be removed. It is best to locate the kiln so that the center of the chimney coincides with the center of a rafter, so that no more than one rafter has to be cut. Drop a plumb line from this rafter, at the point where the center of the chimney will pass through the roof. The plumb bob will touch the floor at the point immediately under the center of the chimney. Mark this point on the floor and plan to situate the kiln accordingly.

To get the proper size roof opening, the 24″ square hole must be measured on a horizontal plane, not on a sloping roof. To locate this hole, begin at the point marking the center of the chimney on the floor. Measure and draw a 24″ square on the floor around this point so that the chimney will be exactly centered in it.

Using the plumb line, experimentally locate points on the underside of the roof that are directly over each corner of the 24″ square, as shown. Drive a nail through the roof from the inside at these four points. Cut this rectangle out of the roof from the outside.

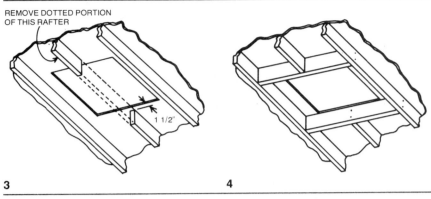

REMOVE DOTTED PORTION OF THIS RAFTER

1 1/2"

3

With a spirit level, mark vertical lines from the edges of the hole cut in the roof onto the side of the rafter that intersects the roof hole. Measure 1 1/2" from these lines (on the side away from the roof hole) and mark lines parallel to the existing vertical lines. Saw through the rafter on the second lines and remove the piece of rafter under the hole.

4

Reinforcing the Roof. Cut two pieces of framing from the same size lumber as the rafters and long enough to fit snugly between the rafters on each side of the hole in the roof. Nail them (using 16D common nails) against the ends of the cut rafter, as shown. Also nail through the two rafters into the ends of the newly installed framing. This will frame opposite sides of the hole in the roof and support the ends of the cut rafter.

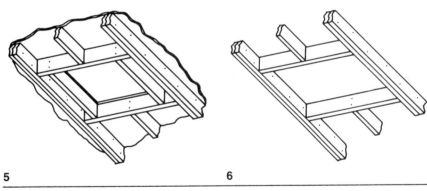

5

To further strengthen the roof, cut 3" off one end of the piece of rafter that was removed. The cut must be parallel to the angled end of the rafter. Fit the cut rafter between the two frame members along one of the unframed sides of the roof hole. If the fit is acceptable, cut another piece of wood the same size for the opposite side of the roof hole. Nail both of these cut pieces in place between the already nailed-in frame members to complete the frame around the roof hole.

Now cut two new rafters the same size as the existing ones. Nail them to the rafters on each side of the hole, as shown. These double rafters will now bear the load formerly carried by the rafter that was cut.

6

If, instead of a rafter, part of a ceiling joist was removed, it should be supported in the same way as the rafter. The framing would then appear as shown.

Building the Chimney through the Roof. Build the chimney right up through the hole in the roof. As a precaution against fire, use 2000°F. insulating bricks for the section that actually passes through the roof. When construction reaches the roof level, the metal hood described previously must be installed, before completing the chimney. To prevent downdrafts, the chimney should extend at least two feet above the peak of the roof and should have a cap like the one in "Building the Chimney" in *Catenary Arch Kiln.*

Outdoor Chimney and Vent System for Downdraft Kilns. In some installations it is best to run the chimney horizontally from the back of the kiln through a wall and then vertically outside the building. If this is done, the area around the part of the chimney that passes through the wall should be constructed of masonry. Castable refractory or insulating firebricks are best because these materials expand very little when hot. Hard firebricks, on the contrary, expand enough so that they may crack the wall around the chimney.

If this type of chimney is used, the damper will have to fit in the horizontal section just behind the kiln. The damper track will be similar to the one for horizontal dampers, but it will be turned on its side so that the damper can be removed from the side of the horizontal chimney section.

The roof or frame wall of a building should not touch the chimney even outside the building. For this reason, it may be necessary to cut back the roof overhang. A minimum of 4" should be maintained between the chimney and the wall or roof of the building. As an additional safeguard, cover any wood near the chimney with a sheet of asbestos board.

Importance of Sealing the Indoor Kiln. A kiln located indoors is more hazardous than one outside, if the flame should fail and the gas continue to flow (see *Burner Systems and Safety Controls*). Therefore, an indoor kiln must have a better seal. To achieve this tight seal, first make sure the kiln parts are fitted together carefully during construction, and, afterward, plug any holes or crevices with either clay or refractory patching material.

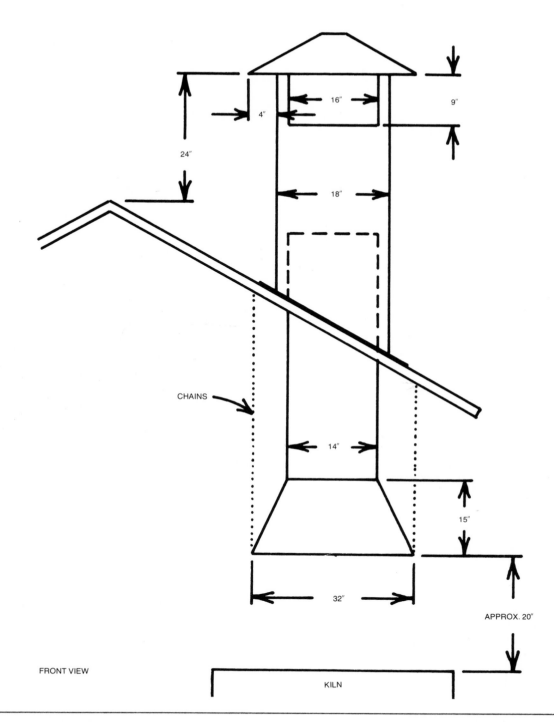

CHAINS

FRONT VIEW

KILN

7

Venting Systems for Updraft Kilns.

The venting system for an updraft kiln consisting of a hood, telescoping flues, and a cap, can be made from 20 to 24 gauge galvanized sheet steel. Since a large volume of room-temperature air is mixed with flue gases, no insulation is required. However, an airspace between the vent and the roof material is required; this space is indicated in the drawing.

It would probably be best to have the parts of the venting system made at a sheet metal shop. Besides the information about the vent given in the drawing, you will also need to know the roof pitch, the height of the chimney above the roof, and the distance from the bottom of the hood to the roof.

The kiln should be located, if possible, so that the roof opening for the chimney can be cut without severing a rafter. This can best be done by locating a point halfway between two rafters. This point must be directly over the center of the kiln's flue opening. Hang a plumb line from that point, and locate another point on the floor direct-

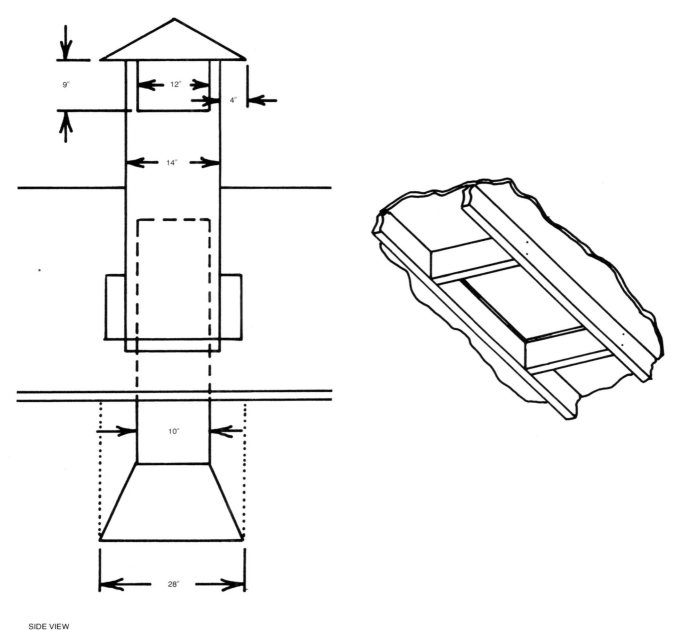

9″

12″

4″

14″

10″

28″

SIDE VIEW

ly below it. Using the point on the floor as center, mark out a 14″ × 18″ rectangle. The 18″ sides should be parallel with the rafters. With the plumb line, experimentally locate the points of the roof directly above the corners of the rectangle. Drive a nail through the roof at each of the four points; then cut out the rectangle of roof material bounded by the nails.

Cut pieces of 2 × 4 to fit between the rafters and nail them in place to box in the hole, as shown above right.

If the kiln must be located so that a rafter has to be cut for the chimney, frame the hole and reinforce the rafters, using the method described in "Reinforcing the Roof," earlier in this section.

Suspend the hood over the kiln from four chains attached to the ceiling. Position it so that there is a 2″ air-space between it and the edges of the hole in the roof. Allow enough chain so that the hood can be lowered, when necessary, to regulate the draft through the kiln. Lowering the hood will increase the draft; raising the hood will decrease it.

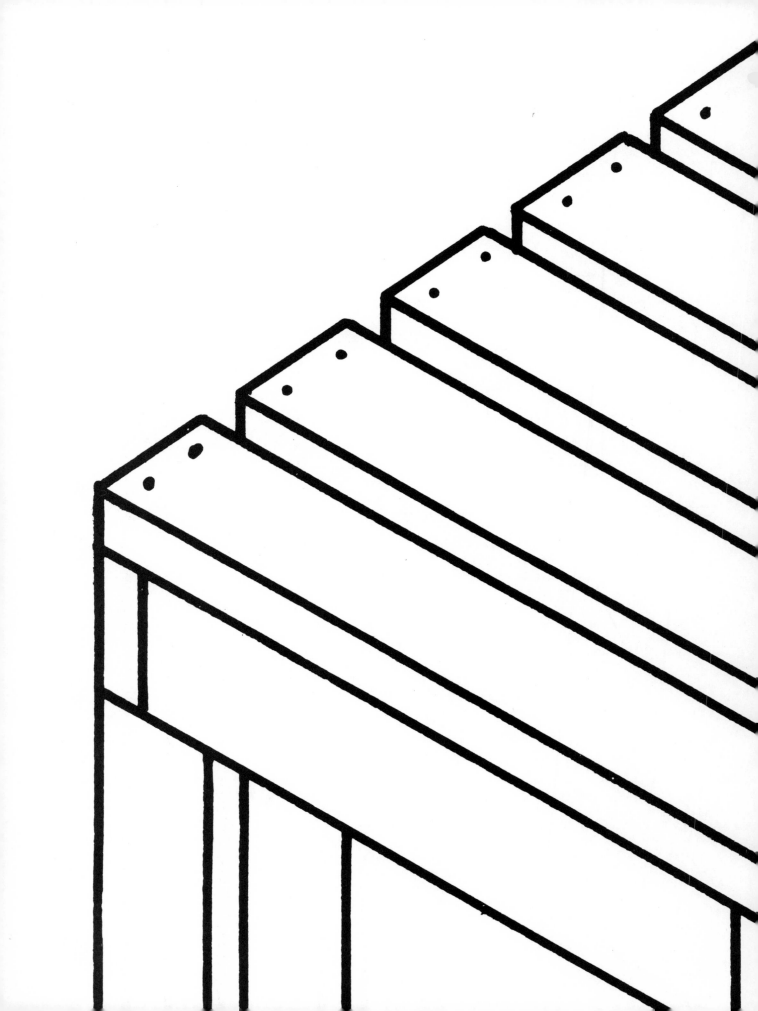

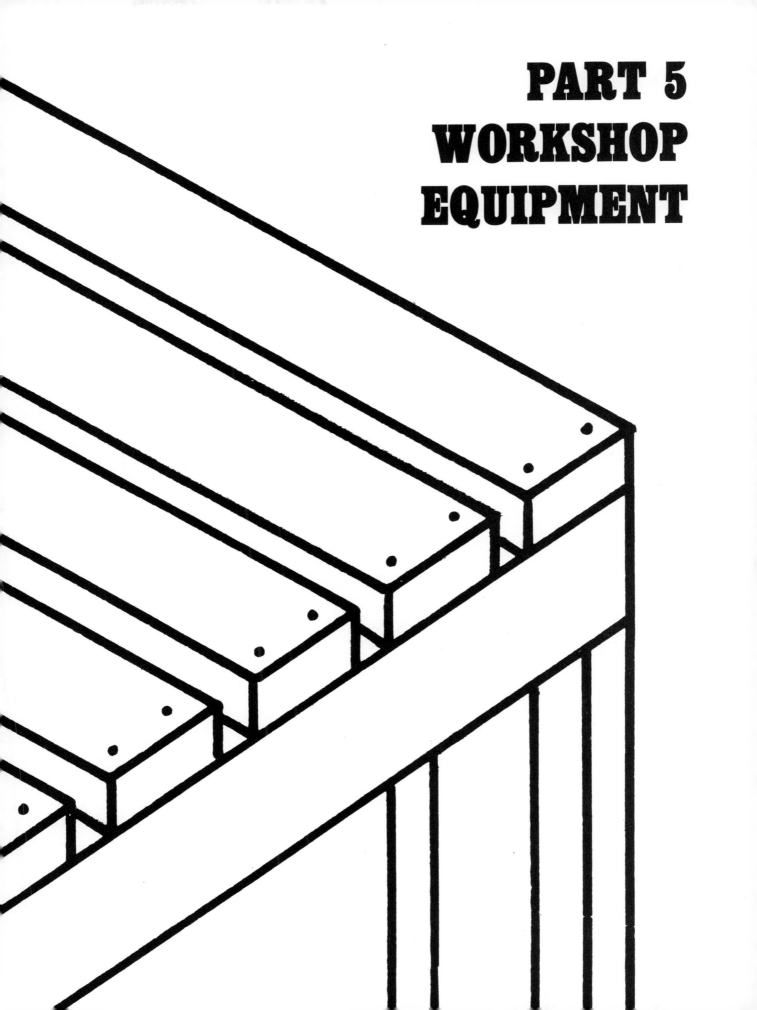

**PART 5
WORKSHOP
EQUIPMENT**

WEDGING TABLE

Wedging the clay to prepare it for use is a strenuous activity, requiring sufficient pressure or impact to force air bubbles out of a chunk of clay. The two methods generally used are: kneading, which involves pressing and rotating the clay, and cutting-and-stacking, which involves slicing the clay and slamming the cut pieces down on each other. Either method requires a strong table capable of withstanding heavy and repeated pounding.

This table is designed to sustain prolonged impact by either method. Planned specifically for wedging, it eliminates the use of plaster and provides a top covering stronger than the often-used canvas. The surface screening also prevents the clay, unless it is extremely wet, from sticking to the table top.

Tools

1. Hammer.
2. Wood-cutting saw.
3. Metal shears.
4. Tape measure or folding rule.
5. Carpenter's framing square
6. Staple gun (optional).
7. Drill with a 1/8" metal cutting bit.

Parts and Materials

Item No.

1. Pieces of 2 × 4 lumber:
   a. Four 22 1/2" lengths.
   b. Eleven 26" lengths.
   c. Four 23" lengths.
2. Nails:
   a. 1 lb. 16D common nails.
   b. 1/4 lb. sheet rock nails.
3. One 26" × 26" piece of 3/4" plywood.
4. One 25" × 25" piece of 18 to 24 gauge sheet aluminum or galvanized sheet steel.
5. One 30" × 30" piece of aluminum insect screening.
6. Staples or tacks.

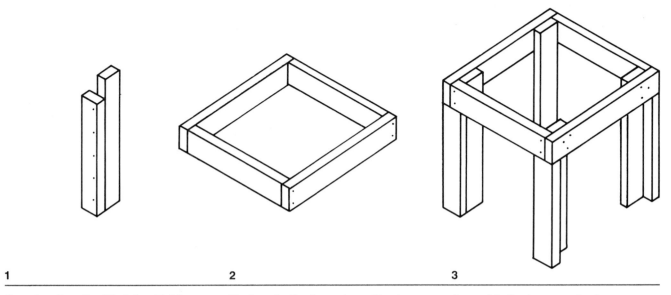

1

2

3

Constructing the Wedging Table. First, make the legs. All four are made in the same way, by nailing together one 22 1/2″ 2× 4 (item 1a) and one 26″ 2× 4 (item 1b), as shown. Use about four or five 16D nails (item 2a) for each leg.

Next, make the frame by nailing together two of the 23″ and two of the 26″ 2× 4s (items 1b, 1c) with 16D nails, as in the drawing.

Assemble the frame on the legs, as shown. Nail through the frame into the legs at each corner with 16D nails.

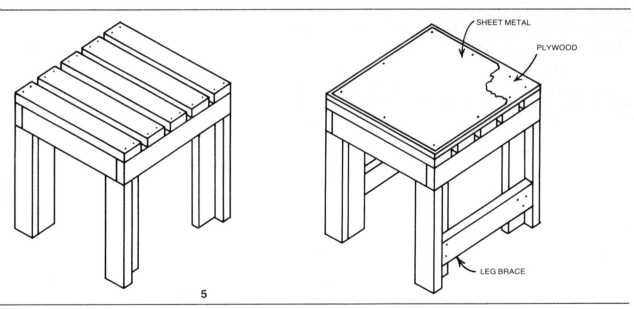

4

5

Arrange the remaining five 26″ long 2 × 4s (item 1b) on the top so that their ends can be nailed to the 26″ long 2 × 4s of the frame. These top 2 × 4s should be laid on their sides and must be evenly spaced, as shown.

Now nail the leg braces in place, as shown, using the remaining two 23″ long 2 × 4s (item 1c).

To make the table top, begin by positioning the plywood (item 3) on the 2 × 4s spaced across the top of the frame. Use sheet rock nails (item 2b) to fasten the plywood in place.

Next, position the sheet metal (item 4) so that a 1/2″ margin of plywood

shows on all sides. Use about three sheet rock nails in each side of the metal to hold it in place. It will probably be necessary to drill holes for the nails through the metal.

Now stretch the insect screening (item 5) over the top. Bend it down over the edges of the plywood and fasten it with staples or tacks (item 6) to the sides of the frame.

WORK TABLE

Although the plans for this 30″ × 8′ × 3′ high work table are as complete and detailed as possible, there are some decisions that will depend on your individual needs and resources. For example, the length of the table you build must fit into the space you have available.

If your workshop has a long wall, this table, which is mounted on the wall, should probably be built to occupy as much of that wall space as your other equipment will allow. It is almost impossible to have too much table-top workspace.

The height of the table presented here is 36″, an average height. As a general rule, this kind of work table should be about waist high. You may wish to adjust this height.

Note: this is a general-purpose work table. It is not designed to be strong enough to be used for wedging clay (see *Wedging Table*).

Tools

1. Wood-cutting saw.
2. Carpenter's framing square.
3. Pencil.
4. Hammer.
5. Staple gun with 5/16″ staples (optional).
6. Drill with 1/4″ bit and masonry bit to fit shields.
7. Screwdriver.

Note: items 6 and 7 are necessary only if the table is to be mounted on a masonry wall with screws.

Parts and Materials

Item No.

1. Pieces of 2 × 4 lumber:
   a. Two 8′ lengths.
   b. Three 25″ lengths.
   c. Three 36″ lengths.
2. Nails:
   a. 1/2 lb. 16D common nails.
   b. 1/4 lb. masonry nails or 5 lead or plastic concrete shields with 2 1/2″ No. 14 wood screws to fit the shields (the shields are necessary only if the table is to be mounted on a masonry wall).
   c. 1/4 lb. 6D common nails.
3. One 30″ × 96″ piece of 5/8″ or 3/4″ plywood.
4. One 34″ × 100″ piece of canvas.
5. Some 5/16″ staples or thumbtacks.

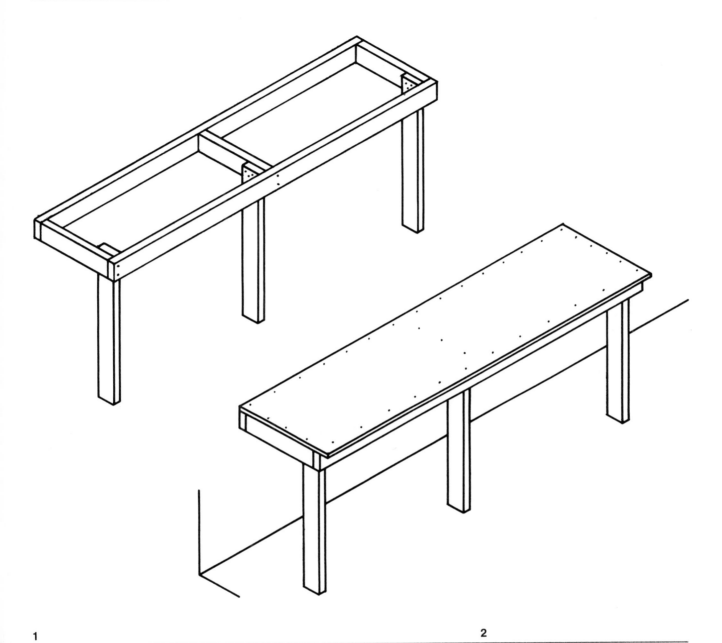

1

2

Assembly. The frame for the top of the work table is made by nailing (item 2a) the two 8′ long 2 × 4s (item 1a), which are the front and back stretchers, to the three 25″ long 2 × 4s (item 1b), which are the cross pieces, as shown. The cross pieces should be spaced about 4′ apart.

When the top frame is completed, the next step is to nail (item 2a) the three 36″ long 2 × 4s (item 1c), that are the legs, to the front stretcher. The assembled frame and legs are now ready to be mounted on the wall.

If you have a wood-frame wall, you can nail (item 2a) the assembled table frame directly into the wall studs. If the wall is masonry, you will need to use either masonry nails or wood screws with lead or plastic shields (item 2b). If you use masonry nails, simply hammer them through the table frame into the wall. To use the wood screws, you will first have to drill 1/4″ holes for them in the frame and matching holes in the wall to accept the shields. Use a masonry bit to drill the holes in the wall. Insert the shields in the wall and screw the frame to the wall.

After the frame is securely mounted in place, nail (item 2c) on the plywood top (item 3). The top should overhang the frame by 1″ or 2″ in the front, as shown in the drawing.

Finally, stretch the canvas (item 4) over the plywood. The canvas will keep wet clay from sticking to the table. Staple or thumbtack (item 5) one edge of the canvas along the back edge of the plywood as close to the wall as possible. Then stretch it taut and smooth across the plywood top and staple it under the front edge of the plywood.

SHELVES AND RACKS

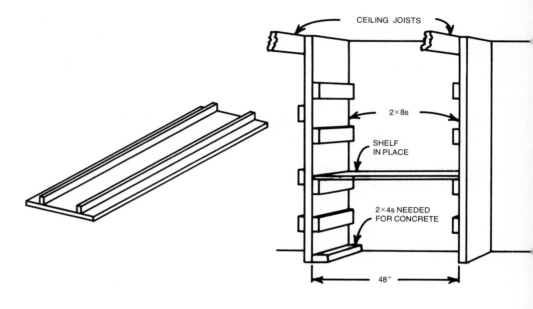

CEILING JOISTS

2×8s

SHELF
IN PLACE

2×4s NEEDED
FOR CONCRETE

48"

Most commercial shelf systems—those supported by brackets, put together in bookcase fashion, or constructed of modular wall units—do not provide adequately for storing pottery ware. Pots must be moved between each phase of production; putting the pots on shelves and then removing them one at a time for each new operation is very time consuming. It also invites breakage. Therefore, special shelves are necessary to speed the safe and efficient handling of ware.

If you have shelves that are portable and small enough so that they can be carried when fully loaded, you can move a whole shelf full of pots at a time. Such shelf units should also be designed so that they can be set into racks rather than on other shelf-type surfaces. This approach often affords substantial savings in material. All of the racks in a workshop should be made to hold a standard size shelf so that shelves can be shifted from one area to another.

It may also be advisable to make some of the racks movable in order to handle accumulations of pots at certain key points during peak production periods.

1

Assembling the Shelves and Racks.
One versatile system can be made using 12″ × 48″ plywood shelves, 3/8″ thick. If these shelves are reinforced underneath with two full-length (48″) braces made of 1 × 2 wood strips (sometimes called furring strips), they can serve two purposes. For ordinary use, the top side provides the customary flat storage surface. However, if plaster bats are used for drying, these shelves can be turned upside down so that their two parallel braces provide raised slats for the bats to rest on, as shown. This arrangement lets air circulate under the bats to speed drying.

If plaster bats are not used in your shop, omit the braces and make your shelves of plywood (3/4″ × 12″ × 48″).

2

Racks for the shelves consist simply of vertical supports made from 2 × 10s that run from floor to ceiling, with 2 × 4 horizontal shelf supports nailed and glued to them at intervals, as shown. The spacing of the 2 × 4 shelf supports can be varied to create storage room of different heights between shelves. The taller spaces should be at the top so that you can place and remove large pots without having to bend over.

Rack supports can often be fastened to the ceiling joists at the top and directly to the floor at the bottom. For permanent racks, nail the supports in place. If the joists are not spaced at the right intervals or if they run in the wrong direction, you will have to nail 2 × 4s to the ceiling perpendicular to the joists to support the top ends of the racks.

If the racks are to be fastened to a concrete floor, nail a 2 × 4 to the bottom, as shown. Drill two holes through the 2 × 4 large enough to take long wood screws. Then, with a masonry bit, drill holes in the floor that line up with the ones in the 2 × 4. These holes should be of a size to accept plastic or lead concrete anchors. Drive the anchors in the holes and then screw the rack to the floor.

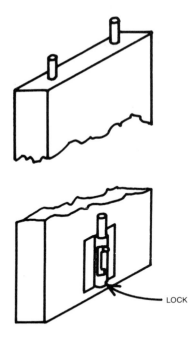

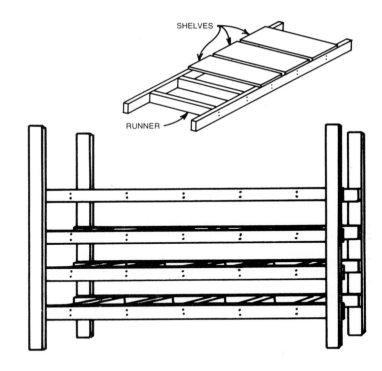

SHELVES

RUNNER

LOCK

3

4

If the racks are to be movable, they will need simple fittings at the top and bottom to hold them in place. To secure the top, drill 3/8″ holes, about 3″ deep, in the top end of the support and insert 4″ lengths of 3/8″ steel rod, as shown. These rods can then be slipped into holes drilled for them in the ceiling joists. To secure the bottom, attach a sliding-bolt type of doorlock, in a vertical position, near the bottom edge, as illustrated; then, drill a hole in the floor in the proper position to accept the sliding bolt. This will work with either wood or concrete floors. You may find it desirable to make some racks permanent and some movable.

Another type of shelf system to consider uses horizontal racks. In this case the racks are permanent and the four shelf units in each one are portable. These shelves are simply flat units made by cutting 5/8″ or 3/4″ plywood into 16″ × 24″ pieces. The horizontal rack that holds them is made of two lengths of 2 × 4 (the length depends on the amount of space you have available), separated by cross-pieces, also made of 2 × 4s. To assemble the rack, arrange the cross-pieces between the long 2 × 4s, as shown, and nail them in place.

Complete the units by nailing the racks to vertical 2 × 4 supports, as shown. Then secure the vertical supports, to the ceiling in the same manner as the 2 × 10 supports for the racks discussed previously. Lay the flat shelf units on the racks, as shown in drawings 5 and 6. The 2 × 4 cross-piece under each unit acts as a runner that lets the shelf slide easily in and out. The spaces between the shelf units, shown in drawing 5, allow pots to extend a bit over the edges of the shelves to let air circulate around them.

No matter what kind of rack-and-shelf system you use, you may want to cover some of the shelves with canvas so that wet pots or slabs won't stick.

DISPLAYING POTTERY

Most pottery forms are best viewed from a particular angle. Bowls are often best seen from above, vases from the side, and hanging planters from below. Items like table lamps that are to be used only at one level should be displayed only at that level. Large or unusual pieces should be prominently displayed, without crowding. If you have a number of similar production pieces, put a few on display and put the others in a less conspicuous place. Everything does not have to be set out on shelves. Groups of mugs can be hung on cords from the ceiling, plates can be hung on the wall in commercial plate holders or they can lean against the wall at the back of a shelf.

Display Equipment for Shows

Display equipment presents a number of problems, including:

1. Use of limited display space.
2. Portability.
3. Strength and stability of display racks.
4. Lighting.
5. Packing convenience and safety.
6. General appearance of the display.
7. Good visibility of your products.

Parts and Materials

Item No.

1. Pieces of 1 1/4" black pipe:
   a. Four 14" lengths.
   b. Two 80" lengths.
   c. Two 92 1/2" lengths.
2. Pieces of 1" black pipe:
   a. Two 36" lengths, threaded on one end.
   b. Two 60" lengths.
3. Four 1 1/4" tee rail fittings.
4. Two 1" cap pipe fittings.
5. Four 94" long 1" × 12" boards.
6. Pieces of 3/16" steel rod.
   a. Two 6" lengths.
   b. Sixteen 2" lengths.
7. Four 60" lengths of chain that will pass through a 1" hole and support 400 lbs. or more.
8. Fourteen steel or brass rings, 2" in diameter, or fourteen 1/4" lengths of 1 1/2" pipe.

There are a number of ways to handle these problems. The display rack described here accommodates shelves and also provides a structure for hanging ware, such as planters and bird feeders, and for mounting display lights. Although the rack is made largely of pipe, fittings should not be used to replace welded joints. The larger diameter of the fittings would make the bottom of the rack uneven and this would make the whole rack unstable.

One asset that makes this type of rack particularly useful is the fact that it can be assembled with only one tool, a 3/16" allen wrench. Disassembled, it can be stored or transported in a minimum amount of space, since it is made almost entirely of separate lengths of pipe.

Tools

1. Hacksaw.
2. Pipe cutter (optional).
3. Welding equipment.
4. Carpenter's square.
5. A 3/16" allen wrench.
6. Wood-cutting saw.
7. Drill with 1" wood bit.
8. Vise.
9. Hammer.

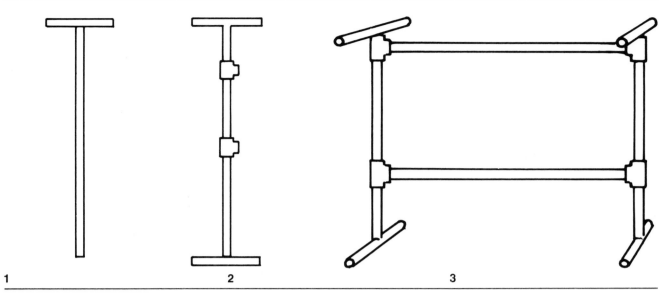

1   **2**   **3**

Constructing the Rack. Begin by welding together the 14″ and 80″ lengths of 1 1/4″ black pipe (items 1a, 1b) to form two T-shaped assemblies, as shown. The two pipes must be perpendicular to each other, so check the angles with a carpenter's square before welding.

Next, slip two tees (item 3) on each of the 80″ pipes and then weld the remaining 14″ pipes onto the ends of the long pipes, as shown. Again, the 14″ and 80″ pipes must be perpendicular to each other. The 14″ lengths must be parallel.

Now join the welded units to each other with the two 92 1/2″ pipes (item 1c), as shown, by inserting the ends of the pipes in the tees and tightening the set screws in these fittings.

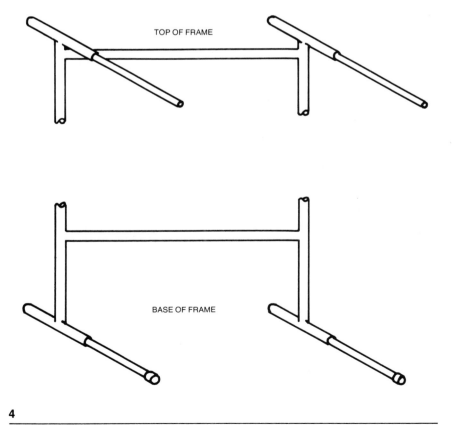

TOP OF FRAME

BASE OF FRAME

4

Next, screw the caps (item 4) on one end of each of the 36″ lengths of pipe (item 2a). Slip the pipes into the welded assembly, as shown.

To complete the display rack, insert the 60″ pipe lengths (item 2b) into the 14″ pipes forming the top of the rack, as shown.

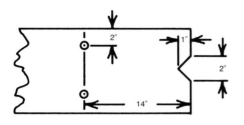 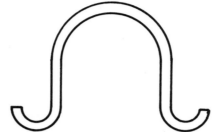 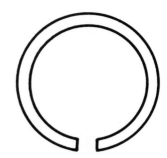

5

Making and Hanging the Shelves.
The shelves used with this display
rack are not fastened in place, but are
hung from the top 92 1/2" pipe with
chains. They are kept from swinging
by the 80" pipes which fit into the
notches in the ends of the shelves.
Prepare the 94" long boards (item
5) that are to be used as shelves by
notching the ends and drilling four
1" holes in each of them, as in the
drawing.

6

To make the hooks for hanging the
shelves in the rack, bend the two 6"
long pieces of 3/16" steel rod (item
6a) to the shape shown in the drawing. The best way to do this is to make
the small bends by putting the rod in
a vise and then bending or hammering the ends into the shapes shown.
The large, center curve can then be
formed by bending the rod over a
piece of 1 1/4" pipe.

Put these hangers on the top 92 1/2"
pipe and hang one end of each of the
four chains (item 7) from one of the
small hooked ends. Pass a chain
through each hole of one shelf and
lift the shelf to the desired height.
Slip a 3/16" × 2" steel rod (item 6b)
through a link of the chain under each
hole. Lower the shelf onto the rods.
Repeat this process for each shelf.
The 80" pipes should now be inside
the notches cut into the ends of the
shelves.

7

To make hangers for planters, bird
feeders, or lights, cut through one
side of about 14 steel or brass rings,
(item 8).

To hang the ware from these rings,
slip the rings onto the 60" pipes at
the top of the rack. Turn the rings so
that the openings in them face downward. Slip a loop of cord, or whatever
you use to hang your ware, through
the openings. Then turn the rings so
that the openings rest against the
top surface of the pipe. This arrangement will permit any item to be removed from the pipe without disturb-
ing the others.

PIPE ROLLERS

The best and cheapest way to move extremely heavy and/or bulky objects around the workshop is to use pipe rollers. There is nothing to construct, and the materials required may already be lying around the shop— or can be picked up for little or no money.

Pipes at least 2' or 3' long and preferably 2" to 4" in diameter are best. You will need three to five of them, depending on the size and weight of the object to be moved. The one other item required is a piece of 3/4" new or used plywood, at least 2' square, preferably larger than the item to be moved.

You will probably need at least one helper to move most heavy objects. Evenly space all but one of the pipe rollers beneath the plywood. Start by tilting or levering one end of the object up high enough to slip a part of the plywood underneath. Then push the object the rest of the way onto the plywood.

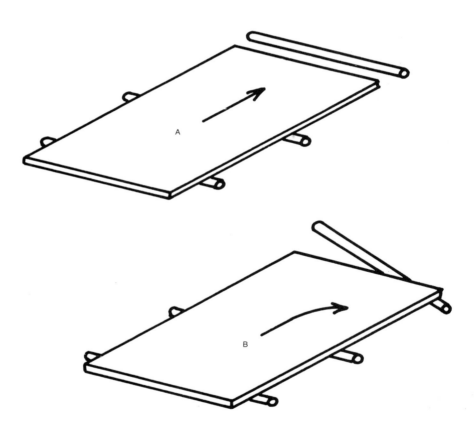

Moving the Object. Push the object and the plywood will roll on the pipes. Pick up each roller and place it ahead of the leading edge of the plywood, as shown in the drawing.

With pipe rollers, you can even move objects around corners. Simply begin angling the rollers, as shown, as you approach the corner.

THE HARVEY HAULER

Wheeled carts are handy for moving pottery from one part of the workshop to another. Wooden or metal carts with casters can of course be built to meet individual needs if desired. However, commercially manufactured carts are available from industrial supply houses and even some mail-order companies at reasonable prices. Check with the supplier to make sure that the carts are designed to handle loads at least as heavy as 300 pounds. If you build the movable shelves described earlier in this part, ware carts may not be required.

The Harvey hauler is a multipurpose cart that lends itself to a wide variety of moving jobs. For example, with just a piece of plywood cut to fit within the front and back angle iron cross-pieces, the cart can be used to carry up to 400 pounds of clay, bricks, or other materials.

With a box in position, many other items around the pottery can be moved. Wooden boxes like these are ideal for packing pottery for transport to dealers or exhibitions. Three of them can be stacked one on top of another on the tricycle cart. You may want to alter the dimensions of the cart to match the size of the wooden box most readily available in your area.

The four-wheel design helps to combine stability with maneuverability—the cart can be turned around within the length of its own wheelbase. Also, the handle swings all the way around for storage under the cart, so that the whole unit requires minimum storage space.

Although making the cart does require welding, the welds are simple. Therefore, having a welder do the job on already prepared parts should not be too expensive.

Tools

1. Welding equipment.
2. Cutting torch (optional).
3. Hacksaw.
4. Pipe cutter (optional).
5. One C clamp (must open 2").
6. Drill with 1/8" and 1/2" bits.
7. Pliers.
8. Carpenter's square.
9. Tape measure or folding rule.
10. Center punch.
11. Wood-cutting saw.

Parts and Materials

Item No.

1. Wooden boxes, as needed, 17 1/2" × 29" × 12" deep (other sizes can be used if the dimensions of the cart are changed).
2. Pieces of 3/8" steel rod:
   a. One 33" length.
   b. One 6" length.
   c. One 1" length.
3. Cold-rolled steel rod to fit the wheels:
   a. One 4 3/4" length (for 6" wheels, item 8a).
   b. One 22" length (for 8" wheels, item 8b).
4. One 6 1/2" length of 1/2" steel rod.
5. Pieces of 1 1/2" × 1 1/2" × 1/8" angle iron.
   a. One 18" length.
   b. Three 6" lengths.
6. Heavy steel washers:
   a. Four to fit the front axle (item 3a).
   b. Two to fit on 1/2" rod.
   c. Two to fit the rear axle (item 3b).
7. Five cotter pins or nails to fit in 1/8" holes.
8. Wheels with rubber tires:
   a. Two 6" in diameter.
   b. Two 8" in diameter.
9. Black pipe:
   a. One 1/2" × 2" nipple.
   b. One 30" length of 1".
10. One piece of 3/4" plywood 29 5/8" × 18".

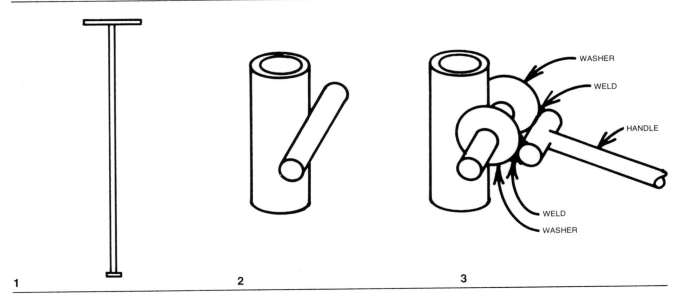

1

Making the Handle. Weld the three pieces of 3/8" steel rod (items 2a, 2b, 2c) together, as shown.

2

Making the Front Wheel Mount. Begin by welding the 4 3/4" steel rod (item 3a), that is to serve as the front wheel axle, to the pipe nipple (item 9a), as shown. Note that the two pieces should be perpendicular to each other and joined at the center point of both pieces.

3

Slip a washer (item 6a) onto each end of the axle. Arrange the washers so that they touch the pipe nipple on each side and are parallel to each other. Then position the shorter cross-piece of the cart handle so that it just touches the outer edges of the washers. Weld the cross-piece and washers together, as shown. The welding should be done so that the washers are able to turn freely on the axle.

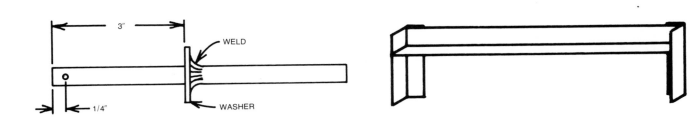

4

Making the Steering Axle. Weld a washer (item 6b) 3" from one end of the 1/2" steel rod (item 4), as shown. Weld only on the side of the washer facing the longer end of the rod. Drill a 1/8" hole 1/4" from the end of the rod, as shown.

5

Making the Cart Frame. Begin by welding one of the 6" pieces of angle iron (item 5b) to each end of the 18" angle iron (item 5a), as shown.

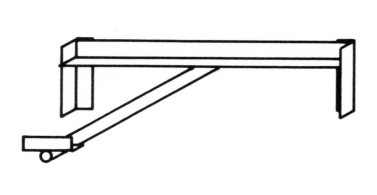

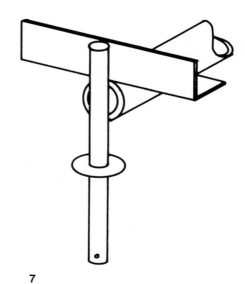

6

Now arrange the 30″ length of 1″ pipe (item 9b) so that it rests on the bottom face of the 18″ angle iron and is perpendicular to it. The end of the pipe should be flush with the back surface of the angle iron. Clamp the pipe and angle iron together and weld, as shown.

Weld the 6″ piece of angle iron (item 5b) to the top side of the other end of the pipe. The 6″ angle iron should be flush with the end of the pipe and parallel with the 18″ angle iron.

7

The steering axle can now be welded to the front end of the pipe and the 6″ angle iron, as shown. Make sure that the steering axle is perpendicular to the pipe and that the end with the 1/8″ hole is pointing downward.

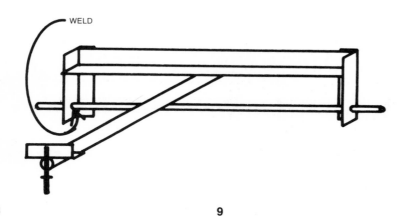

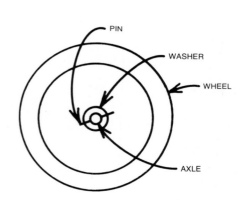

8

9

Making the Axle for the Rear Wheels.
This axle is made from either 1/2″ or 5/8″ steel rod (item 3b) depending on the diameter of the shaft holes in the 8″ wheels (item 8b). Drill or cut whichever size holes are required to accept the steel rod used. Center the holes 3/4″ from the lower ends of the 6″ angle irons already welded to the rear of the frame.

Weld the axle into the two holes, so that the sections of the rod extending out of the holes on each side are the same length as shown.

Attaching the Wheels to the Axles.
Now slip the steering axle down into the pipe nipple welded into the front wheel assembly. Put a washer (item 6b) on the end of the steering axle and fasten it in place with a cotter pin or nail (item 7) bent to keep it in place.

Now slip the rear wheels (item 8b) on the ends of the rear axle; add washers (item 6c) and drill 1/8″ holes through both ends of the axle outside

of the wheels and washers. Put cotter pins or nails (item 7) through the holes and bend to keep them in place, as shown. Use the same method to install the front wheels (item 8a).

The cart is now complete. The wooden boxes (item 1) should now fit within the front and back angle irons. To make a flatbed for the cart, simply cut a piece of 3/4″ plywood (item 10) to fit between the front and back angle irons.

Completed Harvey Hauler.

*Harvey Hauler with crate ready
to be packed with ware.*

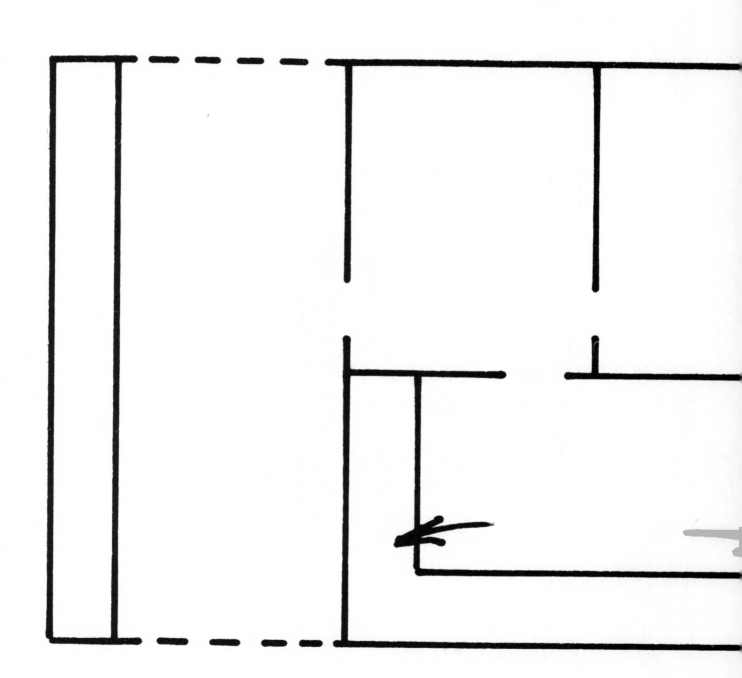

PART 6
WORKSHOP
LAYOUT

Since no two potters are likely to have exactly the same needs, the same working methods, or the same working spaces at their disposal, some aspects of laying out a workshop have to be treated in rather general terms. There are, however, some basic layout considerations that most workshops have in common.

Space Usage and Equipment Storage

Since most workshops are set up in already existing buildings, layout decisions involve not only the overall available space but also structural assets and liabilities. The shape of the interior space, the sources of light, the presence or absence of continuous wall areas are among features that can influence decisions on where to install equipment and keep supplies. The physical environment outside the building—including climatic conditions—can also affect the indoor-outdoor placement of both pottery-making equipment and storage units.

Pottery Production

The kind of pottery you plan to make and the methods you expect to use impose some specific demands on the layout. For example, turning out both low-temperature and high-temperature ware may necessitate allowing space for more than one kiln. Also, throwing and hand-forming techniques set different space requirements.

The number of potters and/or students that will be using the workshop must be considered as well as the proposed level of production. The more people and/or pots, the more space will be required for most production processes. If the workshop will also be used for teaching, it may be necessary to set aside extra or defined spaces for certain phases of instruction.

One-Man Shop

A single potter operating on a full-time, full production basis can function satisfactorily in as little as 500 square feet of space. However, certain varieties of equipment require more room than others. A gas kiln, for example, will generally require more space than an electric one. If finished pottery is to be displayed in an adjacent area, count on allowing at least an additional 300 square feet. All of these figures should be regarded as minimum. Actually, twice as much space could be used.

Four-Man Shop

Counting on a minimum of four throwing wheels, a larger than usual work table, some storage and shelf space, at least 1,000 square feet will be required. Even this estimate may not be large enough if the shop is to be used for teaching as well as production. In that case extra space may be needed near at least one of the wheels and around other equipment

so that students can gather around the instructor during demonstrations. Of course, the sales area for a four-man shop may have to be substantially larger than the size suggested for a one-man shop.

Indoor Shops

Even the workshop that must be enclosed and heated for cold weather can use peripheral areas, that are neither heated nor entirely enclosed, for storage and other needs. During the warmer seasons of the year, this kind of shop may need some kind of cooling arrangement. Ideally, structural flexibility should permit opening doors and windows for natural ventilation. Some activities might even move outdoors; this might be a refreshing change from working indoors during the rest of the year.

Indoor-Outdoor Shops in Mild Climates

This kind of shop also requires protection from weather—not just from sun and rain, but also from those chilly spells that can occur even in semi-tropical climates. On the other hand, the work areas should be kept as open as possible to attain maximum air circulation in hot and humid weather. Provisions for insect screening will probably be necessary.

Perhaps the biggest difference in planning the mild-climate shop is that it is not likely to need protection from prolonged periods of really low tem-

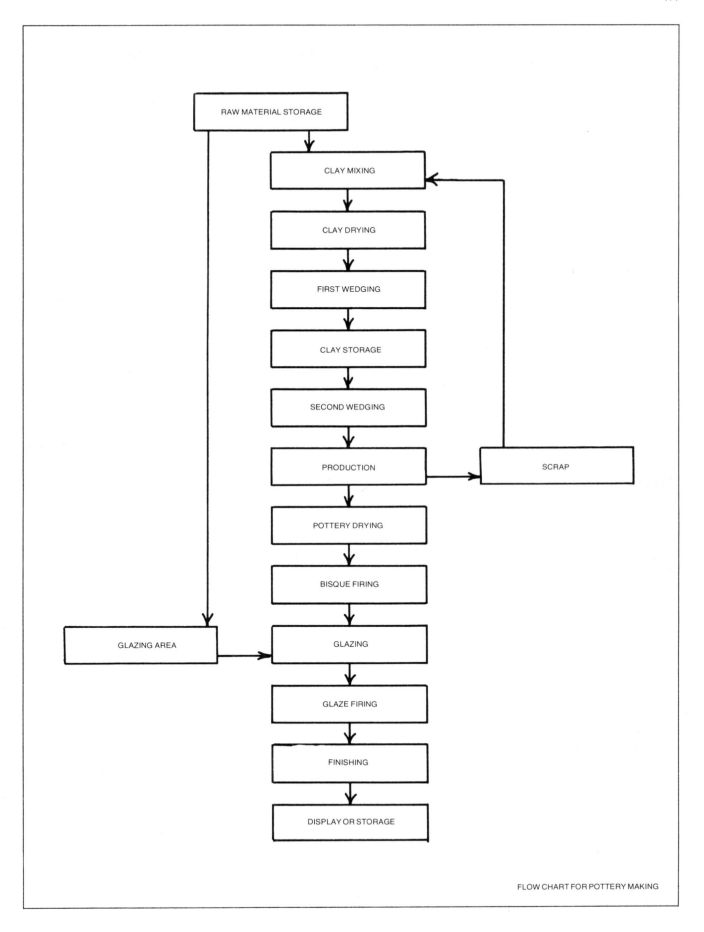

FLOW CHART FOR POTTERY MAKING

peratures that can threaten prepared clay, newly formed pots, and other items that can be harmed by freezing.

Flow of Materials

The flow of materials is the major factor to consider in the overall space planning. Both raw materials and the products of the workshop should move from storage through the work areas to the shipping and/or display area with minimum difficulty.

Avoid situations that necessitate backtracking or those that require lifting and moving the same items more than once. Also avoid arrangements that permit items to accumulate at a place where they become obstacles to circulation or safety hazards, or where one object must be moved just to gain access to another.

Each potter should have his own working area with ample space for equipment and materials so that he can work comfortably, safely, and with a minimum of fatigue. It is also important to provide "traffic lanes" so that people can move easily from one point to another, especially when they are carrying breakable items.

Flow Chart. The flow of materials and products through the typical workshop operations is traced in the flow chart.

Raw Material Storage. The location should allow easy access by large delivery trucks. The floor must be able to support large concentrations of weight. The floor-space requirements will depend on the maximum quantity of materials likely to be stored at any one time. As a rule of thumb, remember that a standard unit of clay weighs about 1 1/2 tons, and it is generally delivered on a 4' × 4' pallet, stacked about 3' high. Each material should be stored so that it will be accessible without moving large quantities of other materials. The surrounding space should be wide enough so that a hand truck, or the four-wheeled Harvey hauler (see *Other Workshop Equipment*), can be wheeled in and out easily for loading and unloading. Items stored in small quantities may be kept on shelves or racks to minimize floor-space requirements. The area must be dry. For lighting, moderate general illumination should be sufficient.

Clay Mixing. Clay mixing should be located near the raw materials storage area and on the same level, so that heavy bags of clay do not have to be carried any farther than necessary. It is especially important to avoid having to carry clay up and down stairs. The floor-space requirements will depend on which mixing methods and equipment you prefer. For example, the dry-mixing drum, described in Part 1, requires a space not less than about 6' × 7'. It also requires a ceiling structure able to support a weight of at least 400 pounds, and a column or post will be needed on which to mount the winch. Powered equipment, like dough mixers and pug mills, may require even more room. Heavy commercial mixing equipment, like a dough mixer or pug mill, will require a floor capable of supporting its substantial weight. It may also require three-phase wiring.

Since clay mixing by any method is a dusty business, plan for an exhaust fan, if possible. General illumination should provide enough light.

Clay Drying. A clay-drying area will be necessary only if you use mixing methods that produce a semi-liquid mixture or slip. Since drying occurs more rapidly in a hot, dry spot, a good location would be near a furnace or some other major heat source. In some climates during certain times of the year, it may be possible to take advantage of favorable conditions outdoors. Clay that is drying in direct sunlight must be closely watched, however, because the clay tends to dry very fast on the surface. If there are no suitable drying conditions available, some can be supplied. A heated, ventilated cabinet can be used; in a small cabinet, the heat from several light bulbs will be enough. If space permits, use a small heated room. In any enclosed area, the drying process generates hot, moisture-laden air that must be exhausted. Good ventilation and moving currents of air are helpful. A dehumidifier may be useful, if it has a large moisture-removing capacity.

Aside from the supplementary equipment, space requirements will depend primarily on the volume of clay to be dried and on the size of the surface (or surfaces) that hold it. If you use the clay drying boxes described in Part 1, you can determine the area you will need by the number of racks you want to install to hold the boxes. Low-level lighting should be adequate.

First Wedging. The location for wedging newly prepared clay should be near the clay-drying and clay-storage areas. The amount of floor space needed will depend on the size of the wedging table, described in Part 5. The floor in and around the wedging area must be able to withstand frequent heavy pounding —day-in and day-out—in a full-production workshop. Since 50 or more pounds of clay can be wedged at once by the cut and stack method, the effects of repeated impact and vibration must be taken into account. In this area, general lighting should be sufficient.

Clay Storage. Clay should be stored, if possible, where it will be near the wedging table, the drying area, and the production area. Often, it can be stored in spaces that would otherwise be wasted—under work tables or on lower shelves, for example. Clay ready for use should always be kept near the floor, because it is usually cooler there, and the clay will tend to dry out less rapidly. The amount of storage space needed will depend on the volume of work and on the aging times required by different kinds of clay.

Second Wedging. Requirements for the area where clay is re-wedged are the same as those for the first wedging. In smaller shops or in those where the layout is flexible enough, it is possible to perform all wedging in the same area. This is a matter that will have to be decided by the needs and facilities of the individual workshop.

Production. Production should be located as near as possible to the clay-storage, wedging, and pottery-drying areas. Since water (both hot and cold) is required in many phases of throwing, a source—complete with sink—should be close by. (For more information on plumbing, see *Plumbing Problems* later in this part.)

Space requirements will be determined by the number of wheels and related equipment you plan to install. A welded frame kickwheel, like the one described in Part 2, occupies a space about 5′ × 5′. Shelves or tables should be placed immediately adjacent to the wheel and to the hand-forming bench. These should be suitable for holding hand tools, slip containers, bats, and other small equipment and supplies. If you use a powered wheel, the electrical system must be able to accommodate it. Since water is involved in throwing, you should use a three-wire grounded system for safety.

In most climates a good source of general heating is important. Working with wet hands can be uncomfortable and even painful.

Good lighting is essential. Fluorescent fixtures assure more even, over-all illumination. However, localized light sources may also be advisable.

While it may not be strictly necessary, a source of music can help to make the production area a more enjoyable place to work. Music is more important in this area than elsewhere because more time is spent at the wheel and the hand-forming bench than anywhere else.

Scrap. Small containers, such as six gallon plastic trash cans, are useful and inexpensive, and they take up a minimum amount of room. One container should be reserved for semi-liquid scrap because it can be mixed into fresh batches of clay. Scrap too hard to wedge should also be put in a separate container for later reclamation.

Pottery Drying. The location for pottery drying should be as near as possible to the production area and the bisque kiln. Shelving is the main requirement here. To accommodate pots of various heights, shelves should be arranged so that the spaces between them vary. Adjustable shelves are best. Additional temporary shelving, that can be set up for periods when production is particularly heavy, is a good idea, if there is space for it. Rolling shelf units are especially handy because they can transport pots directly to the bisque-firing center and eliminate intermediate handling (see *Shelves and Racks* in Part 5).

Bisque Firing. The bisque kiln should be located as near as possible to the pottery-drying area unless rolling

shelf units or a car kiln are used. The space needed will depend on the number and types of kilns you intend to install as well as on the anticipated volume of production. If an electric kiln is to be used, it should be situated near a power outlet and will probably require a 220 volt electrical supply. Safety equipment requirements for kilns are discussed in Part 4. For indoor kilns, good ventilation is essential. Indoors or out, use only fireproof materials in the vicinity of your kiln. Good heating will be needed around this center only in very cold climates.

Glaze Mixing. Many workshops do not set aside a special area for mixing glazes. If it is convenient, the raw-materials storage area may be the best place both for storing the glaze ingredients and for mixing them. Dry-mixed glazes can be carried to the glazing area where water can be added. The only requisite equipment of any considerable size is a triple-beam balance scale, which is a bench-top item.

Glazing. The handiest locations for glazing are near the kiln, if possible, and (of less importance) near the raw-materials storage area. Space allotment will be determined by the number of ready-to-use glazes to be kept here, the size of the spray booth (if any), and kiln capacity. If you plan to have a table that is used only for glazing, allow space for that, too. A low table or a shelf along a wall on which to set glaze tubs is handy. The surface should be high enough so that the tops of the tubs are about 3′ from the floor. Just as for pottery drying, the shelves used for glazed pots awaiting firing should be set at varying heights. These heights should correspond to the heights of the shelf posts in the kiln. The pots can then be grouped according to size as they are glazed. This will facilitate loading the kiln and also make it easier to estimate when there are enough pots to fill the kiln.

Good lighting is as necessary here as in the throwing and hand-forming areas. Electrical outlets will be needed for a glaze mixer, a spray booth, an air compressor, and a ball mill, if you plan to use this kind of equipment.

Water is used in glazing procedures in relatively small amounts. Although

a sink is convenient, it is possible to do without one. However, a hose connection is handy for mixing glaze. A bucket of water may be all that is needed for rinsing used equipment.

Glaze Firing. Glaze firing should be located as near the glazing area as possible. General requirements are the same as those for the bisque-firing area. Often, the same kiln is used for both operations.

Finishing. Finishing consists mainly of grinding off any glaze that may have run down onto the bottom of the pots during firing. The equipment generally used for this is a bench grinder. In the small shop, where there is room for only one, all-purpose work table, the grinding will probably have to be done there. This operation requires some special precautions. It is important to protect anyone in the vicinity of the grinder from flying bits of glaze or pottery that may be thrown off. It is imperative that the person using the grinder wear safety glasses.

Display or Storage Area. These requirements will vary from workshop to workshop. They will depend primarily on how many and what kinds of pots the workshop has to offer and on the preferences and tastes of the individual potter. For example, a comprehensive showing of an entire line of ware will present different requirements from a display that highlights just a few choice pots. In any case, lighting can be a most important element. It should be planned so that it will enhance the distinctive features of individual pots and so that colors, shapes, and textures can be readily appreciated. The use of vertical space is very important. Shelves or other multi-level displays not only increase display space but make the showroom more attractive. Don't overlook outdoor display areas which can be very effective as well as inexpensive. (See also *Display Equipment* in Part 5 and *Production Efficiency* in this part.)

NEWARK MUSEUM WORKSHOP JOHN WATTS, DIRECTOR

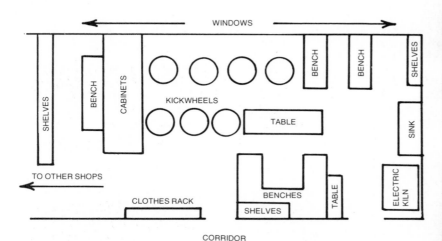

WINDOWS

SHELVES

BENCH

CABINETS

KICKWHEELS

SHELVES

BENCH

BENCH

SHELVES

SINK

TO OTHER SHOPS

TABLE

BENCHES

TABLE

ELECTRIC KILN

CLOTHES RACK

SHELVES

CORRIDOR

Student workshop.

KAREN KARNES
POTTERY

Ware storage.

Salt kiln.

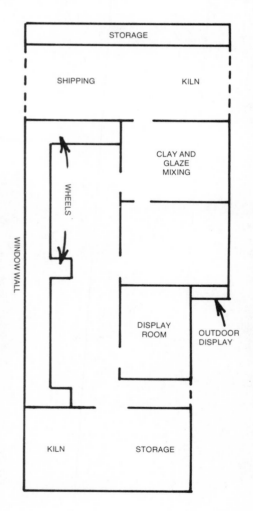

STORAGE	
SHIPPING	KILN
WHEELS	CLAY AND GLAZE MIXING
	DISPLAY ROOM
	OUTDOOR DISPLAY
KILN	STORAGE

WINDOW WALL

Throwing area.

Work benches and tables.

HARRY HOLL
SCARGO STONEWARE POTTERY

Throwing area and greenhouse.

Glazing area.

Outdoor display area.

Indoor-outdoor display area.

BYRON
TEMPLE
POTTERY

Glazing table, ready to use clay storage, and ware shelves.

Salt kiln.

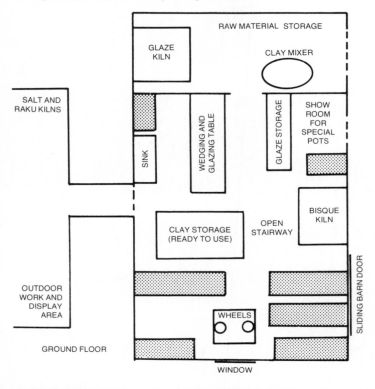

RAW MATERIAL STORAGE

GLAZE KILN

CLAY MIXER

SALT AND RAKU KILNS

SINK

WEDGING AND GLAZING TABLE

GLAZE STORAGE

SHOW ROOM FOR SPECIAL POTS

CLAY STORAGE (READY TO USE)

OPEN STAIRWAY

BISQUE KILN

OUTDOOR WORK AND DISPLAY AREA

WHEELS

SLIDING BARN DOOR

GROUND FLOOR

WINDOW

Throwing area.

Glaze kiln and clay mixer.

Packing area.

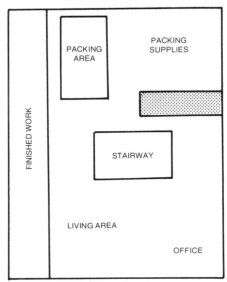

SHELVES

PACKING AREA

PACKING SUPPLIES

FINISHED WORK

STAIRWAY

LIVING AREA

OFFICE

SECOND FLOOR

CAROL CHESEK'S POTTERY WORKSHOP

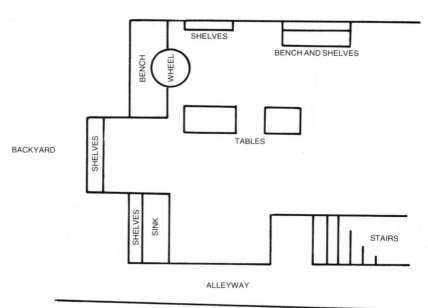

Sprung arch gas kiln.

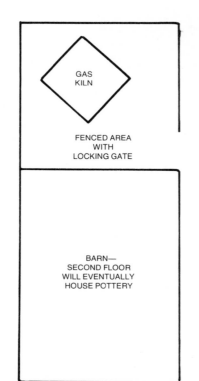

GAS KILN

FENCED AREA
WITH
LOCKING GATE

BARN—
SECOND FLOOR
WILL EVENTUALLY
HOUSE POTTERY

BACKYARD

SHELVES

BENCH AND SHELVES

BENCH

WHEEL

SHELVES

TABLES

SHELVES

SINK

STAIRS

ALLEYWAY

Throwing area and glaze shelves.

Shelves and wheel.

PRODUCTION EFFICIENCY AND SAFETY

Laying out and equipping a pottery workshop are only the first steps in making it productive. Too little attention to working methods and good workshop practice can cause problems ranging from fatigue-engendered accidents to stopped-up drains and even fires. Such mishaps inevitably ruin ware, damage equipment, and keep the potter from his work.

"Potter's Back"

Perhaps the most hazardous aspect of making pottery is lifting the heavy materials. There are many potters who suffer from back injuries that result from lifting too much at a time or from lifting weight improperly. While many materials are sold in large, heavy quantities, they can usually be divided into more easily handled amounts. If you must move heavy materials or objects any distance, always use a hand truck, cart, or rollers, as described in Part 5. Lift heavy objects by keeping your back straight or as near vertical as possible. Bend your knees so that most of the work is done by straightening your legs.

Loading kilns is probably a major cause of strained muscles and back problems among potters. This is especially true when it is necessary to handle kiln shelves or heavy pots at arm's length.

One way to alleviate this problem is to load the kiln in a sequence that will minimize reaching too far when handling heavy items. If the inside height of a front-loading kiln is about 40" to 45", you may find that you can stand in it with your legs slightly bent and your back pressing against the upper portions of the kiln. In that position, handling loads with your arms extended should be easier on your back.

One of the simplest aids in loading a kiln is to have someone stand behind you and hold onto your belt while you are bending over with the load. Then you won't have to strain so much just to maintain your balance.

Handling Hazardous Materials

Some of the materials commonly used in the pottery are highly poisonous; others are harmful if inhaled or ingested. The poisonous materials most commonly encountered are the various forms of lead and barium. Always wash your hands immediately after handling them, even if you work with scoops or other such tools. Also, do not eat or smoke while working with hazardous substances.

Another kind of hazard in the workshop is the prevalence of dry, powdered materials. The dust from some of these substances can be injurious if inhaled. If only small amounts of dust are present, they are not too dangerous as long as the potter is breathing through his nose; the nose has mechanisms for filtering the air. But if, for any reason, the potter breathes through his mouth, the air, laden with dust, enters his lungs. During very dusty operations, such as mixing clay or glazes, wear a respirator.

Avoiding Electrical Hazards

The electrical system for the entire workshop should be of the three-wire or grounded type. If you touch an improperly grounded piece of equipment, especially with wet hands, you may get a dangerous shock.

If the electrical system already installed is the older two-wire, non-grounded type, there is a way to make it safe. Clamp a wire to a metal cold-water pipe in the plumbing system. This pipe must be metal along its entire length to the ground. Be sure to scrape the pipe clean where the ground wire is attached so that good contact is made. There are two ways of connecting this ground wire to the electrical outlets on the power-driven equipment. Run lengths of the wire to each electrical outlet and connect each length to the terminal provided on a three-prong plug adapter used for each piece of equipment. The alternative is to replace all outlets with three-hole types and connect the ground wires to the hex head screw on the outlet. The ground wire does not necessarily have to be insulated. Any grounded system is safe only if the three-wire cords are used on all equipment, or if power tools are of the double-insulated type.

Plumbing Problems

The drain system in a pottery needs special attention. Over a period of time, a large quantity of clay and glaze materials go down the drain unless they are somehow intercepted.

There are three general ways to handle this problem. The standard method is to have a mud trap installed by a plumber. This trap is a box-like device that is installed under the sink and collects much of the coarse material from the water before it enters the drain system. The second method uses a dry-well or cesspool type of pit outside the shop into which all clay- or glaze-bearing water is drained. The water seeps through the porous walls of the pit into the ground and leaves the solid material behind. Some potters recover this material from the pit and use it in raku clay. The third and simplest way to collect the waste material is simply to pour any clay- or glaze-bearing water into a bucket placed in the sink. The heavy materials settle to the bottom and the cleaner water runs over the top and down the drain. The bucket can be emptied outside where the residue of slippery, sticky clay material will cause no problems, or the residue can be saved for raku clay.

APPENDIX

TABLES

TABLE OF TEMPERATURE CONVERSION—CENTIGRADE TO FAHRENHEIT

°C.	°F.	°C.	°F.	°C.	°F.	°C.	°F.
100	212	500	932	900	1652	1300	2372
110	230	510	950	910	1670	1320	2408
120	248	520	968	920	1688	1340	2444
130	266	530	986	930	1706	1360	2480
140	284	540	1004	940	1724	1380	2516
150	302	550	1022	950	1742	1400	2552
160	320	560	1044	960	1760	1420	2588
170	338	570	1058	970	1788	1440	2624
180	356	580	1076	980	1796	1460	2660
190	374	590	1094	990	1814	1480	2696
200	392	600	1112	1000	1832	1500	2732
210	410	610	1130	1010	1850	1520	2768
220	428	620	1148	1020	1868	1540	2804
230	446	630	1166	1030	1886	1560	2840
240	464	640	1184	1040	1904	1580	2876
250	482	650	1202	1050	1922	1600	2912
260	500	660	1220	1060	1940	1620	2948
270	518	670	1238	1070	1958	1640	2984
280	536	680	1256	1080	1976	1660	3020
290	554	690	1274	1090	1994	1680	3056
300	572	700	1292	1100	2012	1700	3092
310	590	710	1310	1110	2030	1720	3128
320	608	720	1328	1120	2048	1740	3164
330	626	730	1346	1130	2066	1760	3200
340	644	740	1364	1140	2084	1780	3236
350	662	750	1382	1150	2102	1800	3272
360	680	760	1400	1160	2120	1820	3308
370	698	770	1418	1170	2138	1840	3344
380	716	780	1436	1180	2156	1860	3380
390	734	790	1454	1190	2174	1880	3416
400	752	800	1472	1200	2192	1900	3452
410	770	810	1490	1210	2210	1920	3488
420	788	820	1508	1220	2228	1940	3524
430	806	830	1526	1230	2246	1960	3560
440	824	840	1544	1240	2264	1980	3596
450	842	850	1562	1250	2282	2000	3632
460	860	860	1580	1260	2300	2100	3812
470	878	870	1598	1270	2318	2200	3992
480	896	880	1616	1280	2336	2300	4172
490	914	890	1634	1290	2354	2400	4352

To convert degrees Centigrade to degrees Fahrenheit: multiply by 9, divide by 5, add 32. To convert degrees Fahrenheit to degrees Centigrade: subtract 32, divide by 9, multiply by 5.

TABLE OF CONVERSION FACTORS

To Convert:	Multiply by	To	From	Multiply by
LENGTH	0.03937	Inches	Millimeters	25.4
	0.3937	Inches	Centimeters	2.54
	39.37	Inches	Meters	0.0254
	3.2808	Feet	Meters	0.3048
	1.0936	Yards	Meters	0.9144
	0.62137	Statute Miles	Kilometers	1.6093
AREA	0.155	Square Inches	Square Centimeters	6.4516
	10.764	Square Feet	Square Meters	0.0929
	1.196	Square Yards	Square Meters	0.83613
	0.0015625	Square Miles	Acres	640.
	2.471	Acres	Hectares	0.40469
VOLUME	0.061023	Cubic Inches	Cubic Centimeters	16.387
		Cubic Feet	Cubic Inches	1728.
	27.	Cubic Feet	Cubic Yards	0.037037
	35.315	Cubic Feet	Cubic Meters	0.028317
	0.03531	Cubic Feet	Liters	28.32
	0.13368	Cubic Feet	U.S. Gallons, Liq.	7.4805
	1.3079	Cubic Yards	Cubic Meters	0.76456
	0.2642	U.S. Gallons, Liquid	Liters	3.785
	1.201	U.S. Gallons, Liquid	Imperial Gallons	0.8327
	0.12	U.S. Gallons, Liquid	Lb. of Water, 62°F.	8.336
	0.554	Ounces (Fluid)	Cubic Inches	1.805
WEIGHT, BULK DENSITY	0.035274	Ounces, Avoirdupois	Grams	28.350
	0.0022046	Pounds, Avoirdupois	Grams	453.59
	2.2046	Pounds, Avoirdupois	Kilograms	0.45359
	2000.	Pounds, Avoirdupois	Short Tons	0.0005
	2240.	Pounds, Avoirdupois	Long Tons	0.000446
	1000.	Kilograms	Metric Tons	0.001
	62.425	Pounds per Cubic Foot	Grams per Cubic Centimeter	0.016019
	17.07	Pounds per Cubic Foot	Pounds per 9″ Equivalent	0.05859
	3.6575	Pounds per 9″ Equivalent	Grams per Cubic Centimeter	0.27341
	0.578	Ounces per Cubic Inch	Grams per Cubic Centimeter	1.73
HEAT, ENERGY, POWER	.003968	Btu	Gram-Calories	252.0
	3.968	Btu	Kilogram-Calories	.2520
	.001285	Btu	Foot-Pounds	778.26
	1.8	Btu per Pound	Gram-Calories per Gram	.5556
	.1124	Btu per Cubic Foot	Kg.-Cal. per Cubic Meter	8.899
	1.341	Horsepower	Kilowatts	.7457
	.02357	Horsepower	Btu per Minute	42.42
PRESSURE	14.22	Pounds per Square Inch	Kilograms per Sq. Cm.	.07031
	14.696	Pounds per Square Inch	Atmospheres	.06804
	.4335	Pounds per Square Inch	Feet of Water at 39.2°F.	2.307
	.4912	Pounds per Square Inch	Inches of Mercury at 0°C.	2.306
	2.0483	Pounds per Square Foot	Grams per Square Centimeter	.4882
	.0334	Atmosphere	Inches of Mercury at 0°C.	29.92
	.0295	Atmosphere	Feet of Water at 39.2°F.	33.90
THERMAL CONDUCTIVITY	.2712	Gm.-Cal. per Sq. Cm.	Btu per Square Foot	3.687
	.6889	Gm.-Cal. per Sq. Cm. for 1 Cm. Thickness	Btu per Square Foot for 1″ Thickness	1.451
	1.24	Gm.-Cal. per Sq. Cm. per Hr. per 1°C. per Cm. Thickness	Btu per Sq. Ft. per Hr. per 1°F. per Inch Thickness	.8064

From: A. P. Green Refractory Pocket Catalog, *issued by A. P. Green Refractories Co., Mexico, Missouri*

TABLE OF DRILL GAUGE AND LETTER SIZE

Drill gauge or letter size	Dec. Equiv. Inches	RECOMMENDED ALTERNATIVE SIZES mm	RECOMMENDED ALTERNATIVE SIZES Dec. Equiv. Inches	Drill gauge or letter size	Dec. Equiv. Inches	RECOMMENDED ALTERNATIVE SIZES mm	RECOMMENDED ALTERNATIVE SIZES Dec. Equiv. Inches	Drill gauge or letter size	Dec. Equiv. Inches	RECOMMENDED ALTERNATIVE SIZES mm	RECOMMENDED ALTERNATIVE SIZES Dec. Equiv. Inches
80	.0135	0.35	.0138	45	.0820	2.10	.0827	10	.1935	4.90	.1929
79	.0145	0.38	.0150	44	.0860	2.20	.0866	9	.1960	5.00	.1969
78	.0160	0.40	.0157	43	.0890	2.25	.0886	8	.1990	5.10	.2008
77	.0180	0.45	.0177	42	.0935	3/32 in. 2.35	.0938 / .0925 }	7	.2010	5.10	.2008
76	.0200	0.50	.0197	41	.0960	2.45	.0965	6	.2040	5.20	.2047
75	.0210	0.52	.0205	40	.0980	2.50	.0984	5	.2055	5.20	.2047
74	.0225	0.58	.0228	39	.0995	2.55	.1004	4	.2090	5.30	.2087
73	.0240	0.60	.0236	38	.1015	2.60	.1024	3	.2130	5.40	.2126
72	.0250	0.65	.0256	37	.1040	2.65	.1043	2	.2210	5.60	.2205
71	.0260	0.65	.0256	36	.1065	2.70	.1063	1	.2280	5.80	.2283
70	.0280	0.70	.0276	35	.1100	2.80	.1102	A	.2340	15/64 in. 5.90	.2344 / .2323 }
69	.0292	0.75 1/32 in.	.0295 / .0312 }	34	.1110	2.80	.1102	B	.2380	6.00	.2362
68	.0310	0.78	.0307 }	33	.1130	2.85	.1122	C	.2420	6.10	.2402
67	.0320	0.82	.0323	32	.1160	2.95	.1161	D	.2460	6.20	.2441
66	.0330	0.85	.0335	31	.1200	3.00	.1181	E	.2500	1/4 in. 6.30	.2500 / .2480 }
65	.0350	0.90	.0354	30	.1285	3.30	.1299	F	.2570	6.50	.2559
64	.0360	0.92	.0362	29	.1360	3.50 9/64 in.	.1378 / .1406 }	G	.2610	6.60 17/64 in.	.2598 / .2656 }
63	.0370	0.95	.0374	28	.1405	3.60	.1417 }	H	.2660	6.80	.2677 }
62	.0380	0.98	.0386	27	.1440	3.70	.1457	I	.2720	6.90	.2717
61	.0390	1.00	.0394	26	.1470	3.70	.1457	J	.2770	7.00 9/32 in.	.2756 / .2812 }
60	.0400	1.00	.0394	25	.1495	3.80	.1496	K	.2810	7.10	.2795 }
59	.0410	1.05	.0413	24	.1520	3.90	.1535	L	.2900	7.40	.2913
58	.0420	1.05	.0413	23	.1540	3.90	.1535	M	.2950	7.50	.2953
57	.0430	1.10 3/64 in.	.0433 / .0469 }	22	.1570	4.00	.1575	N	.3020	7.70	.3031
56	.0465	1.20	.0472 }	21	.1590	4.00	.1575	O	.3160	8.00	.3150
55	.0520	1.30	.0512	20	.1610	4.10	.1614	P	.3230	8.20	.3228
54	.0550	1.40	.0551	19	.1660	4.20	.1654	Q	.3320	8.40	.3307
53	.0595	1.50	.0591	18	.1695	4.30	.1693	R	.3390	8.60	.3386
52	.0635	1.60	.0630	17	.1730	4.40	.1732	S	.3480	8.80	.3465
51	.0670	1.70	.0669	16	.1770	4.50	.1772	T	.3580	9.10	.3583
50	.0700	1.80	.0709	15	.1800	4.60	.1811	U	.3680	9.30	.3661
49	.0730	1.85	.0728	14	.1820	4.60	.1811	V	.3770	3/8 in. 9.60	.3750 / .3780 }
48	.0760	1.95	.0768	13	.1850	4.70	.1850	W	.3860	9.80	.3858
47	.0785	2.00	.0787	12	.1890	4.80	.1890	X	.3970	10.10	.3976
46	.0810	2.05	.0807	11	.1910	4.90	.1929	Y	.4040	10.30	.4055
								Z	.4130	10.50	.4134

Courtesy of Dormer Tools (Sheffield) Ltd., England

TABLE OF ELECTRICAL WIRE COLOR CODING

CODING	WIRE		
	Positive or Live	Earth or Ground	Negative or Neutral
American	Black	Green	White
Old British	Red	Green	Black
European	Brown	Green/Yellow	Blue

TABLE OF BTU OUTPUT FOR DIFFERENT ORIFICE SIZES[2]

Orifice Drill Size	Btu/hr. for Butane or Butane-Propane Mixture Pressure = 11″ Water Column[1]	Btu/hr. for Propane Pressure = 11″ Water Column[1]	Btu/hr. for Natural Gas[3] Pressure = 7″ Water Column[1]
7/64″	94,000	84,000	–
1/8″	122,000	110,000	58,000
9/64″	150,000	138,000	70,000
5/32″	174,000	158,000	82,000
11/64″	225,000	200,000	106,000
3/16″	–	240,000	128,000
13/64″	–	–	144,000
7/32″	–	–	174,000
15/64″	–	–	202,000
1/4″	–	–	230,000

[1]For other pressures consult your gas supplier.

[2]Multiply the Btu/hr. values given in the above table by the values given below to determine the corrected values at elevations above sea level.

Altitude	2000′	4000′	6000′	8000′
Multiply by	1.04	1.08	1.12	1.16

[3]If the burner is very far from the meter, the pressure will be decreased. Therefore the orifice may have to be enlarged. To find the actual Btu output, being by drilling the orifice size suggested in the table above. Fire one burner at full volume while timing a revolution of the fastest moving hand on the meter dial. The table below gives values for a meter calibrated at one cubic foot per revolution. If the meter is calibrated differently, simply multiply the Btu/hr. values given by the number of cubic feet per revolution of the meter.

Seconds for one revolution	60	52	45	40	36	33	30
Btu/hr. Natural Gas	60,000	69,000	80,000	90,000	100,000	109,000	120,000
Seconds for one revolution	28	26	24	22	20	18	16
Btu/hr. Natural Gas	129,000	138,000	150,000	164,000	180,000	200,000	225,000

STANDARD BRICK SIZES

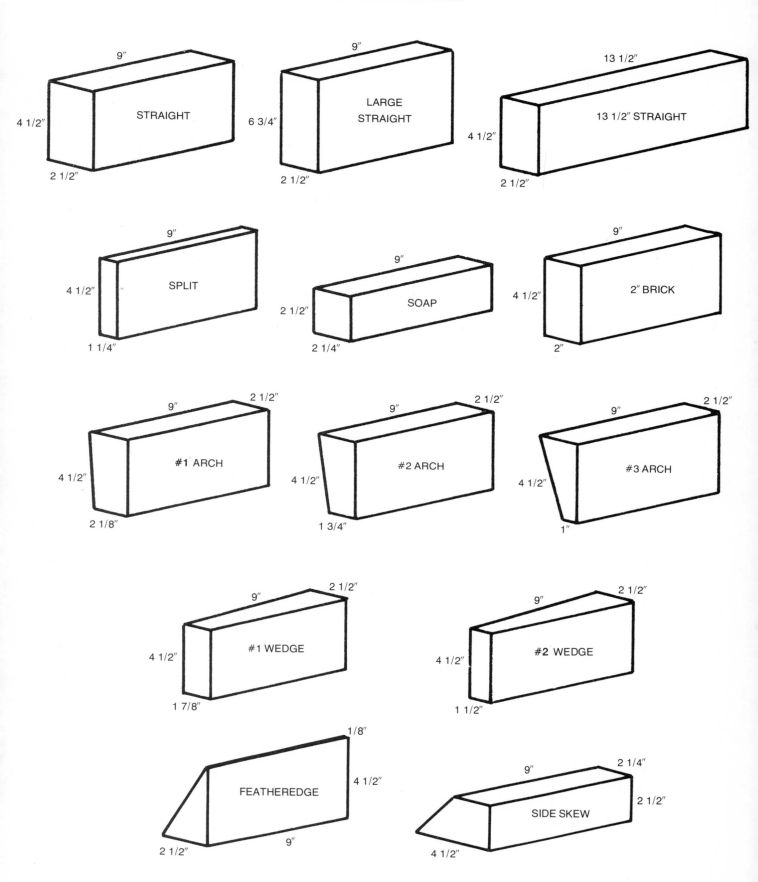

SKEWS BUILT FROM STANDARD 9″ BRICK SHAPES

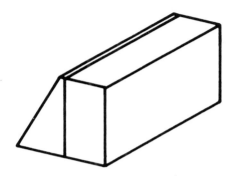

FOR 4½″ ARCH; RISE = 1½″ PER FOOT OF SPAN:
Use one featheredge; 9″ × 4½″ × (2½″–⅛″),
one 2″ brick; 9″ × 4½″ × 2″.

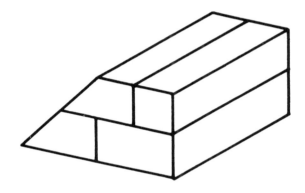

FOR 4½″ ARCH; RISE = 2.302″ PER FOOT OF SPAN:
Use two side skews; 9″ × (4½″–2¼″) × 2½″,
one straight brick; 9″ × 4½″ × 2½″,
and one soap brick; 9″ × 2½″ × 2¼″.

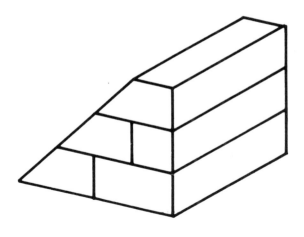

FOR 9″ ARCH; RISE = 2.302″ PER FOOT OF SPAN:
Use three side skews; 9″ × (4½″–2¼″) × 2½″,
one straight brick; 9″ × 4½″ × 2½″,
and one soap brick; 9″ × 2½″ × 2¼″.

TABLES FOR ESTIMATING FIREBRICK ARCHES

FOR 4½″ ARCH: RISE = 2.302″ PER FOOT OF SPAN
Standard 9″ Sideskews Can Be Used for Skew

| SPAN | RISE | INSIDE RADIUS | BRICK REQUIRED PER COURSE | | | | TOTAL |
			NO. 3 ARCH 9x4½x(2½-1)	NO. 2 ARCH 9x4½x(2½-1¾)	NO. 1 ARCH 9x4½x(2½-2⅛)	STRAIGHT 9x4½x2½	
1′ 0″	2⁵/₁₆″	8³¹/₃₂″	1	7	–	–	8
1′ 1″	2½″	9²³/₃₂″	1	8	–	–	9
1′ 2″	2¹¹/₁₆″	10¹⁵/₃₂″	–	9	–	–	9
1′ 3″	2⁷/₈″	11⁷/₃₂″	–	9	1	–	10
1′ 4″	3¹/₁₆″	11³¹/₃₂″	–	8	2	–	10
1′ 5″	3¼″	12²³/₃₂″	–	7	3	–	10
1′ 6″	3¹⁵/₃₂″	13¹⁵/₃₂″	–	7	4	–	11
1′ 7″	3²¹/₃₂″	14³/₁₆″	–	6	5	–	11
1′ 8″	3²⁷/₃₂″	14¹⁵/₁₆″	–	6	6	–	12
1′ 9″	4¹/₃₂″	15¹¹/₁₆″	–	6	6	–	12
1′10″	4⁷/₃₂″	16⁷/₁₆″	–	6	7	–	13
1′11″	4¹³/₃₂″	17³/₁₆″	–	5	8	–	13
2′ 0″	4¹⁹/₃₂″	17¹⁵/₁₆″	–	5	9	–	14
2′ 1″	4²⁵/₃₂″	18¹¹/₁₆″	–	4	10	–	14
2′ 2″	5″	19⁷/₁₆″	–	3	11	–	14
2′ 3″	5³/₁₆″	20³/₁₆″	–	3	12	–	15
2′ 6″	5¾″	22⁷/₁₆″	–	2	14	–	16
2′ 9″	6¹¹/₃₂″	24²¹/₃₂″	–	–	17	–	17
3′ 0″	6²⁹/₃₂″	26²⁹/₃₂″	–	–	18	1	19
3′ 3″	7½″	29⁵/₃₂″	–	–	18	2	20
3′ 6″	8¹/₁₆″	31¹³/₃₂″	–	–	18	3	21
3′ 9″	8⅝″	33⅝″	–	–	18	5	23
4′ 0″	9⁷/₃₂″	35⅞″	–	–	18	6	24
4′ 3″	9²⁵/₃₂″	38⅛″	–	–	18	7	25
4′ 6″	10³/₈″	40³/₈″	–	–	18	9	27
4′ 9″	10¹⁵/₁₆″	42¹⁹/₃₂″	–	–	18	10	28
5′ 0″	11½″	44²⁷/₃₂″	–	–	18	11	29
5′ 3″	12¹/₁₆″	47³/₃₂″	–	–	18	13	31
5′ 6″	12²¹/₃₂″	49¹¹/₃₂″	–	–	18	14	32
5′ 9″	12¼″	51⁹/₁₆″	–	–	18	15	33
6′ 0″	13¹³/₁₆″	53¹³/₁₆″	–	–	18	17	35

From: A. P. Green Materials Handbook, *courtesy of Cutter Fire Brick Co., Cambridge, Mass.*

TABLES FOR ESTIMATING FIREBRICK ARCHES

FOR 4½″ ARCH: RISE = 1½″ PER FOOT OF SPAN
Standard 9″ Featheredge Can Be Used for Skew

SPAN	RISE	INSIDE RADIUS	BRICK REQUIRED PER COURSE			TOTAL
			NO. 2 ARCH 9x4½x(2½-1¾)	NO. 1 ARCH 9x4½x(2½-2⅛)	STRAIGHT 9x4½x2½	
1′ 0″	1½″	1′ 0¾″	5	2	–	7
1′ 1″	1⅝″	1′ 1¹³/₁₆″	5	3	–	8
1′ 2″	1¾″	1′ 2⁷/₇″	4	4	–	8
1′ 3″	1⅞″	1′ 3¹⁵/₁₆″	4	4	–	8
1′ 4″	2″	1′ 5″	4	5	–	9
1′ 5″	2⅛″	1′ 6¹/₁₆″	3	6	–	9
1′ 6″	2¼″	1′ 7⅛″	3	7	–	10
1′ 7″	2⅜″	1′ 8³/₁₆″	2	8	–	10
1′ 8″	2½″	1′ 9¼″	2	8	–	10
1′ 9″	2⅝″	1′10⁵/₁₆″	1	10	–	11
1′10″	2¾″	1′11³/₈″	1	10	–	11
1′11″	2⅞″	2′ 0⁷/₁₆″	1	11	–	12
2′ 0″	3″	2′ 1½″	–	12	–	12
2′ 6″	3¾″	2′ 7⁷/₈″	–	12	3	15
3′ 0″	4½″	3′ 2¼″	–	12	5	17
3′ 6″	5¼″	3′ 8⁵/₈″	–	12	8	20
4′ 0″	6″	4′ 3″	–	12	10	22
4′ 6″	6¾″	4′ 9³/₈″	–	12	13	25
5′ 0″	7½″	5′ 3¾″	–	12	15	27
5′ 6″	8¼″	5′10¹/₈″	–	12	18	30
6′ 0″	9″	6′ 4½″	–	12	20	32

Instructions for Using Arch Tables

To use the arch table, measure the distance between the insides of the walls to be spanned by an arch. This will be the span. Decide the thickness of the arch to be used (usually 4½″ or 9″). Decide which type of skew brick combination to use (see *Skews Built from Standard Brick Shapes*). If the arch has a large span, the 2.302″ rise per foot span combination is more stable than the 1½″ rise per foot. Choose the proper table for the chosen skew combination and find the proper span. Use the corresponding rise and inside radius figures to lay out the arch support form. In keeping with the terminology used in this book, "brick required per course" used in these tables should be taken to mean "number of courses of each brick shape required to complete the arch." When

more than one brick shape is required, the shapes should be uniformly intermixed across the arch to form a symmetrical arc. Multiply the courses required by the number of bricks per course to find the total number of bricks required by the entire arch.

These tables assume that no mortar will be used. If mortar is used, the number of courses will be somewhat reduced.

Note to British readers: U.K. is now standardized on metric bricks which are smaller than the old standards using inches. It may be that more bricks would be required or the job scaled down slightly. The arch bricks referred to in the tables are usually called side arch in U.K. but can be identified by the dimensions. Featheredge would be called

feather end on edge in U.K. Straights are called standard squares in many places in the U.K. There are serious snags in using these tables in the U.K. Undoubtedly brick suppliers could identify the bricks by the measurements given in inches and most manufacturers will advise on the number required.

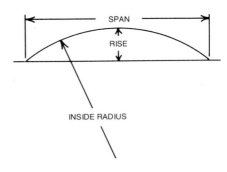

BASIC
INSTRUCTIONS

How to Cut Brick and Concrete Block

Brick: If you have a circular saw, use a blade intended for hard masonry and stone. This kind of blade is available from most hardware stores and building supply dealers. Saw the brick half way through at the narrow side, then turn it over and saw the other half.

These bricks can also be cut with a cold chisel. At the point where the brick is to be cut, chisel a shallow slot all the way around. Then, set the brick on two others so that it is supported only at the ends. Place the cold chisel in the slot and hit it sharply with a hammer. The brick should break in two, more or less evenly. This hammer-and-chisel method is not easy. If you have no experience with this method, it would probably be better to rent or borrow a power saw and invest in the necessary blade.

Insulating firebrick: These bricks can be cut with any coarse-toothed saw, but they are very abrasive and will quickly wear out a blade. For economy, use either an old saw or a hacksaw with a blade edged with silicon carbide chips.

Concrete block: These blocks can be cut by the hammer-and-chisel method described for high-duty firebrick. *Do not* use a circular-saw blade for this purpose.

How to Mix Concrete

Concrete is required in this book for such things as the slabs on which the kilns are built and the flywheels used in some of the potter's wheels. For large quantities of concrete, you may want to purchase the ready-mixed material from a supplier.

The proportions of sand, cement, and gravel in the ready-mix or homemade concrete you use should be:

  1 part portland cement

  3 parts clean sand

  5 parts ¾" gravel

If you are mixing the concrete yourself, use either a regular concrete mixing pan (available from building suppliers) or a child's plastic wading pool.

Spread the gravel over the bottom of the mixing pan first. Next, pour the sand over it, distributing it evenly. Add the cement in the same way.

Mix these dry ingredients together with a garden hoe or other tool good for stirring and blending. When everything is fairly well mixed together, make a depression in the middle of the mixture and pour in about a bucket of water.

Continue stirring in order to wet down all the ingredients. Each time you add water (add it in smaller amounts now), make the same depression in the mixture to receive it.

There is no sure way to know how much water will be required to achieve a proper consistency in the concrete. Most important is to be sure that all the ingredients are thoroughly wetted and thoroughly mixed together.

As a rule of thumb, bear in mind that concrete that tends to be soupy or which pours off the mixing tool is too wet. It should slide off in globs, leaving no dry particles whatsoever.

How to Calculate Castable Volume

Area of the end wall of a catenary arch kiln = ¾ BH

Volume = ¾ BHT (T = thickness)

Volume (in cubic feet) = BHT/2304 (if B, H, and T are measured in inches).

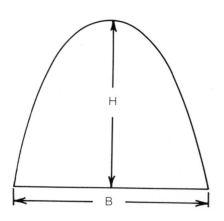

How to Make a Pencil Compass

To build some of the kilns and potter's wheels described in this book, it is necessary to cut out large circular and arc-shaped pieces of wood and plywood. Because drafting instruments capable of drawing large circles are expensive, a compass good enough for the purposes of this book can be made with nails, lightweight wire, and a pencil. And you can use the same length of wire over and over again for a variety of circle sizes.

Let's suppose you have to draw a circle on a sheet of plywood. First drive a nail into the plywood at a distance from the nearest edge equal to the radius of the circle to be drawn, plus about a ½". This nail represents the center of the circle. Measuring from that point, drive a second nail into the plywood at the point equal to the desired radius.

Make a loop in one end of the wire and slip it over the second nail. Stretch the wire taut and tighten the loop. Then, while still keeping it taut, wrap the other end around the first, or center, nail and secure the wire so that it cannot slip.

Remove the nail from the loop and substitute a sharpened pencil for it. Making sure to keep the wire taut, swing the pencil in an arc to draw the circumference of the circle on the plywood.

If an arc must be drawn on a wooden board or piece of plywood too narrow to draw the complete radius needed, use a second piece of wood of the same thickness. Butt it up against the board or plywood on which the arc is to be drawn and secure them together. Proceed to draw the arc over both pieces as though they were one piece of wood. Then remove the second piece and the partial arc will be correctly drawn on the piece you want to use.

How to Bend Steel Rod

There are several simple techniques for bending steel rod. Here are three that are based on using pipe slightly larger in diameter than the rod. (Although not necessary, it will be easier to bend the rod if it is heated until red hot; for heating use an oxyacetylene torch.)

1. This method requires a vise and one length of pipe. Clamp the rod in the vise so that only the end to be bent protrudes. Slip the piece of pipe over the protruding end. Then, grip the pipe firmly and apply enough pressure to produce the required shape.

2. The two-pipe method uses lengths of pipe slipped onto opposite ends of the steel rod so that only the place where the bend will occur is left uncovered. In this case, it is necessary to grip both pipes to apply the pressure necessary to secure the proper bend. This method can be used only when both ends of the rod are and will remain straight, so that the pipes can be slipped off after the bend is made.

3. For this method, only a length of pipe is necessary. To begin, lay the rod on the floor (or any hard surface). Then, slip a length of pipe over one end of the rod. Stand on the uncovered end of the rod, facing the pipe-covered end. Reach down, grasp the end of the pipe, and pull it upward toward you to achieve the desired bend. This method requires less "heft" than the others and can be used if the angle of the bend does not have to be precise.

MATERIAL SOURCES

Suppliers of items that may not be available from local sources

SELECTED AMERICAN SUPPLIERS

Burners and Parts

Flynn Burner Corp.
425 Fifth Ave.
New Rochelle, N.Y. 10802

Johnson Gas Appliance Co.
Cedar Rapids, Iowa 52405

Maxon Corp.
201 E. 18th St.
Muncie, Ind. 47302

Mine & Smelter Industries
(formerly DFC Corp.)
P.O. Box 16607
Denver, Colo. 80216

Pyronics Inc.
17700 Miles Ave.
Cleveland, Ohio 44128

Ransome Gas Industries, Inc.
2050 Farallon Dr.
San Leandro, Calif. 94577

DC Motors

Applied Motors, Inc.
4801 Boeing Dr.
Rockford, Ill. 61109

Graham Transmissions, Inc.
P.O. Box 160
Menomonee Falls, Wisc. 53051

Drive Wheels, Rubber

Metro Supply Co.
1774 Maplelawn
Troy, Mich. 48084

Industrial Equipment

W. W. Grainger, Inc.
5959 Howard St.
Chicago, Ill. 60648
(Warehouses in over 40 states)

Pottery Material Suppliers

American Art Clay Co., Inc.
4717 W. 16th St.
Indianapolis, Ind. 46222

Cedar Heights Clay Co.
50 Portsmouth Rd.
Oak Hill, Ohio 45656

Creek Turn Pottery Supply
Rt. 38
Hainesport, N.J. 08036

A. P. Green Co.
1018 E. Breckenridge St.
Mexico, Mo. 65265

Hammill & Gillespie, Inc.
225 Broadway
New York, N.Y. 10007

Minnesota Clay
8001 Grand Ave. So.
Bloomington, Minn. 55420

The Monomy Potter's Supply Co.
RFD 140E
Chatham, Mass. 02633
This supply house is operated by Roger Harvey and stocks many of the specific parts recommended in this book.

Newton Potters Supply, Inc.
96 Rumford Ave., Box 96
Newton, Mass. 02165

Rovin Ceramics and Pottery
6912 Schaefer Rd.
Dearborn, Mich. 48216

The Salem Craftsmen's Guild
3 Alvin Pl.
Upper Montclair, N.J. 07043

Standard Ceramic Supply Co.
Box 4435
Pittsburgh, Pa. 15205

Stewart Clay Co.
133 Mulberry St.
New York, N.Y. 10013

Trinity Ceramic Supply Co.
9016 Diplomacy Row
Dallas, Texas, 75235

Van Howe Co.
1185 S. Cherokee Ave.
Denver, Colo. 80223

Westwood Ceramic Supply Co.
14400 Lomitas Ave.
City of Industry, Calif. 91744

Jack D. Wolf, Inc.
724 Meeker Ave.
Brooklyn, N.Y. 11222

Power Modules

Cutler-Hammer
Specialty Products Div.
Milwaukee, Wis. 53201

Refractory Suppliers

Also local refractory suppliers and brick producers.

Babcock & Wilcox Co.
Refractories Div.
161 E. 42 St.
N.Y., N.Y. 10017

A. P. Green Co.
1018 E. Breckenridge St.
Mexico, Mo. 65265

Carborundum Co.
Refractories and Electronic Div.
Box 337
Niagara Falls, N.Y. 14302

Denver Fire Clay Co.
2401 E. 40th Ave.
Box 5507
Denver, Colo. 80217

Grefco, Inc.
299 Park Ave.
New York, N.Y. 10017

Johns-Manville Co.
Greenwood Plaza
Denver, Colo. 80217

Metropolitan Refractories
Tidewater Terminal
So. Kearny, N.J. 07032

New Castle Refractories
Box 471
New Castle, Pa. 16103

Norton Co.
Industrial Ceramics Division
Worcester, Mass. 01606

Pyro Engineering Corp.
200 S. Palm Ave.
Alhambra; Calif. 91801

Wheelheads

Many brands of commercially distributed wheelheads will work.

Creek Turn Pottery Supply
Rt. 38
Hainesport, N.J. 08036

Newton Potters Supply, Inc.
96 Rumford Ave., Box 96
Newton, Mass. 02165

SELECTED BRITISH SUPPLIERS

Belts and Pulleys

Listed under Belt Drives and V-Belt Drives in some phone books

J.E. Sexton Ltd
162–164 Grays Inn Rd.
London WC1

Industrial Drives Ltd
Cordwallis Estate
Maidenhead, Berks

Castors

Flexillo Castors and Wheels Ltd
Slough SL1 4ED

DC Motors and Electric Motors

Listed under Electricians Supplies in phone book or Exchange & Mart Weekly

Brook Motors
18 Baldwin St., Bristol 1

Johnson Ltd
319 Kennington Road
London SE11

Insulating Blanket

Fiberfrax from:
Carborundum Co Ltd
Refractories and Electronics Division
Mill Lane, Rainford
St. Helens, Lancs

Caposil 18 from:
Cape Insulation Ltd
Stirling, Scotland FK7 7RW

Kiln Burners

Franklin Furnace Co Ltd
(Dine Burners and Auto Controls)
Baker St., Spark Hill
Birmingham 11

Auto Combustions Ltd
(Swirlamiser Burners)
360–364 Wandsworth Rd.
London SW8 4TF

Nu-Way Heating Plants Ltd
(Nu-Way Burners)
Droitwich, Worcs

Schieldrop and Co Ltd
Stotfold, Beds

Metal (Materials)

Listed under Steel in phone book

Large suppliers are sometimes willing to sell small amounts for cash, but be prepared to cut up long lengths into convenient pieces for transport. This can often be done at the yard by a couple of people with a hacksaw.

Pipe

Available at builders suppliers, also listed under Tubes in phone book

Plastic Laminates

Do-it-yourself suppliers

Refractories

Acme Marls Ltd
Clough St., Hanley
Stoke-on-Trent

Moler Products Ltd
Hythe Works
Colchester, Essex

Gibbons Bros Ltd
Disdale
Dudley, Worcs

Diamond Clay Co Ltd
Hartshill, Stoke-on-Trent

Harris and Bailey Ltd
105 Lower Addiscombe Rd.
Croydon, Surrey

British Sisalkraft Ltd
Refractories Division
Ripple Road, Barking
Essex

E.J. Pearson Ltd
Stourbridge, Worcs

Lafarge Aluminous Cement Co Ltd
73 Brook St.
London W.1.

Temperature Control and Safety Devices

Industrial Pyrometer Co Ltd
66–76 Gooch St. North
Birmingham 5

Kilns and Furnaces Ltd
Kiln St Works
Tunstall
Stoke-on-Trent ST6 5AS

Wheelheads

Pottery Equipment Co Ltd
17–18 Progress Way
Croydon CR9 4DH

Lotus Pottery
Stoke Gabriel
Totnes, S. Devon

J. W. Radcliffe and Sons Ltd
The Old Boro' Works, Rope St.
off Shelton New Road
Stoke-on-Trent ST4 6DJ

Pilling Pottery
Pilling
Nr Preston, Lancs

J.E. Sexton Ltd
(for spindles and flat plates)
162–164 Grays Inn Rd.
London WC1

Wire

Do-it-yourself suppliers, also binding wire from:

Tiranti
72 Charlotte St.
London W.I.

Ceramic Supplies and Equipment

Harry Fraser Ltd
Vauxhall St., Longton
Stoke-on-Trent
ST3 4HP

Fulham Pottery
210 New Kings Road
London SW6 4NY

Moira Pottery Co Ltd
Raw Materials Dept
Moira
Nr Burton-on-Trent

Harrison Mayer Ltd
Craft Division
Meir
Stoke-on-Trent ST3 7PX

Wengers Ltd
Etruria
Stoke-on-Trent ST4 7BQ

Podmore and Sons Ltd
Craft Division
Shelton
Stoke-on-Trent ST1 4PQ

Edwards and Jones Ltd
Globe Engineering Works
Longton
Stoke-on-Trent

Gosling and Gatensbury
Atlas Foundry
College Road, Hanley
Stoke-on-Trent

William Boulton Ltd
Providence Engineering Works
Burslem
Stoke-on-Trent

TABLE OF PRODUCTS AND SOURCES

	Auto parts suppliers	Bearing suppliers	Department stores (Sears, Wards)	Hardware stores	Heating and air conditioning shops	Industrial equipment suppliers	Lumber yards	Machine shops
ANGLE IRON				•				•
ASBESTOS BOARD							•	
BEARINGS		•				•		•
BRICKS, FIRE								
BRICKS, LOW DUTY							•	
BURNERS AND PARTS								
CANVAS			•	•			•	
CASTERS		•	•	•		•	•	
CHANNEL IRON								•
CLAY								
CONCRETE AND BLOCKS							•	
CONCRETE, READY-MIX								
DC MOTORS								
DRIVE WHEELS, RUBBER								
ELECTRIC MOTORS			•	•		•		
ELECTRICAL SUPPLIES			•	•		•	•	
ELECTRODES, PORCELAIN								
FIBERGLASS MATERIALS	•		•	•			•	
FITTINGS, PIPE			•	•	•	•	•	
"HYDRA" SPONGE			•	•				
IGNITORS, BURNER						•		
INSULATION, BLOCK								
INSULATION, CASTABLE								
KILN FURNITURE								
LOCTITE	•	•						•
PIPE AND FITTINGS			•	•	•	•	•	•
PIPE JOINT COMPOUND			•	•	•		•	
PLASTER, MOLDING								
POTENTIOMETERS								
POWER MODULE								
PULLEYS		•	•	•		•	•	
PULLEYS, V (SHEAVES)		•	•	•		•		•
REFRACTORIES						•	•	•
SHEET METAL				•	•		•	
SPONGES, "HYDRA"			•	•				
SQUARE STEEL TUBING								•
STEEL/DRUMS								
STEEL ROD			•	•			•	•
THERMOCOUPLES						•		
TRANSFORMER								
VALVES, AUTOMATIC						•		
VERMICULITE							•	
WHEELS, RUBBER		•	•	•		•	•	
WHEELHEADS								
WINCH, BOAT			•					
WIRE CLOTH (hardware cloth)				•			•	

Local sources for parts or materials can often be located in the Yellow Pages under the headings at the top of this table.

Masonry suppliers	Manufacturers or distributors	Plumbing parts suppliers	Pottery suppliers	Refractory suppliers	Sheet metal shops	Steel distributors or warehouses	Welding shops	Barrel and drum suppliers
						•	•	
•				•				
			•	•				
			•	•				
•	•	•	•					
						•	•	
			•	•				
•								
•								
	•							
	•		•					
		•						
		•						
		•						
			•	•				
			•	•				
			•	•				
		•					•	
		•						
•			•					
	•							
	•							
			•	•				
					•	•	•	
						•	•	
								•
					•	•		
		•	•					
		•						
		•	•					
	•		•					

INDEX